What's the Story? T Meets Their Screenplay

A structured perspective on the crucial interface of director and screenplay, this book encompasses twenty-two seminal aspects of the approach to story and script that a director needs to understand before embarking on all other facets of the director's craft.

Drawing on seventeen years of teaching filmmaking at a graduate level and on his prior career as a director and in production at the BBC, Markham shows how the filmmaker can apply rigorous analysis of the elements of dramatic narrative in a screenplay to their creative vision, whether of a short or feature, TV episode or season. Combining examination of such fundamental topics as story, premise, theme, genre, world and setting, tone, structure, and key images with the introduction of less familiar concepts such as cultural, social, and moral canvas, narrative point of view, and the journey of the audience, *What's the Story? The Director Meets Their Screenplay* applies the insights of each chapter to a case study—the screenplay of the short film *Contrapelo*, nominated for the Jury Award at Tribeca in 2014.

This book is an essential resource for any aspiring director who wants to understand how to approach a screenplay in order to get the very best from it, and an invaluable resource for any filmmaker who wants to understand the important creative interplay between the director and screenplay in bringing a story to life.

Peter Markham is a creative consultant, teacher, author, and former directing head at the American Film Institute Conservatory. His alumni, award winners at major festivals, have notable careers in film and TV. Prior to teaching, he was a director in the UK, and worked with filmmakers including Anthony Minghella and Martin Scorsese.

What's the Story? The Director Meets Their Screenplay

An Essential Guide for Directors and Writer-Directors

Peter Markham

LONDON AND NEW YORK

First published 2021
by Routledge
2 Park Square, Milton Park, Abingdon, Oxon OX14 4RN

and by Routledge
52 Vanderbilt Avenue, New York, NY 10017

Routledge is an imprint of the Taylor & Francis Group, an informa business

© 2021 Peter Markham

The right of Peter Markham to be identified as author of this work has been asserted by him in accordance with sections 77 and 78 of the Copyright, Designs and Patents Act 1988.

All rights reserved. No part of this book may be reprinted or reproduced or utilised in any form or by any electronic, mechanical, or other means, now known or hereafter invented, including photocopying and recording, or in any information storage or retrieval system, without permission in writing from the publishers.

Trademark notice: Product or corporate names may be trademarks or registered trademarks, and are used only for identification and explanation without intent to infringe.

British Library Cataloguing-in-Publication Data
A catalogue record for this book is available from the British Library

Library of Congress Cataloging-in-Publication Data
Names: Markham, Peter, 1952– author.
Title: What's the story? the director meets their screenplay :
an essential guide for directors and writer-directors / Peter Markham.
Description: London ; New York : Routledge, 2020. | Includes index.
Identifiers: LCCN 2020024639 (print) | LCCN 2020024640 (ebook) |
ISBN 9780367415891 (hardback) | ISBN 9780367415877 (paperback) |
ISBN 9780367815363 (ebook)
Subjects: LCSH: Motion pictures–Production and direction. |
Motion picture plays.
Classification: LCC PN1995.9.P7 M327 2020 (print) |
LCC PN1995.9.P7 (ebook) | DDC 791.4302/32–dc23
LC record available at https://lccn.loc.gov/2020024639
LC ebook record available at https://lccn.loc.gov/2020024640

ISBN: 978-0-367-41589-1 (hbk)
ISBN: 978-0-367-41587-7 (pbk)
ISBN: 978-0-367-81536-3 (ebk)

Typeset in Sabon
by Newgen Publishing UK

To Barbara Tfank, for her unwavering belief and support

Contents

Acknowledgments ix

Introduction 1

PART A
The approach 3

1 What's the story? 5

2 Premise 10

3 Theme 16

4 Genre 21

5 World/setting 39

6 Cultural, social, and moral canvas 43

7 Tone 49

8 Structure 55

9 Passage of time 63

10 Character 69

11 Narrative point of view 85

viii Contents

12 Introduction of the protagonist and main characters 99

13 Key images, objects, and motifs 106

14 Opening image, frame, shot 110

15 Closing image, frame, shot 119

16 Endings 124

17 The 5-step creative analysis of the screenplay 131
    17.1 *A brief summary of the scene* *131*
    17.2 *The journey of the protagonist* *131*
    17.3 *The journey of the audience* *132*
    17.4 *The turning point of the scene* *133*
    17.5 *The function of the scene* *134*

18 The director's statement 135

PART B
The case study—*Contrapelo* screenplay by
Liska Ostojic and Gareth Dunnet-Alcocer 137

19 Screenplay 139

20 *Contrapelo* case study 162

21 Conclusion 181

    References 182
    Bibliography 183
    Index 184

Acknowledgments

I would like to give my thanks to the following, without whose inspiration, insights, guidance, and encouragement I could not have written this book: Dubois Ashong, Ari Aster, Zal Batmanglij, Pieter Jan Brugge, Lee Citron, Richard Cottan, Paul Cronin, Neil Dickson, Aihui Dong, Sabrina Doyle, Joseph Garrity, Julian Higgins, Dean Israelite, Mick Jackson, Asher Jelinsky, Leqi "Vanessa" Kong, Stefan Kubicki, Perry Lang, Tal Lazar, Moya Lee, Shiyu "Rhyme" Lyu, Rebecca Maddalo, Manjari Makijani, Theoline Maphutha, Jim McBride, Joel Novoa, Chloe Okuno, Joseph Oppenheimer, Matthew Pancer, Philiane Phang, Charlie Polinger, Asaph Polonsky, Justin Rhodes, Barry Sabath, Daniel Sawka, Chris Schwartz, Omer Ben Shachar, Matthew Specktor, Rob Spera, Courtney Stephens, Greg Takoudes, Tomas Vengris, Max Weissberg, Amelie Wen, Hao Zheng, Quan Zhou, Shu Zhu, Dr Mahlet Zimeta, others whom, with my apologies, I have no doubt omitted to mention, and the many Directing Fellows and those of other disciplines I was fortunate to come to know during my career at AFI Conservatory. I also wish to express my gratitude to Dr. Steven Holt for his meticulous, informed, and enlightening copy-editing.

I am indebted to Gareth Dunnet-Alcocer and Liska Ostojic for allowing me to use their screenplay of *Contrapelo* as the case study.

Note: several categories in chapters 5 and 6 are taken from the class handout of Robert Boyle (1909–2010), AFI Conservatory Production Design Faculty and Production Designer whose credits include *North by Northwest*, *The Birds*, and *Marnie*. Of all the remarkable guests to my class, Bob was surely the most distinguished, and I owe him a debt of gratitude for the insights I was able to put to use in these chapters. I hold the memory of AFI Conservatory colleagues Gill Dennis and Frank Pierson, who taught me so much, similarly dear.

Introduction

There are many who imagine the director's job is restricted to directing the actors, that above all it is about getting good performances. There are those would go on to say it's about deciding how to shoot those performances, in the process "covering" the action of a scene adequately so that its footage will cut together. Among directors, some approach their craft by deciding on a moment in the screenplay and working towards, then away from it—as if those gradients might be the sole contours of dramatic narrative. Indeed, although most filmmakers acknowledge the task of bringing the screenplay to the screen, they perhaps do not entirely appreciate the nexus of dramatic construction and filmic discourse—by which I mean the visual and auditory language of cinema and TV, the tone, the rhythm, the aesthetics, the manipulation of time, and the nature of a film's address to its audience. I used to believe that when a director considers a screenplay, if they are doing their job, they think about the merits and demerits of its story, what the characters want, what their goals might be, what is text and what subtext, and how, artistically, logistically, and fiscally, the film might be made. I knew they should know how to "break down" a scene. I knew they should have opinions and insights as to how good or bad the script was, and what elements might need fixing, but I did not know of any structured approach by which the director could engage with the screenplay in order to understand it at both the granular and the architectural level, to mine the deep strata and foundations of its narrative, to trace its connectivity and fathom its identity in order that this comprehensive understanding might inform each and every subsequent area of filmmaking craft. It was in teaching Directing at AFI Conservatory in Los Angeles, as Discipline Head for eight years and as Senior Lecturer for over six years beforehand, that that shortcoming, thankfully, evaporated ...

While working with the directing "fellows"—some directors, many writer-directors—in the thesis presentation class throughout those fourteen years, also as an adjunct before that, and in teaching some 450 young, talented, and diverse filmmakers from around the world, I developed more clarity and greater method, one that has been proven to work. Indeed, many of the "fellows" in my classes have gone on to achieve great success in film and TV, winning awards at Cannes, Sundance, the Motion Picture Academy, Busan and other major festivals throughout the world.

Writing *What's the Story? The Director Meets Their Screenplay* has given me the opportunity to evolve that process considerably and to present—untrammeled by time constraints and the limitations of a three-hour class—a guide to the essential understanding that, by way of forensic analysis of story and screenplay, together with an accompanying imperative of creative vision, must inform the director's approach to all areas of their filmmaking. This book provides a key to the director's and writer-director's engagement with their film, whether feature or short, or their TV episode or season, at the fundamental levels of story, screenplay, character, and image, these forming the bedrock of all subsequent processes—creative, technical, logistical, and budgetary.

While there are many books about screenwriting, and many about directing that focus on performance, on camera, on physical production, and on the industry, and while many of them are very good indeed, it seems to me there is a dearth of guidance when it comes to considering how the director might engage with the screenplay at the key creative level. *What's the Story?*, by contrast, looks in both directions—at the screenplay one way, at the shoot and the cut the other. With some twenty-two essential topics, explored and then applied to the case study of the included screenplay of the short film *Contrapelo*, co-written and directed by my alumnus Gareth Dunnet-Alcocer, this book addresses the problematic lacuna of much filmmaking literature, with each topic being explained in its own right while the various topics are tied together through their connection to the overarching craft of the visual storyteller.

Here is an approach that will appeal not only to students but to practiced filmmakers too. It will be of value not only to directors and, I hope, screenwriters, but to filmmakers of all disciplines. Cinematographers, production designers, costume designers, editors, and producers (in no particulate order) all practice crafts rooted in story and storytelling. I hope that *What's the Story?* can be not sectarian but unifying. Feeding our commonality as filmmakers, it's a foundation on which to build the mutual trust and insight that going forward makes for a coherent and productive collaborative process, understood by everyone.

A note on references

Specific films are referenced in order to illustrate specific points. While it is recommended that the reader go on to watch those films, they will not need to have seen them in order to understand the points made within their particular context. Few will have seen each of the films mentioned—this book is not a test for cinephiles but an exploration pertinent to all filmmakers.

Part A
The approach

1 What's the story?

Directors are storytellers. In order to tell the story in their screenplay, they need to understand what a story is.

When filmmaking students (and some teachers too) are asked to tell the story of a film, they will often begin by saying "It's a story about …" or even simply "It's about …" Say Wong Kar-Wai *In the Mood for Love* is the film under consideration, they might offer "It's a story about two lonely people," or "It's a story about two lonely people in a relationship," or simply "It's about loneliness and love." None of these sentences describes a story. "Two lonely people" refers to the film's main characters. "Two lonely people in a relationship" describes characters in a particular circumstance. "It's about loneliness and love" is more of a thematic than a narrative notion, a concept, an abstraction. Of course it's important for the director to know their characters, to grasp their condition, their circumstances or state of being, and of course it's helpful to have a sense of the thematic aspects of their movie or TV episode and what these may be *about*, but unless the director understands what a story is, they won't be able to tell one, and if they can't tell one they won't be able to incorporate those other aspects—characters, circumstances, theme—into the elements of their craft.

The Shorter Oxford English Dictionary (OED) defines story thus: "A narrative of real or (usu.) fictitious events, designed for the entertainment of the hearer or reader; a series of traditional or imaginary incidents forming the matter of such a narrative, or a succession of significant incidents."

A story is a progression. Two lonely people fall unexpectedly in love but, faced by their mutual sense of guilt, find themselves unable to maintain their romance, so they go their separate ways. That's a story.

Evident in this progression, as it pertains to dramatic narrative, is an element of *conflict*. There is an *obstacle* that the lovers face—their sense of guilt, which conflicts with their mutual attraction. A tale of the couple meeting, falling in love, and living happily ever after might be a story but would be unlikely to prove a very compelling one. Devoid of suspense and dramatic tension, it would pose no questions and would leave an audience with nothing to want for the characters, whom as a result it would be unlikely to care about. Also integral to story, at least in its manifestation of dramatic narrative, is the element of *sacrifice*. Something is lost in order that something might be gained, the togetherness of lovers, for example, so that their love might be affirmed, or the life of a protagonist, so that their sense of meaning might be encapsulated.

The Shorter OED further defines story as *plot* or *storyline*, thus begging the thorny question as to whether plot and story are the same or, if they are not, what the difference between the two might be. Views on this are contradictory.

Plot can be seen as the *causality* of events, how one thing *leads to* another. Story can be understood as the *delineation* of events, one thing *after* another. Here plot is *why* what happens happens, whereas story is simply *what* happens.

This would appear not to take into account the emotional core of dramatic narrative, however, so in order to accommodate this lack, the distinction might be reversed, plot defined as the listing of events, story as the underlying emotional journey(s) of the character(s). Here, plot is surface, story essence.

The term *plot* might also be applied to a *non-linear* sequence of events in the *storytelling* as opposed to the *linear* sequence of the underlying *story*. The audience journeys through the plot's reorganization of incident in order to discover the story and its chronology, as it does for example with Quentin Tarantino's *Pulp Fiction* or Christopher Nolan's *Memento*.

(*Plot* can also mean *conspiracy*, suggesting perhaps the formulation of a transgressive act—a fundamental ingredient of drama.)

For the purposes of the director meeting the screenplay, however, either as writer-director encountering it wearing the director's hat for the first time, or as director encountering it simply for the first time, the following distinction might prove the most useful.

Story is the essence that underlies the narrative, the character's journey of wants, needs, and motivation at the heart of the film. It's the emotional and cognitive journey that the narrative embodies.

Plot is the mechanism by which the story moves forward.

Thus, to relate the plot of a screenplay or film is to relate the raw events, one after the other. To relate the story is to reveal the emotional narrative of the main character(s). Plot prompts the audience to ask "What is going to happen next?" Story engages emotionally. Both compel, but whereas the audience may never have experienced the specific events of a movie, will rarely have lived through its plot, it will, to a greater or lesser extent, have experienced the emotions, wants, needs, and fears of the film's characters as manifested in the story. Indeed, in *Lessons with Kiarostami*, master director Abbas Kiarostami says "What happens on the screen has no impact without past experiences brought by audiences."

Returning to *In the Mood for Love*, its plot might be set out as follows:

Hong Kong. 1962. Chow Mo-wan, a journalist who aspires to write martial arts serials, rents a room with his wife in the same building and on the same day that Su Li-zhen, secretary to a shipping manager, arrives with her husband. The spouses of both tend either to work late or travel away from home so that, although their neighbors have formed a bustling social group, the two find themselves solitary in their respective apartments. When they go to the noodle shop, however, they encounter each other. Their loneliness, accentuated when Chow's gambler friend Ah Ping takes advantage of him, and when Su has to cover up for her boss's extra-marital affairs, brings them together. In realizing that their spouses are having an affair with each other, they decide to re-enact its possible beginnings in order to learn how the relationship might have started. By spending time together, however, they find themselves falling in love. Chow is to leave Hong Kong for Singapore and suggests Su should go with him, but, after waiting for her, leaves without her so that when she arrives late, she finds him gone. Some time after, she goes to Singapore, where she calls him. He picks up but says nothing. When he returns to his apartment, he discovers lipstick on a cigarette butt, so he knows she's visited. He tells a friend how, in the past, people would whisper their secrets into holes in trees, which they'd block with mud. Years after, Su returns to the apartment building in Hong Kong, asking her former landlady if her room is for rent. Chow returns later, to be told that a woman and her son are now resident in the building. He leaves, not realizing that this is Su (with a boy who is perhaps his own son). Later, visiting the ruined temple of Angkor Wat in Cambodia, he whispers unheard words into a hole in a wall, which he then plugs with mud.

The story of the film might be described thus:

A man and a woman, lonely because of the absence of their respective spouses, discover a painful truth—that their unfaithful mates are having an affair. In trying to work out how this began, they re-enact the possibilities, but by doing so fall in love themselves. Shamed in the realization that they're behaving in the same illicit way as their spouses, they contrive to end their romance although remaining unable to deny it.

As is the case above, the description of a plot is usually much longer than that of a story. Such is the case with Andrea Arnold's short film *Wasp*:

Zoë takes her three girls and baby son along with her when she reprimands a neighbor who has intervened in a scrap between their children. On her way home after fighting with the woman, Zoë encounters Dave, who invites her for a drink. Claiming her children are not hers but belong to a friend, she agrees, saying she will meet him in the pub once they have been picked up. At home she calls a friend to ask them to take care of the children, only to learn she's unavailable. A wasp buzzes at a window, which she opens in order to free it. Zoë then sets off for the pub with her children. Leaving them outside, she enters to find Dave. He invites her to a drink but then suggests she buy the first round. Zoë buys crisps for the children as well as Dave's lager but without sufficient cash foregoes her own drink. When, outside the pub, the children complain that they wanted fries, not crisps, she changes the subject, inviting them to dance to the pub's music. After she's gone back inside to take Dave his lager, darkness falls and the children run wild in the street, while in the pub Zoē and Dave grow more intimate. Dave suggests they go to Zoē's home, which she says is not possible. He lives with his mother meanwhile, so his home is not an option either. When Zoē sees one of the children tapping at the window, she pretends to Dave that she needs the restroom and leaves him, passing her adversary from earlier in the day, who repeats her threat that social services will take her children. Angered when one of them asks if she's going to have sex with Dave, Zoē tells them that they must wait a little longer for her while keeping out of sight. In his car, Dave wants to drive off, but Zoē asks that they remain *in situ*. While they make out, the children spot a passer-by discarding a takeaway and one of them collects it. When a wasp from the garbage lands on the baby's face, one of the girls screams, prompting Zoē to leave Dave and rush over. The wasp crawls into the baby's mouth, terrifying Zoē, but after a while flies out. On seeing the food around his mouth, Zoē blames the girls for the wasp, upsetting them but then comforting them when they cry, an action Dave witnesses on arriving at the scene. Shortly after, while the children eat fries, he tells Zoē he will take them all home so that they can chat.

The film's story, on the other hand, might be described as follows:

Lonely and trapped in impoverished single motherhood, Zoē, who is desperate to engage the affection of Dave, frees a wasp trapped in her kitchen before taking her children along with her as she goes to meet him. Neglecting them, she tries to win his love, but is interrupted in her efforts when she finds a wasp about to sting her baby son. The threat prompts Zoē to realize that her love for her children is paramount, which in turn moves Dave, who at last shows concern for her.

The director should not only know both the story and the plot of their screenplay but also be capable of telling them to their creative team—producer, production designer, cinematographer, costume designer, editor. They might initially ask these key collaborators themselves to tell the story. If they can't, perhaps this is because they're not right for the film, perhaps they simply don't know how to tell a story, or perhaps the screenplay does not make the story clear. Should they all happen to tell the *same* wrong story, either the screenplay is suggesting this or the director's sense of the story is mistaken. If they tell *different* wrong stories it may mean that the screenplay is leaving itself open to individual interpretation and that its story needs to be made clearer.

The director should be able to tell the story to themself too. If they can't, how are they going to tell it to their audience? How are they going to find the *means* of telling it? The visual and aural language, the staging, the style, the modulation of energy, rhythm, tension, suspense, and drama?

Ideally, the director should *need* to tell the story. They should feel an urgency that motivates them. The challenges of the physical production of a movie or a TV show for the director are considerable indeed, but if the filmmaker is *possessed* by the need to tell the story, coming to see it as a story that *must* be told, this can sustain their energy and focus through the multiple difficulties of the pre-production and the shoot.

The director might be telling a story close to their own, or to that of someone they know, admire, care about, or are in some way fascinated by. They will be drawn to the protagonist. They will find the world of the story compelling, whether or not they're familiar with it. They will feel the story "speaks" to them. The most powerful reason for telling a story is that only through its articulation might the answer to the questions it poses be found, although they may remain ever elusive—mystery at the heart of a story affords it a resonance to render it compelling in ways a philosophical treatise or a moral lecture cannot match.

A plot should be clear. A story should engage. A mystery should have no answer.

2 Premise

In its usage, the term *premise* has more than one meaning. This can lead to confusion, so it's important to understand the implications of each interpretation.

> **Meaning 1:**
> The premise is the foundation of your story—that single core statement, says James N. Frey, "of what happens to the characters as a result of the actions of a story." For instance, the premise of *The Three Little Pigs* is "Foolishness leads to death, and wisdom leads to happiness."
>
> (Writers' digest.com, March 11, 2008)

Similarly, in *The Art of Dramatic Writing*, long a mainstay of manuals on dramaturgy, Lajos Egri maintains that premise is the truth that writers seek to prove, at least to themselves, by way of their stories: "poverty leads to crime" or "bragging leads to humiliation," for example. But is this what the director should be looking for in their screenplay? Do the best stories really *prove* anything? Don't they instead pose questions, perhaps questions that have no solutions? Anton Chekhov, master of both theatre play and short story, said that the job of the writer is not to *solve* the problem but to *present* it. More recently, writer and director David Mamet wrote that drama is about *irreconcilable opposites*. Indeed, the French word *dénouement*, which we use in English and tend to interpret as the *wrapping-up* of a story, translates in fact as the *unraveling*—the *opening up*, *unwrapping*, or *untying*.

The problem so often with a story that attempts to prove something is that it can lend itself to moralizing, to teaching the reader or audience how to behave. It can tend to be judgmental, proselytizing, banal even, and ultimately limiting in its dramatization of contradictory human nature and the inner paradoxes that make for the most compelling characters. Most importantly perhaps, it can undermine drama, reducing the inevitable and perennial friction and conflict of life and human interaction to a foolish mistake, something that a moral lesson could have put right all along if only the characters had been lucky enough to know it or be allowed to put it into practice. This can be an approach that soothes and reassures rather than engages and challenges. It sends out a message rather than posing a question, reinforcing a sense of certainty instead of leaving the audience to figure out their own solutions after the film or TV show is over. Another danger this risks is the tendency of the story to conform to conventional wisdom. The best stories, perhaps, help us to find revelatory and even transgressive insights we wouldn't have understood or even thought of without having undergone the intense emotional experience of watching or reading a narrative as it plays out. The best stories do not confirm the beliefs we have, left-wing, right-wing, rational, mystical, but lead us instead to those we did not know we have.

On the other hand, a proof, in the Egri fashion, might indeed lend itself to the uncertainties of paradox. Here's an example of a dictum that contains an interesting contradiction: "One finds one's destiny on the path one takes to avoid it" (Carl Jung). Doesn't this apply to Sophocles' *Oedipus Rex*, one of the earliest of known plays, in which Oedipus, in attempting to avoid marrying his mother, ends up committing that very act? The sentence seems indicative of so many protagonist journeys, in which character, goal or objective, and fate are intertwined. Another way of saying that "poverty causes crime" might be "paupers are fated to become criminals"—and when they try their hardest to become upstanding citizens along the way, then there is a story. Such a *premise* might more usefully be thought of as a *theme*. But more of that later ...

> **Meaning 2:**
> The premise of a film or screenplay is the initial state of affairs that drives the plot. Most premises can be expressed very simply, and many films can be identified simply from a short sentence describing the premise.
> (Premise (filmmaking), Wikipedia)

Thus:

> A chemistry teacher is diagnosed with terminal cancer ... (*Breaking Bad*)
> A photojournalist immobilized with a broken leg becomes convinced a man across the way has murdered his wife ... (*Rear Window*)
> A woman is the sole survivor of a car crash in which she has lost both her husband and her daughter ... (*Three Colors: Blue*)

This is the easiest kind of premise to articulate. It's the germ of the story, the starting point for the sequence of events to follow. It's the *set-up*, the thing that *goes wrong* in the story's world and needs to be put right in some way or other so that order can be reinstated, or it's a crime that's been committed so that justice needs to be done in order that moral equilibrium be restored. The director needs to understand the set-up their screenplay establishes. When they tell its story they must be sure to make this crucial component crystal clear. Novice screenwriters and directors often set about being deliberately vague or try to be clever because they're afraid of being too "on the nose." They imagine that obscuring basic information is a sign of sophistication. Not only are they wrong, but they are failing in their first duty as storytellers—the communication of the information an audience needs in order to remain engaged with their film. The nature of a set-up is essential information the audience must have. The fact that it needs to be clear does not imply that it has to lack drama or emotion. When such information is delivered forcefully, it can seal the audience's connection to the movie or TV show; and when, in particular, that audience is in the protagonist's *narrative point of view* (see chapter 11), it will have no choice but to ask itself "What is he/she going to do now?" (see the example from *Three Colors: Blue* in chapters 11 and 12).

> **Meaning 3:**
> This next definition, which can be expanded to *premise* as *log-line*, includes both the *set-up* and the course of action the protagonist takes in order to rectify its consequences. This is the *hook* of the story, after which the audience should be unable to tear its eyes away from the screen. "Where is this course of action going to lead the character, and can they make it work?," it wonders. A story will be all the more compelling if such a course of action is one audiences both want and do *not* want the character to take, one they even fear them *succeeding* in taking. Does the viewer want Walter White in *Breaking Bad* to be able to provide for his family after his death? Yes! Does the viewer want him to cook crystal meth, with all the misery that will inevitably follow for his customers? No. At least, one assumes, that will be true for most viewers.

Now the premise begins with the word *when*:

> When a chemistry teacher is diagnosed with terminal cancer he resorts to cooking crystal meth in order to provide for his family after his death ...
> When a photojournalist immobilized with a broken leg becomes convinced a man across the way has murdered his wife, he seeks proof of the crime ...
> When a woman is the sole survivor of a car crash in which she loses both her husband and her daughter, she resolves to bury her grief by destroying all traces of them ...

> **Meaning 4:**
> This leads to the sense of premise that's perhaps the most useful for the director in understanding the narrative drive of their story and its shifting of impetus, which is a combination of the above two elements plus the question the protagonist comes to confront as a result of the *new* and *worse* problem their action causes. (In trying to make things better they make them, at least at this stage, worse.) In Genre 1 (see chapter 4), thrillers, action movies etc., this frequently involves physical, often mortal danger.

Thus:

> When a photojournalist immobilized with a broken leg becomes convinced a man across the way has murdered his wife, he seeks proof of the crime. As his discoveries bring him to the attention of the killer, how can he keep from becoming a murder victim himself? (Mortal danger).

In other dramas, the peril might be emotional or moral—in other words, the character faces some figurative death.

> When a woman is the sole survivor of a car crash in which she loses both her husband and her daughter, she resolves to bury her grief by destroying all traces of them. As she's forced to confront the emerging truths of her husband's betrayals, how can she find a way to overcome their implications? (Emotional danger)

A combination of the former and latter can pack a powerful punch indeed:

> When a chemistry teacher is diagnosed with terminal cancer, he resorts to cooking crystal meth in order to provide for his family after his death. As he battles with murderous rivals, how can he keep his family ignorant of his worsening crimes? (Mortal and emotional danger).

As premise in Meaning 1 relates to theme, so the narrative progression of Meaning 2, Meaning 3, and Meaning 4 relates to structure—how the story is put together. (See chapter 8.)

The director should distinguish the question the protagonist faces from the question the story poses. The former often invites a black or white answer, and is related to what the protagonist's goal is, so it is usually plot-related. For example, "Can the hero succeed in their mission to fit in?" Or: "Can they get the girl/boy?" Or: "Can they win the battle?" In a TV season, or succession of seasons, such a question can grip viewers for weeks, months, or years on end. It's an ongoing question that sustains the tension of the narrative from episode to episode and season to season. Perhaps it's never to be answered—as the journey taken transpires in the end to be everything ... (This may be even more the case when a show is cancelled; the story remains unfinished and viewers are denied a conclusion, a predicament that in many cases does not entirely diminish the pleasure thus far derived, the journey of the show proving more important than its destination.)

The next question, the big question, to which the film or TV show or season itself leads an audience, is a philosophical/moral/existential question, a universal one that applies not just to photojournalists, the abruptly widowed, or crystal-meth-cooking chemistry teachers. It's one that at its best denies the audience any easy answer: "Is fitting in really that important?," "Is love worth fighting for?," "Is the battle to be fought at home or in the field?," etc.

This question, the *thematic question*, again takes us, as its name suggests, to the concept of *theme*, which follows on from *premise*.

The director should write down the premise of their screenplay. They should try the first approach, Meaning 1. Is there a moral lesson? Is an easy judgment being passed, or is there a paradox that will leave the audience thinking and wondering? They should write down the others, taking them step-by-step. The s*et-up*. The s*et-up* and *action*. The *set-up*, *action*, and the *question* the protagonist confronts.

This is *not* an academic exercise but a preparation for filmmaking. A director is a storyteller who needs to understand every element of the story they are telling, its emotional and tonal path, its surfaces, its depths, its foundations, and its drive. They need to know the connections between character and narrative, film and audience, story and "message" or question. Equipped with a strong grasp of premise, the director can set about designing an aspect of what might be described as the broad *punctuation* of their film. In Krzysztof Kieślowski's aforementioned *Three Colors: Blue*, for example, the director gives weight to the predicament the protagonist Julie faces by cutting from a hyper close-up of her eye to a big close-up of her face—the first time in the film he has shown this—before cutting abruptly to the loud and graphic smashing of a mirror (literally what many a screenwriter might describe as a *smash cut*!). The arresting shots and the transition between them mark the end of the movie's prologue and the beginning of its next act or *movement*. In Martin Scorsese's *Gangs of New York* the director marks the conclusion of the film's prologue, after the imperative of protagonist Amsterdam's revenge on Bill the Butcher has been introduced, through a virtuoso crane shot (achieved before the era of drones), starting on Priest Vallon's face and rising to a dizzying view from the stratosphere of the entirety of the island of Manhattan, embellished by the title "Manhattan 1846." The amalgam of bravura camera movement, shift of scope and scale from the micro to the macro, from a human to a god-like perspective, and the bold announcement in words of the film's historical period constitutes a proclamation on the part of the director of the epic genre of his film.

Most directors, even if gifted with Scorsese's profound understanding of, and creative agency in the richness and constant reinvention of, visual language and storytelling, may not have such logistical, technical, or financial resources at their disposal, but with other, more available capabilities—patience in the creative process, imagination, thoughtfulness, and collaboration with their creative team—can explore the many means by which they can bring to their work the punctuation that premise (and structure) invites. Camera—movement, composition, lensing—lighting, transitions through rhythm and pace, through tone, through place, through scale, through emotion expressed maybe through performance, through sound and/or music are some of the resources of directing craft available as the means to announce a significant step in the progression of the premise.

When a director has a strong grasp of their premise, as with the other topics covered in this book, they will be well set to plan and direct their film or TV show. Indeed, they need to know this *connective tissue*—all of the aspects of story and dramatic construction and how they fit and function together—better than anyone else, better perhaps than even the screenwriter, who, if they have been successful in their writing, and even when they've been meticulous in their craftsmanship, will have tapped into much of their best work through their creative subconscious. It is the director's obligation to protect that precious realm while also unleashing it to best effect as they make their movie.

3 Theme

> An idea that recurs in or pervades a work of art or literature.
> (oxforddictionaries.com)

Central to its story, the *theme* is the truth a film embodies. It is expressed through drama and conflict, imagery and visual language, and the journeys of the characters, and it is encapsulated in the sense or question of meaning the story comes to reveal. How we see the constitution of this truth, how we define it, follows different opinions and takes different forms.

Lajos Egri, in *The Art of Dramatic Writing*, talks of theme as something to be expressed by a single abstract noun. Isolation, war, love, greed, power, faith, courage, honor, rivalry, revenge are some examples. Krzysztof Kieślowski's *Three Colors: Blue* might be said to have as its theme the concept of *liberty*, while Alfred Hitchcock's *Rear Window* might have *voyeurism* as a theme. One might also consider a combination of such concepts: secrecy and romance, friendship and loyalty, selfishness and cruelty, justice and law. These notions might be thought of as too general, too obvious to help the director in the fashioning of their film, however. They serve the purposes of academic study, perhaps, while affording minimal insight into the creative processes of filmmaking, tending to close down rather than open up a question. Certainly the director should be aware of such broad concepts running through their film's story, but the insight they need in order to understand the truth at its heart might be better served by a phrase or sentence conveying a universal truth, one that crosses geographical, cultural, and ethnic boundaries and traverses any line of division constructed between one human being and another. This might be understood to correlate with what Egri sees in his book as a *premise*, his commonplace, if arguably simplistic "Poverty leads to crime" a case in point.

Theme in dramatic narrative might be more effectively expressed in terms of *conflicting* concepts such as *crime* vs. *justice*, *individual* vs. *community*, *revenge* vs. *mercy*, *love* vs. *hate*, although again this might seem somewhat general from the perspective of the director setting out to understand their screenplay in ways that will inform their craft. What it does, though, is provide a broad sense of the nature of a film's underlying thematic conflict, an insight that invites representation in the movie's visual discourse and the contrasts it incorporates whether through imagery, location and production design, costume, lighting, casting, sound (which pertains to "the screen of the mind" and can therefore be construed as a visual resource), or other elements of craft. In Hitchcock's classic spy thriller and romance *Notorious* such broad conflict might be described as *espionage* vs. *romance, dissimulation* vs. *honesty, or manipulation* vs. *intimacy*—contrasts manifested as much within the shifting power play of protagonists Devlin and Alicia as between the two strands of the film's narrative: their journey as lovers from suppressed sexual attraction to emotional intimacy and their journey as secret agents seeking to uncover a Nazi conspiracy. When Devlin first rescues Alicia, giving her a pick-me-up to help her overcome a hangover, Hitchcock shows him, as he approaches her, from her point of view so that, as he towers over her, he's shown upside down. Devlin's motives at this point are far from kind; he's dissembling, in the process of recruiting Alicia for a mission that may place her in lethal peril—so the skewed angle transpires to have been appropriate. At the end of the film there's a scene that mirrors this, when Devlin again rescues Alicia, on this occasion saving her life. As this later scene echoes the first, so its staging reflects the earlier blocking, but on this occasion, as Devlin approaches the prone Alicia, she's suffering from the effects not of alcohol but of a poison administered by antagonist Alex Sebastian. Now Devlin's motives are unimpeachable—he's no longer acting as an agent but as lover. As he approaches Alicia, the director chooses *not* to upend him. He remains as upright as his intentions. Romance wins out over deception, at least in the *story*. In the *plot*, on the other hand, it's the deception inherent in espionage that triumphs. Although the opposites are mutually exclusive, the film seems to be saying that both are necessary. Irreconcilable opposites provide the foundation of drama, so the lack of easy answers, of any readily *definable* message, renders a film less a vehicle for moral instruction and more a vision of the human condition. Most importantly, it makes it all the more compelling.

There can be more than one set of thematic opposites in a film, and another in *Notorious* is *love for the parent* vs. *love for the lover*. The former loses validity and function, the latter gains in both. For the male, so the film suggests, mothers such as Alex Sebastian's become encumbrances, entrapping their sons, whereas, through romance, sweethearts such as Alicia promise maturity. The thematic concern here is universal, not only to much of this director's work (think of the mother and son in *Psycho*), but also to life in general, not only from Hitchcock's male perspective—love for parents generally superseded at some point or points by love for a partner. In scenes between Alex and his mother, production design, shot composition, and framing are *increasingly* employed to entrap the hapless Nazi son. The director traps the lovers cinematically too, but finally releases them while shutting the door on Alex.

Another way of positing theme is to think of it as *issue*: ethnic oppression, the dangers of social media, corruption in politics, the "War on Drugs," and other contemporary concerns—although, as with Egri's abstract noun, this fails to get at a story's core, the heart of meaning that nourishes narrative and drama.

More useful for the director is to have insight into theme in yet a further sense: the combination of thematic opposites to yield the single truth of a *contradiction* or *paradox*:

> In vulnerability lies strength (Barry Jenkins' *Moonlight*)
> Love will tear us apart (Derek Cianfrance's *Blue Valentine*)
> The identity that affords us life, kills us (Darren Aronofsky's *The Wrestler*)

The previous chapter on premise raised the notion of the question a film asks not of the protagonist but of the audience. This might be called the *thematic question*, and relates to this idea of thematic conflict or paradox. "Do we find meaning in life through duty or transgression?" might be a theme in *Breaking Bad*. "Do we find freedom through our relationships or ourselves?" is perhaps the quandary posited by *American Honey*. A film does not need to give an answer to the thematic question. Indeed, it should avoid solutions, leaving the audience to ponder. The best films, like the best novels or short stories, live on in this way, their narratives, characters, events, images, and questions capable of haunting for a lifetime.

Just as a theme of this nature may surprise the viewer or audience when it reveals itself, it may have surprised the writer when they discovered it in their story. Perhaps the director was the writer, and was surprised to discover it after they had been writing for a while. Often, because the subconscious plays a fundamental part in the creative process, the most powerful themes are found as the writing of a story develops. Starting work on a story with a clear theme in mind can lead to an overly schematic and didactic film. When the director "meets" the screenplay, they should beware of any narrative erected on the foundations of philosophical or political certainty or noble intention. Story is sovereign. It needs to talk back to the filmmaker with its own sense of theme as it talks back through its characters and their actions. If it surprises a screenwriter, or a director, when it emerges, the chances are a theme will surprise an audience.

Thinking back to Sophocles' *Oedipus Rex*, theme might also be considered as a *warning*. Unlike a moral, such an admonition is not so much didactic as chilling. One might see the ambiguous and shocking ending of Lee Chang-dong's *Burning* as one such example. Take this path of obsession and look where it will lead you! The emotional experience of engaging with the film lends the warning a force that a simple caution would lack, the result for the audience being somehow both chastening and gratifying at one and the same time.

A theme can, and maybe should, be encapsulated in a final image. A crucifix in the palm of the hand of the protagonist, a Jesuit missionary in seventeenth-century Japan, at the end of Martin Scorsese's *Silence* expresses the idea that meaning in its cosmic sense can be *grasped* only personally—an exquisite paradox. Marion Crane's car pulled from a muddy swamp at the end of Hitchcock's *Psycho* perfectly articulates the notion of a chilling truth emerging from the mess of the psyche. (See chapter 15.)

There is yet a further consideration, and it's one to challenge these suppositions. Just as a film may convey emotions hard to articulate in words, so its theme may be difficult to define. If a theme can be written as a sentence, why make a movie in order to express it? Some directors, moreover, might be afraid that in attempting to articulate their theme they may kill their film. If it's a thematic obsession that drives their career and they come to realize what that is, they may fear that their output will wane. It may indeed be that the most powerful motivation for some filmmakers, many great ones among them, is the need to find out *why* they need to make their film. (See chapter 18.) They may never entirely understand the evasive thematic question, and might prefer not to. This approach might be construed as an "anything goes" abdication of the storyteller's duty to tell their story well, but it need not be—the director may come to know that their story works as it is and cannot work in any other way, follow any other path, or culminate in any other ending. They may not understand its meaning on a conscious level, but they nevertheless know that it works. What, after all, are the precise meanings of Homer's *Odyssey* or Shakespeare's *Hamlet*? And if epic poems and stage plays that work so formidably can achieve such longevity without definable meanings, why not films or TV shows? What do Terrence Malick's *Tree of Life*, both existential epic and family drama, or David Lynch's neo-noir *Mulholland Drive* mean? What are the thematic questions they pose? One might suggest resistance vs. acceptance in the face of nature's randomness for the Malick maybe, or glamour's promise vs. toxic decay for the Lynch, yet would either of those directors wish to reduce their movies to such ready encapsulations, to a single sentence, to a couple of abstract nouns, a single one? For these filmmakers, to misquote the words of sixties cultural commentator Marshall McLuhan, it is the mystery that is the message. And how can one articulate a mystery except through a poem, a story, or a film? The Italian novelist Italo Calvino said that the greatest stories were the folk tales and myths passed down through generations, each generation of storytellers excising what wasn't working in the story while keeping what was. The result of this revision over centuries is a story that works in and of itself. It isn't that the theme grows clearer, it's that the mystery and power of the story become unassailable.

Should there be obvious thematic elements in a screenplay, the director has to understand them, however. The director should ensure that all elements of their movie, its narrative, drama, visual discourse, and imagery, serve to reveal that theme. If it's hard to pin down, the director needs to acknowledge that also, and embrace the mystery. Should the story seem strong and work on its own terms, and the director know they have to make their film, a thematic core may become apparent in the making of the movie. Some filmmakers may need a clear sense of theme, some may eschew it—what counts is what works for the individual screenplay and the individual director. Ludwig Wittgenstein wrote that "Whereof we cannot speak we must remain silent." Perhaps he was wrong. Perhaps whereof we cannot speak we must tell a story.

4 Genre

What, exactly, is meant by the word *genre*? In film, TV, and fiction, genre is usually thought of as referring to various types of predominantly commercial storytelling—thrillers for example, horror, crime, spy movies and novels. In this context the word suggests a story that takes place in a world of heightened reality and often at some level of fantasy, even complete fantasy—the science fantasy genre of the *Star Wars* saga is a case in point. In such realms the world of the film tends to have its own rules, codes, and logic, either devised by the writer or inherited from previous movies and novels of similar type. The film follows certain narrative conventions, fulfills particular expectations, utilizes recognizable tropes, and perhaps embraces a level of "action" and violence above and beyond what one would generally encounter in everyday life (at least in relatively stable societies) or in other kinds of story. Such mayhem is used for the purposes of entertainment—the word *thriller* itself suggests visceral, sexual, and adrenal gratification, afforded by mortal danger, cruelty, and lethal violence. Not all genre is geared to such thrills, however, and examples of genre in this first sense (Genre 1, the main sense in which the term is used) cover a broad range, including buddy movies and romantic comedies (romcoms) as well as westerns, heist movies, noirs, and neo-noirs with their more "muscular" material.

The term genre can be used in a general sense too (Genre 2). Its origin, the Latin *genus*, meant *gender, descendancy, kind, sort, class* (The Latin Dictionary). In this sense genre can be seen as a means of categorizing *any* and *all* films, not only those among the Genre 1 classification but social realist movies and everyday dramas also, as well as any considered *sui generis* (of their own genre or kind)—for example, Apichatpong Weerasethakul's *Uncle Boonmee Who Can Recall His Past Lives*, a *metaphysical drama* perhaps.

The Merriam-Webster Dictionary defines genre as "a category of artistic, musical, or literary composition characterized by a particular *style, form,* or *content.*" All films adopt a *style*, whether they are "stylish" or not, whether that style is intentional or not. Ken Loach's *Kes*, Richard Linklater's *Boyhood*, or Andrea Arnold's *American Honey* (like *Wasp*, her aforementioned vignette of the everyday struggle of a single mother) may appear to eschew expressionist conventions of lighting, camera angle, and performance often embraced in Genre 1. They remain couched in their filmmakers' distinctive visions of reality and its representation, however, with styles derived from documentary, Italian neo-realism, and French cinéma vérité. "The art that conceals art" might be a useful description of such approaches. Such films also have *forms* to which their style relates. *Kes* is structured around the relationship protagonist Billy Caspar develops with his falcon. *Boyhood* follows central character Mason Evans Jr. through key periods when his circumstances change—the film is structured around these. *American Honey* follows protagonist Star through a series of episodes on the road trip she takes with a group of outcasts. The *content* of *Kes* and *American Honey* might be described as everyday life plus something extraordinary—a Yorkshire schoolboy and a falcon, a road trip and a gang of petty criminals. Linklater's film, meanwhile, relies on elements of a young life over several years to which many in the audience might relate—a *slice of life* movie in a sense (as well as a *coming of age*).

(*Kes* and *Boyhood* are *coming of age* films too, also known as *Bildungsromane*, while *American Honey* is at once a *coming of age*, a *romance*, and a *road movie*—its episodic form is characteristic of the latter genre. Given the love of Billy for his falcon, *Kes* might also be considered a romance—see the note on multiple genres at the end of this chapter.)

But isn't all of this, one might ask, merely academic, a tool for the critic, the teacher, the marketer, no more than a simple and quick way to define what type of film a film is? If it's relevant to filmmakers in any way whatsoever, isn't it simply a matter of them ticking off one genre or another before moving on to more important creative and practical issues? The answer to this is that a director's understanding of the genre, or more probably, the *genres*, of their film, is of critical importance to all aspects of its execution. The director should have a strong sense of where their movie stands within the complex spectrum of genre—in the Genre 1 sense certainly, and if not within that arena then in the broader sense of Genre 2—because the genre or genres of a movie will have a profound impact on its style, narrative, and tonal coherence, and on its very identity. Genre might be thought of as the coat a film wears, its human truth donning a particular outfit for a particular occasion. In that sense, the nature of a film's genre will have impacts on the following areas.

Expectations

These form what might be thought of as a central facet of the *contract* the director draws up with the audience. Expectations of either escapism or gritty realism, the nature of the film's conflicts, of the restrained or graphic presentation of sex and/or violence, of their inclusion or exclusion, of justice or injustice are all dependent on the genre of a film. A single murder in an intimate drama of family relationships will prompt a profoundly different reaction in an audience from the lavish carnage in a James Bond movie and will need to be presented in a different manner—the killing witnessed in Alfonso Cuarón's *Roma* is a powerful example, which, presented to the back of the shot, comes across as sudden, arbitrary, and harrowing. A filmmaker might choose to subversively represent a murder in a thriller style in an otherwise realistic movie, or naturalistically in a thriller (as in the brutally protracted slaying in Alfred Hitchcock's *Torn Curtain*), but this would tend to suggest a *meta* approach, a critical and moral comment on the audience's engagement with screen violence—as in the complex and transgressive films of Michael Haneke, a filmmaker who uses depictions of violence to critique depictions of violence—his *Funny Games* is perhaps the definitive example.

The intended audience

A strong sense of genre prompts a strong sense of the movie's audience. This is not to suggest that the director pander to any particular socio-economic group, more that an awareness of the nature of the audience their film addresses is important—a good storyteller surely takes note of to whom they are telling their story. Paul Feig's romcom *Bridesmaids* and Michael Haneke's historical, social, and family drama *The White Ribbon*, for example, although both considered fine films by many, hardly anticipate the same audience. The calculation might be seen as a cynical bid to play to the tastes and demands of one particular group, but genres incorporate their own cultures and play their own *cultural games*. Audiences attend movies or watch TV seasons expecting those games to be played—the trials and tribulations of the outsider cop, the struggle of the superhero with a human flaw, the female assassin in a male world. These may be carried through to the gratification of the audience or may be subverted to the approving delight of some members and displeasure of others, but when such a game is ignored, or has not been fully grasped by the director, the result can be disorientating and alienating for the audience.

Suspension of disbelief

The credibility of the events, characters, conflicts, and drama of a story rests in large part on its genre foundations, on the world in which it takes place, and on the spectrum of its moral universe. Expectations and acceptance of the nature of scenarios in a superhero movie and of those in a gangster movie are different (although physical confrontation will doubtless play a part). In one the suspension of disbelief is greater than in the other. In both it's greater than what an audience will be prepared to accept in an everyday domestic drama. Plausibility in film and TV is not an absolute but varies according to the degree of realism. A character in an action movie might jump off a roof with impunity. One in a more naturalistic drama would break a leg and be ambulanced to ER. The extremity of a story's events too is modulated according to genre. The family of Mike Leigh's *Another Year* undergo credible although deeply affecting travails far less sensational than the vicissitudes encountered by the hapless household in his admirer Ari Aster's horror genre *Hereditary*. Here the audience is presented with occurrences altogether more drastic but which, in the context of Aster's sure-footed navigation of genre (the film is also a family tragedy), its audience is powerless to dismiss as implausible.

A movie's genre or genres give it authority, providing a cultural provenance to validate the events of its narrative. Like the soccer field for soccer or a baseball field for baseball, genre establishes the playing field for a movie. But if the story needs to be plausible within the confines of its genre(s), its logic still needs to be plausible, within its framework, to an audience—Genre 1 does not offer carte blanche for lack of narrative logic.

The depiction of events

When a jeep runs over a landmine in Anthony Minghella's *The English Patient*, the audience witnesses the result from the same distance as Juliette Binoche's Hana. The heart of the drama, emotional rather than explosive, lies not with the destruction of the jeep, nor with its unfortunate occupants, but within her. If this were an action movie, such an event might be seen from much closer, would be covered from many angles, shown perhaps partly in slow motion and cut with gusto. When an SUV comes to grief in Ryan Coogler's *Black Panther* the event is shown from dynamic angles, the duration of the action expanded, its energy and danger manifested in the thrilling proximity to the violence and in the director's control of the dynamic energy both within the frame and in the editing. In other words, a sense of genre helps the filmmaker establish the locus and nature of their movie's drama, its style and its discourse—the staging, size, and placement of elements in the frame, how it is cut, and how its sound design is modulated. This has an impact on the requisite filmmaking, of course. In superhero or action movies, dynamic incidents, which can be thought of as *set-pieces*, will need intricate storyboarding, use more camera set-ups, employ more crew, take more time to shoot, involve more post-production processes and be very much more expensive than the moments of personal cataclysm in less hyper-realistic films. Even the latter, however, may warrant meticulous planning and storyboarding; the incident in *The English Patient* required a second, expendable jeep, tracks along which to pull it (it had no engine), dummy occupants, an explosive charge, a special effects crew, two cameras—one in the truck with Binoche, one by the roadside—and many hours to set up and shoot.

In this respect, and in relation to the later topic of how genre might inform cinematography, one might consider three types of camera:

the *observing* camera
the *complicit* camera
the *critical* camera

Is the audience invited to watch, participate in, or reflect in a way the characters do not, upon the action? In the above example of *The English Patient*, it watches (then feels along with Hana), in an action sequence in an action movie, with a dynamic moving camera, or in a moving POV shot, it might be said to participate in the scene; and at the end of a film such as *The Irishman*, with the senescent Frank Sheeran seen alone through a door that's been left ajar, it's placement and framing might be seen as a sobering comment on the tragedy of his soul, not moralizing but revealing.

Tropes and conventions

The amnesia of a central character, an example of a trope, is a common go-to of thrillers, a device to prompt the unraveling of backstory (The *Bourne* franchise, TV's *Homecoming*, from Sam Esmail), while in a realistic drama such a condition might evoke more painful emotions. Genre 1 tends to play knowing games with an audience familiar with its conventions and traditions—the bad guy who does bad things to worse guys (trope) in order to rescue a child (trope) and discovers a corrupt politician (trope) and in killing him comes to an unexpected realization (trope), in Lynne Ramsay's *You Were Never Really Here*, are examples. (No amount of directing mastery on Ramsay's part can disguise her derivative material, so ossified in genre convention it defies subversion.) Validity in such cases is predicated not so much on lifelike behavior in any usual sense but on a marriage of artifice, transgression, and expectation, or, in the case of the romcom genre, for example, on rituals of courtship informed by the caprices of the lovers combined with the audience's desire to see the forging of a satisfactory bond by the movie's end. Films need to engage their audiences, but whereas some embrace accepted methodologies to do so—at their worst merely regurgitating, at their best constantly and ingeniously reinventing and reworking them—others seek to hold theirs by forging new paths, telling stories that captivate on their own terms, whether through the truthfulness of their humanity and evoked world (Abderrahmane Sissako's *Timbuktu*, set in a Mali beset by extremist Islamists) or by their heretical insights (Yorgos Lanthimos' *The Lobster*, a black comedy set in an absurdist dystopia). Some (Ari Aster's *Hereditary*, both family drama and horror movie) do both. The director should know which approach their movie needs to take, whether they are playing a game and if so which game, so they might modulate their craft and filmic language accordingly.

Directors of note are worth considering in this respect: Kubrick, whose films can appear almost aggressively naive or indifferent as to the conventions of their respective genres; Tarantino, who is the knowing opposite; and Polanski, who perhaps steers a path in between.

Moral universe

This is often authorized by the "coat" of genre. The variance from the norms of daily life in a gangster or spy movie will be greater, for example, than that of a romcom or most buddy movies. (For a more detailed consideration of this aspect, see chapter 6.)

Characters

Coming of age films tend to involve mentor or parental characters, movies set in worlds of organized crime will invariably involve bosses, other characters who step outside enforced codes, and crooked lawyers, while spy movies often make use of a fiendish antagonist, a treacherous secret agent, and a romantic partner for the protagonist. Romcoms self-evidently require a pair of lovers. A specific genre, in others words, often utilizes specific character types and a specific character configuration.

The journey of the protagonist

Then there is the question of victory or defeat, triumph or tragedy in the film insofar as this pertains to the path the protagonist takes. In Genre 1, should the hero always win, or are there times when they might not? Should they even survive or not? In a noir or neo-noir, a protagonist often fails, or at least succeeds in attaining their objective only at great cost, or evil may triumph. In Clint Eastwood's *Mystic River*, to take one chilling example, justice is not done, and iniquity carries the day.

What kind of hero might there be in a movie not in the Genre 1 category? Can such a film have a hero? If so, is the nature of their heroism determined by the film's genre? The protagonist James Gillespie in Lynne Ramsay's *Ratcatcher* follows what might be regarded as a "hero's journey" when he takes a bus out to the fields of wheat beyond the city limits of a grim, oppressive Glasgow, and later when he immerses himself in the waters of a canal at the very spot where his friend had drowned, where he failed to raise the alarm. He's a vulnerable, frightened boy, not an action hero or warrior, yet his journey encompasses a sequence of escape and personal restoration along with atonement and redemption.

There are, it's often posited, archetypes of narrative that underlie all stories. This may be true, but the director nevertheless needs to recognize the relationship between the genre(s) of their film and the nature and dramatic terrain of the journey taken by its protagonist.

Casting

The genre of a film can affect its casting profoundly. Apart from the fact that a low-budget indie, taking place in an "everyday" setting among "everyday" people, is unlikely to be able to bear the costs of a star, such a known actor, with their charisma and "baggage" from a prominent career, can undermine the credibility of the film's world and milieu. (Michael Fassbender in Andrea Arnold's *Fish Tank* and Shia LaBeouf in the same director's *American Honey* offer notable exceptions.) If, moreover, such a star has acted in Genre 1, there might also be, in the minds of the audience, the memory of more sensational goings-on that could diminish a movie's less heightened drama. It may well be that casting a star will help raise much needed finance for a low-budget film, but a director should beware of the impact this can have. One star in a movie that uses non-professional child actors can undercut the freshness of the entire work if their more schooled performance is not carefully pitched. Casting unknowns in the major roles of a commercial genre piece with its familiar elements of plot and character could well prove equally unwise—a known star gives a certain perspective to the heightened nature of action and violence, rendering it as entertainment, safely unreal and "distanced" rather than as some unbearably grim trauma. On the other hand, a star known for playing heroes or villains might, when playing against type, invest a character with significance an audience might not otherwise initially register.

Performance

This is to a great extent linked to casting—when a director casts an actor, they may well be casting a performance—but is not quite the same. A skilled star or actor might be capable of giving a heightened performance, one more naturalistic, or something positioned elsewhere within that complex spectrum, while a non-actor will rarely have the skills to offer such a range. (In Dexter Fletcher's *Rocketman*, for example, Taron Egerton gives a central performance in tune with an exaggerated register appropriate to this musical bio-pic, with director, actor, approach, and material at one. Adam Driver in Jim Jarmusch's *Paterson*, by contrast, offers understated poignancy completely in harmony with his director's masterly vision of dramatic pitch and visual style.) Although eliciting seemingly spontaneous performance is the aim of most directors across all genres, there exists a contrast between the accomplished artifice and knowingness of actors in movies such as *Mission Impossible*, *Fast and Furious*, or *Harry Potter* and the apparent and invariably deadpan naturalism of the acting in a film such as Lynne Ramsay's *Ratcatcher*, set in a deprived working-class Glasgow, or Nadine Labaki's *Capernaum*, which follows the story of a Syrian refugee boy living in the slums of Beirut.

When it comes to understanding how the genre of a film can determine the nature of performance, the director would be well advised to be apprised of the various schools of acting. Method and Meisner, for example, draw on inner resources on the part of the actor that can nourish the emotional depth of a drama of social and psychological realism, but clash with the filmic discourse of a movie of the Genre 1 kind. Hitchcock struggled to manage Paul Newman in his spy thriller *Torn Curtain*, demanding from the actor a neutrality of performance that would not interfere with the director's exacting cinematic language. On the other hand, it could be argued that, since genre might be understood as a "coat" for a story, there needs to be a truth at the heart of performances within the Genre 1 context that will resonate with the emotions of the audience, even if it is not itself largely comprised of action heroes, intrepid warriors, or hired assassins.

The demands of comedy bring other factors to bear on the pitch and nature of performance. The broad comedy of the Farrelly Brothers' *Dumb and Dumber* sees Jim Carrey in full comedic throttle and in command of every purposefully exaggerated expression and gesture, while an actor as nuanced throughout his career as Jeff Daniels revels in the amplified palette of comic performance. Jacques Tati in his *Monsieur Hulot's Holiday* or *Mon Oncle* provides another example of comedic virtuosity, his acting as precise in its restricted emotional and psychological dimension as it is broad in its clownish absurdity. Whereas other performances in his films reflect this central artifice also, other comedies, less broad maybe, might incorporate secondary performances flatter and less caricatured in nature—the straight characters who function as foils to the leading comic. In a dark comedy such as Bong Joon-ho's *Parasite*, on the other hand, performances are geared to emphasize the traits of the characters, whether this be ruthless opportunism, sheer malevolence, or witless gullibility.

Conflict, friction, tension

Is the conflict of the film simply between the good characters and the bad? Is it *Manichaean* (good vs. evil) or are its moral polarities less comfortably defined? Is there ambiguity in the moral merits of the opposing forces? Is it physical or is it psychological? Generational or cultural? Territorial or emotional, or both? (It had better become emotional in all cases.) Is it to be resolved by combat or by more subtle means, by strategy or by guile? By realization and understanding even? Or is it never to be resolved? Is the conflict purely external or is there an internal struggle within the protagonist's heart and soul? Is the conflict rooted in the vulnerabilities of the characters or in their strengths? In their emotional needs or in their professional, social, or romantic obligations and imperatives? Is it manifested by action, by combat, sword fights or gunfights, or are its maneuvers more subdued, dramatized through subtext, looks, emotional, and psychological subterfuge?

Note: another useful word in this respect is *friction*. Less suggestive of direct confrontation than *conflict*, *friction* describes conflict under the surface, the incompatible differences and mutually exclusive needs, wants, and objectives of the characters that give rise to the *anticipation* of conflict, with the resulting *suspense* a major contributor to a story's *tension*. (In suspense genre movies such as *Rear Window* and *North by Northwest*, Alfred Hitchcock proved himself a master of friction without action—although he never balked at the dynamics of physical drama when the call came.)

Pitch, register, tenor

As with conflict, a sense of genre is key to the modulation of these elements. High-energy car chases in action movies would seem out of place in an intimate, domestic drama, while the primordial terrors of a slasher movie would be incongruous in a social realist "issue" drama—although Luis Buñuel's magnificent, gritty *Los olvidados* (so much more than social realism, admittedly) contains what is surely one of the most terrifying nightmare sequences ever, a mesmerizing study in primal dread worthy of any horror film. There is also the consideration of the ratio of the emotions experienced by characters up on the screen and those undergone by the audience. Melodrama, in its worst sense, suggests material in which the emotions of a film or novel are more heightened than those an audience or reader feels in response. When, on the other hand, a character on screen is attempting to repress or deny intense pain, and when consequently that pain has no release, audience members might themselves have trouble containing their feelings. This also begs the question as to whether the pain might be physical or emotional. What, to come to the point, are the stakes? Does the film deal with life or death literally or metaphorically? Is survival the challenge? Is finding or affirming identity? Is it pride that's under threat? Is the sense of personal meaning in peril? (See the case study of *Contrapelo*.) And does the film shout or does it whisper? If it shouts, does it leave echoes in its wake? (Paulo Sorrentino's *The Great Beauty*—a male life-crisis movie, like Fellini's *8½*). If it whispers, does it grip? (Lucrecia Martel's *Zama*—a historical drama, also a life-crisis movie.)

Tonality

The degree to which an audience might be expected to empathize with the characters on screen or that to which it might find itself distanced or at odds can be dependent on a film's genre. Stanley Kubrick's *Barry Lyndon* is a period movie, a historical drama, but it's also an example of what in literary terms is described as the *picaresque*, a story of a ne'er-do-well character drifting or machinating their way through life, often with dubious moral integrity. The film exudes irony, dry and droll wit with the inimitable virtuosity of its filmmaker. Invariably the tone runs counter to the emotions of the characters, often seeming to mock their predicament, a stratagem founded both in the voice and vision of Kubrick and in the nature of the picaresque novel as a genre in itself—Thackeray's original *The Luck of Barry Lyndon*, as well as his *Vanity Fair*, are cases in point. A self-aware thriller might also make use of knowing irony; James Bond's mordant wit comes to mind, for example, in the way a quip from him might render the violent dispatch of a bad guy an entertaining interlude. Or, in other espionage movies, emotion may be deliberately understated, as in various adaptations of John Le Carré's novels in which the inner pain of a protagonist is muted by their involvement in seemingly inescapable *Realpolitik*. A spy movie with factual roots, such as Steven Spielberg's *Bridge of Spies*, might offer a similarly deadpan approach.

From restraint to exaggeration and on to the point of archness, where does the movie's tonality sit and how does that mesh with its genre? A family drama (of sorts) such as Hirokazu Kore-eda's *Shoplifters* delivers its emotional punch wrapped in a warm and compassionate tonality, whereas Lars von Trier's *Melancholia*, part family drama, part sci-fi, part *sui generis*, brings more chilling currency.

A director's voice, evident or barely discernible, also comes into play, although that director needs a clear sense of the genre in which they are working. (See chapter 7.)

Pay-offs, closed and open endings

The genre of the film will suggest the nature of its pay-offs—the consequences or outcomes of incidents and questions occurring as the story develops—and whether these should be unnecessary or obligatory. In a film or TV show in the Genre 1 category, an audience might be frustrated if expected pay-offs never materialize. In a whodunit, clues lead to explanations: the mud on the shoe connects to the muddy location of a murder, or the oil on the driveway connects to the leak from a particular car. The director needs to make such details crystal clear, making sure they "mark" them—both the initial "question" (what does this mean?) and the eventual answer (oh, it means this!)—using clear, unambiguous compositions and shots. Vagueness is unhelpful, an obstacle to the audience's understanding of the story. Obscuring the information, so that only the most perceptive member of the audience spots it, is a dereliction of the director's duty as regards the communication of necessary information. In a film or TV show not within the Genre 1 category, such as a drama of family life or social interaction, such details may not be clues that lead to answers but features of the lives of the characters, elements in the fabric of their lives to enrich the authority of the movie's world.

Generally speaking, the most important pay-off is the ending. Is this closed or open? Does it answer every question? Resolve every conflict? Settle every issue? Or are matters, at least some of them, left without conclusion? What is it in these respects that the genre of the film demands? Which imperatives can be subverted? Which outcomes will satisfy the audience's expectations, which would frustrate or disappoint them? What is true to the film and what might be a wrong move?

A superhero movie or any movie that's part of a franchise might leave a thread unresolved in order to seed a sequel. A TV season might offer an open ending as a conduit into a following season, a means by which the story can continue and a teaser for its fans. A post-modern detective movie, for quite different reasons, might allow the criminal to escape justice yet promise no follow-up (David Fincher's *Zodiac*), or the drama of a missing child might, without explanation, allow the child to remain missing (Andrey Zvyagintsev's *Loveless*). Dramas outside the canons of Genre 1 might be less likely to organize plot and resolution mechanically, denying their audience the satisfactions of neatness and solution. Questions will be left unanswered. A set-up may lead to little or no development. A thread may tease but find only an oblique pay-off that works emotionally, perhaps, rather than through the ingenuity of a plot twist. Indeed, an excessively rigorous observation of the demands of plot might undermine the authority of such a movie, rendering its dramatic and narrative construction too obvious for the representation of what it proclaims as reality. (Perhaps Asghar Farhadi's *Everybody Knows* is less successful than his *A Separation*, *About Ellie*, or *The Salesman* for that very reason.) (See chapter 16.)

Production design

As with other members of their creative team, the director needs to make clear to their production designer the genre(s) of their film. Locations, sets, and set dressing are integral in establishing its world and instrumental in setting tone and atmosphere. A world needs to ring true within the film's particular genre(s), and consideration should be given as to how this might this be conceived along the axis of reality and heightened reality or fantasy. Should the filmmakers go for locations or sets? Might the former bring a greater sense of realism, even if the latter, more controllable, more amenable to camera placement, movement, and lighting, can bring greater ease of shooting? How will the genre affect the level and nature of any preparatory research into the physical world and setting of a film? How much research is needed, and what will be its nature? A historical maritime drama such as Peter Weir's *Master and Commander* would have required entirely different research and implementation of such research from that of a fantasy swashbuckler movie such as Gore Verbinski's *Pirates of the Caribbean*.

An interesting example of how production design is related to genre can be seen in the work of Dante Ferretti in Martin Scorsese's *Gangs of New York*. The film is an epic historical drama, a chronicle of New York City at a particular period in its history, but is a revenge thriller too and also the myth of a son and his two fathers. (Amsterdam has a blood father, Priest

Vallon, and an adoptive second father, Vallon's killer, Bill the Butcher.) It is this mythical element which is incorporated into Ferretti's designs of both "The Old Brewery" with its subterranean and labyrinthine caves, and the floors and boldly conceived open-plan rooms of its teeming tenement, and "Satan's Circus," the twisted roots of a tree snaking down around its bar to intimate the realm of fairy tale. The reconstructions of the Manhattan streets where the draft riots later take place are, by contrast, meticulously researched replicas of the originals, perfectly creating the world of *Gangs* as historical drama. Lucrecia Martel's *Zama* includes a similar differentiation in the work of its production designer, Renata Pinheiro, when, in the second part of the film, a party of soldiers is set upon by natives who take them into an undefined, hellish place of punishment. Historicity is abruptly abandoned in favor of a timeless Hades, apocalyptic and nightmarish, that severs protagonist Don Diego de Zama from the colonialist trappings that have constrained his life—although not in the manner he's been seeking—as what has thus far been a period drama becomes what might be interpreted as the allegory of the collapse of an entire culture.

Such instances of sure-footed correlation between a film's navigation of genre and its modulation of production design offer useful guidelines to the director and production designer as they embark on the vital understanding and execution required to control the connective tissue of a movie or TV show.

Note: while it's important not to let the vital constraint of budget shut down creative imagination, it's only realistic to acknowledge that historical dramas invariably make more of an imposition on financial resources, while thrillers and action movies are going to invite greater demands on locations and incur higher production design costs than modest domestic and social dramas. *Ratcatcher*, even with its delightful mouse-on-the-moon sequence, was never going to require the expense of Kathryn Bigelow's *Zero Dark Thirty* with its global setting. On the other hand, *Zama*, with its modest budget of $3.5 million, handles its eighteenth-century world with adroit and productive economy, while Steven Spielberg's historical epic *Lincoln*, with a budget of $65 million, realizes an astounding canvas that money alone could not buy without the skills of production designer Rick Carter. In both cases the directors were keenly aware of their film's genre, and the scale that dictated, and made use of their resources accordingly. The imagination costs nothing, while the limitations of budget are not necessarily drawbacks, but can be a catalyst for the creative process.

Cinematography

As with production design, genre gives context to the approach of the director and cinematographer. Perhaps this will adhere to what might be expected. Perhaps it will run counter to previous strategies. Perhaps it will fall somewhere in between or draw on conventions from different, even dissonant genres that are in some way relevant. But whether heightened or more naturalistic, the nature and texture of the image on screen should be informed, one way or another, by precedent or by the reworking and reinvention of a film's genre conventions. Mise-en-scène, lensing and depth of field, saturation or desaturation, and camera placement, angle, and movement need careful deliberation within this context. Perhaps the most fundamental consideration is the difference between comedy and drama. The mantra once commonly stated, that the cinematography of comedy should be bright and white, whereas drama should utilize contrast, no longer seems to hold sway. The masterly comedy of Jacques Tati, his *Mon Oncle*, demonstrates precisely that aesthetic, but then so does Roman Polanski's *Chinatown*, not by any stretch of the imagination a comedy, but a neo-noir, yet one frequently bathed in the harsh light of Los Angeles rather than portrayed through the contrast common to its predecessors. Paul Feig's *Bridesmaids*, broad in its comedy meanwhile, seems hardly brighter or whiter than many dramas. A similar wisdom of contrary style was once deemed important in the *lensing* of comedy and drama, the former given to the use of wider-angle lenses that yield greater depth of field, the latter to the neutral or tighter lenses that narrow it. True of *Mon Oncle* maybe, but also true of much of Stanley Kubrick's work, his horror masterpiece *The Shining* a case in point, every focal plane laced with terror.

At this point it's worth considering the assumed imperatives of Genre 1, in which the heightening of reality generally correlates with the lighting employed, and the contrast and saturation of the image. Directors and cinematographers of superhero and action movies ramp up their approach to intensify the pitch of their films and invest their worlds with a visual artifice above and beyond the flatness of "reality." Movies in other genres also achieve this—Chan-wook Park's existential thriller *Oldboy*, for example, brings rich saturation and bravura lighting to its filmic palette. A more realistic film such as the Dardenne Brothers' *The Kid with a Bike*, on the other hand, an intimate, all too credible story of a young boy's rejection by his father, embraces a flatter, more neutral approach, the measure of its cinematography tied closely to the everyday nature of its drama.

One example of how an individual director might adopt contrary approaches to lighting in movies of essentially the same genre can be seen in Ari Aster's horror duet *Hereditary* and *Midsommar*. In the former film, the shadows fall on the outside—the world of the Graham family, the rooms of its house cloaked in darkness and much of the action taking place at night. In the latter, the conventions of horror are subverted, and the world of the Hårga, the ancestral cult in Sweden visited by a group of young Americans, is bathed in an unsettling perpetual light. The shadows here, dark as any, remain, by contrast to the earlier film's, firmly on the *inside*, psychological and figurative rather than visual. (It's worth noting that there's a precedent in the absence of literal darkness in Carl Dreyer's 1932 *Vampyr*, although here the quality of the light is altogether softer—lambent rather than fierce.)

Yet just as *Gangs of New York* and *Zama* follow a close correspondence between genre and production design, so *Midsommar* demonstrates a transition from the tenebrous menace of its urban prologue to the unmerciful effulgence of its rural rituals.

Sound design

The genre(s) of a film presents a major factor in decisions as to how exaggerated, how naturalistic, how complex, or how simple its sound design should be. An action movie replete with car chases and crashes, explosions, and mayhem in general is going to require more extensive and expensive sound design to match its abundance of hyper-dramatic incident, and to achieve the physical and visceral impact such a genre promises. Horror or ghost stories also require a calculated and intricate approach, the creaking floorboard, the groaning hinge, the hiss of a draft to rustle the curtains are all coinage in the currency of sound in the genre, heightening an audience's sensory awareness and thus rendering it more susceptible to "jump scares" and *frissons* in general. But less sensational genres also bring their own demands in terms of sound. In any movie, sound design is an essential resource in creating the texture of verisimilitude of its world. Traffic, planes, the trundling of carts, the clip-clop of hooves, a distant steam locomotive, a police siren can create the subliminal sense of a particular time and place, but there is more to consider. A sound evokes an image that appears on the screen of the mind. This may be an image of an object, a character, an action, a windswept landscape, or whatever. This image may in turn prompt a further image. The squeal of brakes will conjure the image of a vehicle braking, but, if the audience knows a child is present, that sound will conjure the image of the child being knocked down. This relates to the nature of a movie's genre, which can help determine what is seen and what only heard. An audience seeking high-energy entertainment will feel cheated if spectacle is denied them in favor of auditory information, just as only the distant glimpse of a jeep exploding would disappoint it. On the other hand, an audience engaged in intensely intimate drama will usually be disorientated by spectacular displays of mayhem. When, in Krzysztof Kieślowski's *Three Colors: Blue*, the audience, knowing a little girl is a passenger, hears a car crash, it envisages—for a fleeting instant before rejecting the picture, which is too distressing—her fate. Not seeing the car crash into a tree makes the image of it all the more powerful, an image on the screen of the mind. In other instances, a sound might be connected with a particular image and then used later to create that image in the minds of the audience without the director having to show it again, a potent effect in the creation of suspense or under-the-skin horror—Charlie's *tock* sound does exactly this in *Hereditary*. In short, the auditory becomes visual. (Whereas the visual somehow fails to become the auditory—the silent *image* of a steam locomotive comes across as strangely lacking and dead, failing to prompt any sound in the mind, but the *sound* of one prompts a mental image. There never was a "silent cinema," only one without a sound track and accompanied in its place by live musicians playing music, mimetic of sound and rhythm absent from the film itself.)

Sound design can also be used to create mood and tone subliminally. The sound of children playing or birds singing, to give two obvious examples, although so distant that an audience may barely register them, may in some contexts create an air of well-being, joy even, although in other contexts they might layer a moment with threat. Sirens, bells, wind, the cawing of crows, the shriek of seagulls, jackhammers, and train whistles, along with so many more elements, can be used to calculated effect even in the most apparently naturalistic of genres to enrich and intensify the engagement of the audience. They can also be used to convey specific messages that drive narrative and tone. Alfred Hitchcock was a past-master of this technique—listen to the train whistles beckoning a journey early in *Notorious*, when the momentum of the thriller needs to pick up speed, or the sinister rumblings of the subway in *The Wrong Man* that imply dark and unseen depths in a character accused of armed robbery. In neither case is the audience aware of how its thoughts and emotions are being directed, its manipulation all the more effective as a result.

A further consideration for the director, one that to an extent depends on the genre(s) of their film, is whether a sound should be heard by its audience as if in the third person or perceived through the conduit of one particular character, the protagonist or a secondary character who is the focus of a scene. (This relates to the topic of the narrative point of view—see chapter 11.)

Music

Genre is a crucial consideration when a director is determining their approach to the music in their film. For movies of the Genre 1 category, scored music, generally the norm, is often a major resource in conveying tone and emotion, working closely with image to heighten the experience of the audience. Composers such as John Williams, Hans Zimmer, Alexandre Desplat, and others contribute considerably to the power of commercial movies. At its best, the grandeur of a score can raise the epic canvas of a film, heightening emotion and immersing the audience in its drama. At its worst it can work as a kind of insurance policy, attempting to bolster moments lacking in true emotion. It might also prove unnecessary, the emotion already present being in no need of reinforcement, so that the resulting redundancy diffuses its impact rather than enhancing it. Most superhero movies, though, most science fantasies such as the *Star Wars* installments, most franchise thrillers or spy movies, and most horror movies or romcoms would nevertheless seem inconceivable without a musical score. The level of artifice this brings correlates with the heightened reality and visceral palette of many

Genre 1 films. The tone, mood, and emotion of the music most often mirror what's happening on the screen, and the audience will be unaware of it as a separate element. Such scores frequently work within the nineteenth-century orchestral tradition, emphasizing middle registers, filling out all registers, as they leave no stone unturned in the delivery of emotion. Their effect may be sweeping, or it may result in auditory overkill.

A film may employ an original score, may make use of source (readily existing) music, may include only diagetic music (music deriving from within the world of the film itself and heard by the characters as well as by the audience, as in Alfonso Cuarón's *Roma*), or may exclude music altogether. Where a genre tends towards naturalism, an original score needs to be handled with care. Musical accompaniment can undermine the intimate scale of a domestic drama, suggest emotional safety, lead to sentimentalism (false emotion), or render the drama overblown. Source music, on the other hand, can be particularly effective—the opening bars of Beethoven's *Adagio un poco mosso* from his Piano Concerto No. 5, Op. 73, which repeat at moments during the Dardenne Brothers' *The Kid with a Bike*, pack a potent emotional punch derived in part from their repetition but also from the dissonance of music and world, the cultural counterpoint of music of one period and social class with what the audience expects to hear from the world of the characters. Working in the opposite direction, Sophia Coppola begins her historical drama *Marie Antoinette* with the UK's post-punk Gang of Four's *Natural's Not in It*, mixing as the film progresses songs of related bands with more apposite eighteenth-century works by Rameau, Scarlatti, and Vivaldi. In much the same manner, an original score might be conceived with incongruity in mind. Martin Scorsese, in his *Gangs of New York*, for example, has composer Howard Shore do exactly that. Although set in 1846, the opening battle scene is accompanied by an altogether modern score, while elsewhere in the film, which takes place in the early 1860s, blues harmonica is used, in a story taking place decades before it existed.

Thus music, source music especially, can also be employed to counterpoint emotion and tone, yielding irony, critical comment, or ambiguity of meaning, and the director should consider how far a film's genre determines whether their choices should run in tandem with the emotions of the characters and events depicted, or run counter, subverting the mood of their world. In Stanley Kubrick's war movie *Full Metal Jacket*, for example, a scene in which weary and wounded soldiers are lying down resting is accompanied by Sam the Sham and the Pharaoh's *Woolly Bully*, the uneasy languor of the scenario at odds with the song's celebratory urgency. In Quentin Tarantino's heist and crime movie *Reservoir Dogs*, the bouncy *Stuck in the Middle with You* by Stealer's Wheel plays while a criminal severs the ear of a hostage cop. In *Zama*, Lucrecia Martel makes use of source music from the 1950s Brazilian guitar duo Los Indios Tabajares, the dissonance between the smooth tunefulness and rhythms of such strains and the marginalized discomfort of the listless Don Diego de Zama serving to emphasize his alienation while tempting the audience to dance. In TV's period gangster series *Peaky Blinders*, punk guitar, bass, and drums accompany the beaten-down milieu of post-World War One Birmingham, proclaiming the show's contemporary sensibility, rather than its period credentials.

Such bravura use of music is a mark of the "Indie" too, and of genres allowing for a directorial voice more evident than might be the case in less personalized mainstream vehicles. Here the music has a subversive connection to the narrative that's skewed according to the director's attitude to their material and is intended to be noticed by the audience as a comment that throws the narrative into a new light. One might say it has a "distancing effect," affording the audience an objective perspective while at the same time immersing them in the richness the movie offers. In most mainstream movies, on the other hand, the music is to be accepted as part and parcel of the drama being presented, in perennially effective fashion.

The use of a score in TV shows requires consideration above and beyond the manner in which music works in movies. The unifying themes of the show build in tonal and emotional resonance as a season progresses, gaining cumulative power and shifts of meaning that their counterparts in even a long movie rarely achieve. Integral to the viewer's delight in returning to a show, they require diligent application. Whether pertinent or dissonant to a show's subject matter and genre, themes and stings require the potential to express the range of contrasting emotions and tones a long-running show will employ in order to sustain its narrative.

Note on multiple genres

Two questions:

> Can a film combine more than a single genre?
>
> Are single-genre films possible anymore?

Just as the classical tragedy of Ancient Greece has no precise parallel today, genre is rarely the absolute it may have been decades ago. Quentin Tarantino, in an opening class for AFI Conservatory in 2017, commented that noir no longer exists in its pure form. His insight is well taken. We are too aware, too knowing, too versed in the conventions of what were once individual genres to cleave to purity. There has been an osmosis or cross-pollination of genre through the decades that has led to what might be described as *hybrid genre*. Alongside this evolution has developed *meta genre* and a post-modern self-awareness giving a charge to movies such as Charlie Kaufmann's *Adaptation*. Westerns, for example, went through a process of reinvention in the late seventies en route to their current self-aware manifestation. Contemporary culture, being post-modern, meta-modern, is perhaps too knowing for the innocence of Genre 1 in its pure sense, too interconnected for its former simplicity. The constant reworking and cross-referencing between one genre and another, the accumulation of referential baggage and the sense of a culture in a state of radical shift through each decade since the early 1900s—when genres in cinema were born kicking and screaming but vibrant and universal in their themes and emotions—renders attempts at movies of a single genre now often more a form of living archaeology than living art, a phenomenon perhaps best described by the term *retro genre*. (Maybe in an age of multiple platforms cinema itself can no longer exist in its purest manifestation. It cannot be created, cannot be shown, without its makers' and audiences' awareness of other visual media.)

Another term introduced over recent years is *elevated genre*. This seems to refer to some extra level of sophistication, intelligence, or self-awareness being applied to what was once regarded as the standard fare of entertainment. Jordan Peele's *Get Out*, an example, melds horror with the issue of racism. Ryan Coogler's *Black Panther* is both superhero and black consciousness movie. An example of historical drama combined with fantasy is Guillermo del Toro's *Pan's Labyrinth*. *Genre bending* is another term used to describe films with such self-aware approaches.

In order to understand the nature and potential of their film, the director would be advised to list the possible genre categories into which it might fall, be influenced by, or touch upon, whether centrally or tangentially. This comprehensive list can then be applied to all of this chapter's categories in order to determine the most effective approach to each.

Note: the director should on occasions be prepared to name one genre only. Many studio executives favor the single-genre approach as being preferable from a marketing perspective, but they have a point as regards story also—the screenplay that jumps genres simply because a writer has not found any other way of moving the story on, fails. Hybrid genre should not be seen as an excuse for inconsistency.

5 World/setting

Because the physical and cultural settings of a film interact (the latter is discussed in the next chapter), the director needs to grasp the implications of both fully. In respect of the former, they should understand what the screenplay reveals of the following:

1. The period in which the story takes place (also related to its cultural setting).
2. The nature of its world(s)—general/specific locale, geography, and terrain, urban or rural, or both, its constructed environment, its architecture, the degree and configuration of its density of settlement, its living conditions, its ratio of interior and exterior locations.
3. The climate, weather, seasons, and conditions, the light, heat, or cold (pertinent to the ease or difficulty of everyday life).
4. The manifestation of "the four elements": earth, air, fire, water. (See the opening sequence of Fellini's 8½—smoke emitted from a car's dashboard: fire, clouds in the sky: air, the sea: water, a sandy beach: earth).

The director should understand how the screenwriter has incorporated these many aspects into their narrative, and, should they be not merely a backdrop to the action, what their effects on the story and characters might be. Do they complement the drama (a romance in idyllic surroundings) or do they counter, perhaps subvert them (a romance in a brutal prison)? Then, in working with the production designer—who will bring informed insights—the director needs to understand what the setting (particularly if constructed) says about the lifestyle of the characters. What does a moated castle suggest? What does a decrepit row house suggest? A pristine state-of-the-art office? A coffee shop on a busy city thoroughfare? A Victorian city hall? A shantytown on a hillside? The detail of a particular character's life and their backstory can be visually and economically communicated through the physical world also, through the nature and state of the environment and the articles that fill or do not fill it, pictures or photographs, objects necessary to life, objects unnecessary. A child's bedroom replete with their artwork. The interior of a Manhattan apartment crammed with gold fittings. Such specific detail will be described in the proficient screenplay, a pointer to further work to be undertaken in the production of the film. So much of character and story can be revealed through the detail of the physical world, and the director needs to work closely with the production designer to ensure the coherence of understanding and vision that facilitates this economical but powerful element of visual storytelling. Founded in the specific detail the screenplay may suggest, this is a resource to inform and deepen the audience's sense of a character's emotional journey.

Screenwriters, what's more, may employ a physical setting as an element integral to the core of the narrative. The nature of a physical world may embody a *thematic* dimension, a deep connection to what the story is about— and when this occurs, the visual and the dramaturgical come together in cinematic unity. During the pre-production of *The English Patient*, writer-director Anthony Minghella posited the story's desert landscape as a visual metaphor. The true map of the world that the film's story reveals, he said, is the map not of nations but of humanity, so he thought there should be moments in the film when the desert resembles the human body, when it might even be mistaken as such. The opening of the movie presents that very concept (reinforced by the painted human figure of the opening titles), the camera high above a desert vista as it tracks over its rolling dunes. With nothing to give context, either to the nature of the image or its scale, there is visual ambiguity until the shadow of a plane appears (even that at first resembles the human form), followed by the plane itself, glinting in the sun as it flies below the camera. The audience might see the terrain as desert or as human flesh, as vast or intimate. Thus the theme of the film is encapsulated in a single shot while at the same time one of its two worlds—the other is rural Tuscany—is deftly established.

Settings may also echo stages in the emotional journey of a character. In Lynne Ramsay's *Ratcatcher*, the rundown streets of working-class Glasgow present an oppressive setting that gives visual force to James' emotional entrapment. The field of wheat he discovers after he's taken a bus out of the city to a housing estate seemingly abandoned mid-construction (a symbol of lost hope?), in which he rolls around gleefully, provides a powerful visual contrast to the streets of his home and marks a crucial step along his journey towards a degree of self-understanding. In Lucrecia Martel's *Zama*, the setting of the seashore at the film's opening, the claustrophobia of the interiors in which Don Diego lives and works, the open spaces seen in the story's second section, and the strange hell into which the protagonist and his companions are taken by their indigenous captors each encapsulate a stage of his emotional journey—his longing to return home, his desperation in the face of the lack of that possibility, his temporary sense of freedom, and the hell of his soul, ever incapable of self-awareness.

Apart from the essence of aspects of narrative and character that a physical setting can embody, the nature of an environment also brings important *practical* considerations to filmmaking craft. A rural, exterior world will render smooth camera movement less convenient than might be the case in an urban, interior world (just as it might leave the film's characters less mobile—making one's way through a tropical forest will take more time than walking along a street). Confined spaces will not prove so conducive to shooting as larger spaces—small rooms make it harder to get wider shots without resorting to wide-angle lenses, the problem being that this tends to make spaces appear bigger than they actually are. It can be easier to shoot in a more capacious location or set which, through the use of neutral or tighter lenses, can be made to look smaller than more constrained spaces.

If the world can have an impact on the telling of the story, the story and its telling can equally have an impact on the world, and not only in the obvious manner—gladiators need a coliseum, ghosts need a house to haunt—but in relation to some of the practical requirements to be considered in respect of the design of the sets or the selection of locations. There's frequently a sense of staging intrinsic in a scene on the page, of the positions of the characters in relation to each other, as well as clear indications of their movements and interaction. The flow of action in a scene or sequence can thus determine the nature and configuration of the sets or locations needed in order to accommodate it. There may be other ways of blocking a scene in order to achieve the screenwriter's intentions, however, so when a location is found that presents other merits, whether authenticity, aesthetic value, proximity to another essential location, or simple availability, there can sometimes be a different approach to be found in order to make the story of the scene work.

The scope and scale of the world of a movie or TV show will obviously have a crucial bearing on its costs and schedule. Expansive locations, sets, lots require greater production design effort, materials, and labor, more extras to populate the vistas (who need more costuming and feeding), more set PAs and assistant directors, while shots will take longer to set up and retake. Digital post-production has over the last two or three decades made ambitious visions easier to realize, and worlds once impossible to create are now within ready reach, but even here the expense can be considerable. The budget of a period film such as *Zama* was, however, a relatively modest $3.5 million—the physical scale of the film contained while its creative vision of a doomed colonialism generates a huge resonance; an intimate narrative can be vast in its implications while an epic might not always bear sweeping implications. Then again, it might—Martin Scorsese's *Gangs of New York*, with its meticulous, extensive, and largely actual (rather than virtual) recreation of mid-nineteenth-century Manhattan, offers an epic physical environment that mirrors its mythic dimensions and epic themes—another example of how world and setting can be integral to story and drama. (From Fritz Lang's dystopian *Metropolis* to Ridley Scott's *Blade Runner* with Lawrence Paul's futuristic and potently oneiric Los Angeles, from the *Harry Potter* films to the *Lord of the Rings* movies, sci-fi and fantasy make similarly daunting demands on budget and inventiveness.)

Note: screenplays are exercises in economy of writing. The director should research thoroughly the world and setting of the film. The screenwriter has probably carried out more research than is evident, or they should have, and it behooves the director, whenever possible, to discuss this with them as well as conducting their own research while working in tandem with the production designer.

6 Cultural, social, and moral canvas

Closely connected with the physical and geographical setting of a film, and with its period, is its cultural environment, its *human* universe in all of the social, political, economic, religious, and moral aspects this includes—the rules, codes, imperatives, lifestyles, and activities that form the foundational factors and context for story, character, and the register and stakes of the drama. Thus the director needs to understand and incorporate in their approach what the screenwriter has constructed (or perhaps has failed to) with regard to this.

Social milieu and rules

Is the movie's milieu at one with the larger society or is it a group within this or outside of it? Is it based on shared ethnicity, nationality, commerce, culture, or religion, or what? Is it old, deep-rooted? Is it new, not yet settled? Is the society/community/group stable or unstable, set in its ways or in a state of flux, and how aware of its condition is it? What are its attitudes to love, violence, death, guilt, pride, shame, identity, gender, intimacy, sex, privacy, space, and territory? What are its prevalent threats, fears, conflicts, contradictions, strengths, and weaknesses? What generational tensions might there be? What degree of friction is there between individual and family, individual and community, tribe and other tribes, one gender and another? What are the governing ideas and concepts that determine day-to-day behavior and common assumptions? Is the society portrayed based on one in the contemporary world or one in the past, or is it invented, maybe within the realm of fantasy? If invented, does it have predecessors in its genre or others to which it might be related? If invented, are its rules clear? Do they follow a logic the audience will understand? Even in more naturalistic movies, the rules of the society may need to be made clear, especially when there are two sets, one in conflict with the other. In Ken Loach's *I, Daniel Blake*, for example, set in the contemporary northeast of England, the doctor of the unemployed eponymous protagonist forbids him from taking certain jobs on the basis of his medical condition, while the bureaucracy of the UK's welfare state demands that he remain flexible in his search for work.

Economics

How is this regarded? How much are the characters' actions determined by economic factors? How much by other considerations? How easy or difficult is it to obtain money and property? What is the degree of wealth or poverty? How "old" is the money or how "new"? What are the attitudes to money in terms of hoarding or spending? Is it used for good or for evil? Is it respected or not, resented or enjoyed? How stable is the economic framework? How unstable?

Status

On what criteria is status based? Wealth? Power? Achievement? Celebrity? Gender? Ancestry? Physical attractiveness? Physical prowess? Education? (Formal or "street"?) Courage? Duty? Transgression? Tradition? Wisdom? Guile? Providence? Ability? Sex? Brute force? Participation? Intellect? Charisma?

Morality

What are the factors that determine the morality of the characters and how does this compare with the moral preconceptions of the audience? What are the taboos, what are the transgressions? (The word *mafia* cannot be spoken, a character says the word *mafia*.) Is the moral validity of an action judged on its face, on its context within an accepted social/ethical framework, or on its consequences and effectiveness? What is the value given to principle and what to expediency? What is the dramatic potential for the disparity between the socially accepted or imposed morality and that which the protagonist, in the course of their journey through the screenplay, discovers for themself? What is the moral conflict in the story and what are the moral choices the character faces? Is this conflict simply between good and evil? Or maybe between morality and *a*morality, or between two positions, each compromised, so that victory for either comes at a moral cost? How much is the audience put in the narrative point of view (NPOV) of characters with whom they share ethical preconceptions? Is it put in the NPOV of a protagonist whose precepts are *not* its own and, if so, what impact will this have on its relationship with that character? How far does the genre determine the moral terrain of the screenplay? Is there a moral "surprise"? (Paul Thomas Anderson's revelation of mutual abuse as a form of love in his fashion designer drama *Phantom Thread*, for example). Does the screenplay use its moral canvas to proselytize or to explore? Is it judgmental or does it tell its story without prejudice?

The moral universe of a film, intractably connected to its genre, also provides context for the nature and plausibility of its events, veering from what might be generally accepted in daily life to more extreme compasses. Superheroes kill, soldiers kill, hitmen or hitwomen kill, although all perpetrate their slaughter, in fiction at least, according to codes that audiences to some extent come to accept. The more transgressive the moral universe, the more likely it is to be found in Genre 1, although that is not always true by any means—László Nemes' *Son of Saul*, set in a concentration camp, its hapless protagonist forced to drag away the bodies of the innocent multitudes the Nazis have murdered, could hardly be construed purely as a vehicle for entertainment. A thoughtful and harrowing evocation of one man's nightmare, the film uses its 4 × 3 aspect ratio to encapsulate the protagonist's attempt to shut out the moral entropy in which he finds himself. Extreme moral universes, what's more, can be socialized arenas—the internecine transactions of Francis Ford Coppola's *The Godfather* reflect those of the organized criminality on which it is based, revealing in turn the dark side of "The American Dream" and "American Family Values." Thus it works as a gangster or crime movie, but also as both a family and a social drama, and a national epic. Another Genre 1 type of film noted for the unsettling ethics of its worlds and characters is noir (or its contemporary manifestation, neo-noir), which originated in a forties America of disintegrating moral certainty and was defined and named soon after by French film critics. A playground for the "shadow" described by psychologist Carl Jung, and, depending on one's view, either a celebration of cynicism or a quest for humanity in an imperfect and cruel world, noir and neo-noir (the latter a term used liberally and hard to define with precision) take the moral cosmos of film to the dark side.

Meaning

What is it that gives *a sense of meaning* to the characters, and what is the sense of meaning the protagonist or any other character gains in the course of the film? Is this derived from the milieu or is it personal, rooted in character? Is it reassuring ("we need love") or less comfortable ("we need danger")? Is meaning founded in *a sense of identity*? If so, does the protagonist find a new sense of this at the end of the story? Do some characters need a sense of meaning that offers little palpable reward, while for others expediency, success, and power are life's sole benchmarks? How much is honor a factor? How much duty? How much tradition? How much hope? How integral is a sense of meaning to sustenance? What is the balance between meaning and death? Is life more important than meaning or is meaning more important than life?

The journeys of morality and meaning in a story, intrinsically linked as they are, and their place against the context of the broader cultural and social canvas, are founded in the decisions and actions the characters take. When that backdrop itself shifts, the moral (or amoral) agency of the protagonist is highlighted—the collapse of systems of operational and moral rules in the face of shifting circumstances and growing forces of antagonism provides a potent mechanism for dramatic narrative. In Hirokazu Koreeda's *Shoplifters*, the moral rule, a variation of "honor among thieves," presented by Osamu, the leader of the movie's gang (or family), is that only goods not yet sold should be stolen as supposedly they do not belong to anyone—a claim to a measure of integrity in a predicament of moral compromise dictated by the family's situation. Later in the film, it is Osamu himself who, through force of circumstance, breaks his own maxim as, in a bid for survival, he sacrifices the very sense of meaning that's sustained him by stealing from a parked car. In Andrea Arnold's *American Honey*, protagonist Star believes initially that the gang of miscreants she's joined makes its living by selling magazine subscriptions door-to-door, only to discover they tell lies to customers to boost their sales. She learns that her boyfriend Jake steals from the houses he visits, and she herself is forced into prostitution in order to survive. Thus, although she's escaped the misery of life as an abused nanny, she finds herself morally compromised by the sub-culture she has entered, its unspoken activities at odds with its declared code. Only through a brief and inconclusive moment of solitude does she finally attain a degree of freedom. The overarching irony of *Breaking Bad* is that Walter White finally admits his motive for taking his criminal path was not after all concern for his wife and son's future, but his own gratification. His moral transgressions, he comes to acknowledge, have given him the agency, the sense of being alive, that his day-to-day existence as a chemistry teacher had failed to provide. It was thrill that was driving each increment of his downward moral gradient, not duty.

The cultural world of a film also informs that film's discourse, speaking to its style and language. The oft declared duality of "style and substance" (or "form and content") is no duality at all but a misunderstanding of the word *style*, which need not mean a merely cosmetic veneer but may rather denote a means of discourse to be drawn, one way or another, in concert with or counter to *substance*. The period in which a story is set, for example, will have consequences for the style of the movie, the aesthetic of its cinematography, and the approach of the production designer and on performance, editing, and music. The look of the film might be influenced by the aesthetics of the time or it might adopt the cultural counterpoint of more contemporary modes, but with no awareness of those original aesthetics the director is at a disadvantage and their movie or TV show will miss out on a rich dimension of visual language and address. While Lanthimos' *The Favourite*, to take one example, in its style eschews the classicism and formality of its

England's eighteenth-century Augustan period, the film embraces the irreverence of its contemporary satire, a sensibility illustrated by the cartoons and paintings of Thomas Hogarth. Although Hogarth flourished slightly later, the grotesquery of his work might easily have been a reference for the visual mischief of Lanthimos' cinematographer Robbie Ryan, whose use of wide and fish-eye lenses isolates the movie's lonely characters in vast, distorted spaces as disrespectful to the period's architecture as Lanthimos and his screenplay by Deborah Davis and Tony McNamara are to its rigid social order. (This approach might usefully be termed *subversive style*.)

In Kubrick's *Barry Lyndon*, set also in the eighteenth century a few decades later, the director adopts by contrast a more formal style, one that corresponds to the contemporary sensibility. The work of cinematographer John Alcott is famous for his use of candles to light scenes set in a time when candles were of course the only means of illumination—a scrupulous observance of historical accuracy and an instance of the unity of style and substance. In Kubrick's *2001* also, the cold precision of cinematographer Geoffrey Unsworth's work provides the perfect counterpart to the impersonal culture of its sci-fi futurist world. (These approaches might be termed *complementary style*.)

How far the editing of the film mirrors what one understands as the rhythm and pace of the time is also a consideration. The subtext of a scene may flow faster than its culturally imposed surface. The tension may be more drawn out than the freneticism of its world. The emotions may be more jagged than any ostensible decorum, or the tone more downbeat than the brightness of the characters. On the other hand, a degree of adherence to the "straightjacket," so to speak, of a cultural environment might, by force for irony, heighten conflict and emotion. Should actors deliver performances appropriate to the period, maybe stilted and unnatural in some cases, or should they be contemporary and spontaneous? Terrence Malick has been criticized for according the characters of his *The Thin Red Line* diction quite unlike that employed by soldiers fighting at Guadalcanal in World War Two. Why though? The language Malick gives his characters is consistent—it isn't that he's introduced some incongruous idiom through ignorance or carelessness. In any case, why should filmmakers be bound by the shackles of literalism? Is any film, any fiction, literal truth? How much, then, should the filmmaking craft of a period movie or TV show strive to work like "living history," attempting to recreate as faithfully as possible what is known of the time, and how much should it acknowledge the artifice of period drama and go with that instead? The same questions can be applied to any cultural canvas. In the context of a staid and static cultural environment, should the director eschew camera movement? In the context of a shifting culture, should the camera be equally fluid? Might the architecture of an urban world determine the geometry of shot composition? Might the irregularity of a rural setting suggest less stringent approaches? It may be that only the degree of visual sensibility on the part of the director can decide these questions. Just as every film has its tone, however, so every film has its style of discourse. Better the director is aware of that. Better they understand how the cultural canvas of their screenplay is central to both the story of their film and the means by which they might tell it.

7 Tone

When talking about tone one is thinking of the attitude of the filmmaker, whether screenwriter or director, to their material. A tone may echo the world of the film and its atmosphere, its moods, the emotions of its characters, the pitch and stakes of the drama, or it may be at odds with those elements. Tone is not so much rooted in the characters and their predicament as in the screenwriter's and director's disposition towards them, which may or may not be sympathetic. What's more, at any moment there may be a single tone or there may be two dissonant tones. Tones may be heightened or muted. A tone suggests an emotional dimension, although it may equally undercut or suppress emotion. In some ways it can be similar to the voice of a filmmaker and it certainly informs it, but it is not the same thing—*voice* suggests more a perspective on material, a vision of life and humanity particular to the filmmaker. A screenwriter or director might maintain such a perspective throughout their careers but write or direct films of contrasting tones, which in themselves employ tonal shifts. (Voice might also be manifested in a distinctive approach to storytelling—as is the case with Quentin Tarantino and Wes Anderson.) No story can be told without a tone. Even no tone is a tone, deadpan maybe, or matter of fact, but a tone nonetheless.

Some examples of tone might be: tender, angry, warm, cold, comedic, foreboding, poignant, satirical, bitter, heartfelt, callous, suspenseful, dreamlike, mystical, haunting, happy, hectic, serene, frantic, brutal, ominous, sinister, celebratory, bittersweet, deadpan, ironic, bleak, unflinching, trenchant, gentle, lyrical, tense, humorous, harrowing, desperate, melancholy, mysterious, harsh, compassionate, dispassionate, heartbreaking, wistful, dark, light, sadistic, loving, urgent, languorous, mournful, bright, somber, serene, menacing, calm, erotic, paranoid, contemplative, clinical, violent, matter-of-fact, dry, heady, martial, whimsical, breezy, fearful, claustrophobic, ecstatic, nostalgic, playful.

Writers of novels and short stories convey tone both through their material and through their prose. Choice of style and idiom, vocabulary, syntax, rhythm, and punctuation can afford an event a particular tone that may or may not correlate with the emotions or implications of the event itself. The prose may be intricate or it may be terse, dense, or minimal. The discourse of the screenwriter tends to be more restricted. Using simple but deft language, the screenwriter conjures setting, story, and mood with economy. Efficiency is paramount, precision mandatory. Yet within such apparent limitations the language of screenplays proves enormously agile. One word, successive words, pace, style, image upon image, the crispness of description, harmonious elements, dissonant elements, a terse or jagged address, a flowing mellifluous address, choice of idiom, modulation of rhythm and energy can prompt varying and deep tonal resonances for the reader of a script. Many screenwriters think in terms of imagery, and this comes across in writing that becomes a verbal storyboard. (They are after all *screen*writers.) A director should be sensitive to the tones in a screenplay, as they also need to grasp all other elements of dramatic narrative. Much of the tone of a completed film nevertheless depends on the approach of the director. If that director has misunderstood the intentions of the screenwriter there may result a clash of vision. When the intentions of both mesh, however, the craft of the director will be all the more effective.

That said, it should be recognized that filmmaking is an evolutionary process. What works in a screenplay may not work in a film, or may not work as well as what might be discovered in the course of making the film. The opening of the (apparently fourth draft) of the screenplay to *Three Colors: Blue* by Krzysztof Kieślowski and Krzysztof Piesiewicz is largely descriptive, detailing "a crowded motorway. Eight lanes of cars speeding in both directions. The rumble of lorries, roar of engines, drone of motorbikes as they weave their way among the cars. Hell." After a general description of the scene that last word "Hell" indicates the attitude of the writers to the noisy and busy environment they conjure. It's efficient. It's precise. Yet the film itself begins in a very different fashion that rather than conveying a general sense of pandemonium instead evinces an ominous feeling of dangerous isolation, setting the tone for the entire opening sequence, which the lines in the screenplay do not do. (See chapter 14 for a description of the first shot of this film.) The hell of the crowded motorway was nicely evoked in the screenplay but not related to the film's connective tissue. The sense of danger Kieślowski chose by contrast foreshadows the tragedy that begins Julie's story.

The screenplay to Alfonso Cuarón's *Roma*, written by the director, describes graphically the sex in the scene in which Cleo and Fermin make out in the Metropolitan Cinema, Fermin coming across as aggressive in a way he does not in the film itself at this point. Cleo reveals that she is pregnant, and Fermin makes his excuses as the film ends, ostensibly leaving for the restroom but in actual fact fleeing. The tone of the written scene is menacing, which may be powerful in itself but does not serve the storytelling, instead foreshadowing Fermin's betrayal—given his hostility, what else would the audience expect of him? The tone of the scene in the movie is very different. The lovemaking is not graphic and appears more affectionate, so that Fermin's reaction to Cleo's revelation comes across as all the more shocking. What gives the scene its emotional punch, however, and undercuts any potential sentimentality that might suggest warmth in Fermin's character, is the tonal element Cuarón adds. The screenplay does not specify the film playing but, in *Roma* itself, Cuarón opts for a farcical British comedy replete with a ludicrous action sequence. The dissonant tone this introduces to the scene affords the couple's lovemaking an awkwardness entirely appropriate to their doomed relationship, while leaving the audience unprepared for the shock of Fermin's callousness. Tone in the screenplay was set to direct the audience to the end of the scene. Tone in the film *misdirects* the audience so that its end is all the more uncomfortable.

The scene in the film that follows, however, remains largely faithful to the scene as written in the screenplay. A brief vignette of the lonely Cleo walking through the lobby is omitted but then comes the moment when, outside the entrance to the Metropolitan, she sinks to her knees among a bustle of noisy and animated street vendors. The audience feels her devastation all the more keenly because of the contrast between her sudden isolation and the vibrant activity around her. If she were alone in the frame, silent in a surrounding silence, the effect would have less impact. In both screenplay and film, the juxtaposition of opposites—Cleo's personal grief with the lively, unstoppable, and indifferent dailiness of the city—conveys the dissonance of tone within the frame by which Cuarón renders her predicament palpable. (Lulu Wang's *The Farewell* is another film that makes frequent and effective use of such designed tonal dissonance within the frame.)

The first sequence in Ari Aster's screenplay to his *Midsommar* effectively conveys tone by the juxtaposition of image and a voice-over. After a montage of icy forests in low light, together with mournful singing, a phone abruptly rings as the night vista of a large town appears, a contrast but hardly one to render the audience uncomfortable. With the following scene, however, the writer's intention becomes clear. A man and woman in their sixties are asleep in bed as the phone rings and, while they show no signs of response, a woman's voice is heard from the answer phone: "Hey Mom and Dad, it's Dani. Sorry I'm calling so late. I'm just checking in to make sure everyone's okay. I got kind of a scary email from Terri and it sounded like you guys were having some sort of conflict? Anyway, I just got a little worried, so call me when you can, and if there's anything I can do, just please know that I'm here. Okay. All right. I love you." The stillness of the couple and the unease of Dani's voice evince the ominous tone of both screenplay and film, an example of how the screenwriter's storytelling craft can successfully dictate the work of the director. What was clear in the screenplay becomes clear in the film.

Agile dissonance or contrast of tone can also work when scenes of parallel action *alternate* one tone with another—tenderness with violence, for example, as in the opening sequence of Steve McQueen's crime thriller *Widows* in which affectionate amours are interposed with the crescendo of mayhem that follows an armed robbery. The effect is jarring to say the least and a forceful illustration of what the Soviet cinema pioneer Sergei Eisenstein described as a "collision of shots." When screenwriter and director interweave one story strand with another, leaving each thread hanging as they cut back and forth, they create additional suspense, one part of which rests on the audience's need to know what is going to happen next in each story, another on how the two threads will connect, while a third part rests on the dissonance prompted by the contrasting tones of the two narratives. In the case of *Widows* this might be described as tender vs. violent, or tranquil vs. urgent. (The full irony of the *Widows* opening sequence is not appreciated until much later in the film.)

The classic example of this tonal dissonance through juxtaposition is the baptism/murders sequence that comes towards the end of Francis Ford Coppola's *The Godfather*, although it is designed also to link the protagonist to the murders he has ordered as they are carried out—narrative glue as well as tonal dissonance.

When tone in a screenplay is not clear, and when the director has not worked with the screenwriter to make it clear, or not had the opportunity to, time may be lost in the shoot as a result. The famous "Singing in the Rain" scene from the dystopian *A Clockwork Orange* came about, according to Malcolm McDowell—Alex the Droog—in a Q&A at AFI Conservatory in 2005 only after a couple of days of uncertainty on set when the director was uncertain how to make the beating-up of the writer work to appropriate effect. Simple brutality was not enough. The mischievous devilment of Alex and his Droogs that melded violence with playfulness needed to be sustained. When, in a moment of ennui, McDowell began to hum the tune, Kubrick found the solution, a dissonance of tone that has been emulated by many directors since. (Source music can indeed be a powerful means for the director of modulating tone. Lynne Ramsay, Quentin Tarantino, and Martin Scorsese are three examples of filmmakers who use this technique to great effect. Often, it isn't until a scene has been shot and cut, however, that a song can be found that works tonally.)

The modulation of tone on screen is one of the most challenging aspects of the director's craft. They must first be clear as to the intention of the screenwriter, then they need to realize those intentions in their filmmaking while remaining open to the evolutionary nature of the creative process through which better options may become evident, and then, even if they have been successful thus far, they may discover that the reaction of a test audience is very different from what they've been anticipating, so that a scene may need further modulation. Screenplay, shoot, cut, screening—the director's grasp of tone has to be sure-footed at each stage.

As with genre, the sense of tone will have an impact on many elements of filmmaking craft.

Production design

The director's tonal approach can determine the nature of sets and locations, their spaciousness or otherwise, of confined spaces and composite spaces, of landscapes and vistas, the play of light upon and within them, and variations on possible architecture, its materials and state of repair—new, aged, decrepit, imposing, ordinary, distinctive, familiar, different. Colors and hues, compositions and textures can convey tone. How much nature plays a part in a world and how much it is excluded is an important consideration. How much sky is visible and how little. How beautiful the environment is, or how ugly. Much of this will be determined by the story and the world it inhabits, but the *presentation* of the world of a film has an impact on the tone it projects, just as the intended tone of a film needs to inform its production design. As with so many of the elements of connective tissue in filmmaking, the relationship is symbiotic.

Cinematography

If production design, like casting and performance, is intrinsic to the authority of the tone within the film, cinematography, along with sound and editing, is fundamental to how that tone is perceived by the audience. Lighting, framing, camera placement, angle, and movement, lensing, contrast, and the degree of saturation or desaturation of the image are all resources that if used in different combinations can change the tonal message of a scene. Tight lenses, restricted framing, and heavy shadow might, for example, in the expressionist tradition, convey the claustrophobia or menace appropriate to a psychological thriller, whereas filming with a wide-angle lens, generous framing, and an absence of shadow was once the accepted mode for a comedic tone, although in *Midsommar* this becomes a language of horror.

Editing

The frequency of the cuts, the kind of cut—imperceptible, jarring (jump cuts), matched or unmatched cross-cutting—and the motivation for the cuts, perhaps promoted by one character in particular, or to give an increment of information or a revelation, or for reasons of rhythm or pace—will have an impact on the tones communicated to the audience. Also worth considering is whether the cuts should mirror the emotions and actions of the characters and the mood of a scene or run counter as a kind of critical comment tonally at odds with the material.

Sound design

A powerful resource for creating tone subliminally, the background soundscape of a scene, rooted in the film's world but distilled and heightened for particular effect, can give rise to either tonal reinforcement or counterpoint of the tone of the drama itself. This resource is especially helpful to the director since, as with music, it can be added during post-production either as a corrective to material that is not working or as an element of a previously conceived strategy. The emphasis or muting of sounds within action can also dictate tone—footsteps, the rustle of clothes, the ringing of a phone, the movement of a chair, the creak of a hinge, the loudness or quietness of a breath or the hum of light fittings are some examples. Again, much of this is work to be done in post-production, once the detailed journey of tone has been honed and more fully understood.

A final note on overkill

A temptation of the director, in order to ensure that the tone they intend is being conveyed, is to use every resource available—setting, performance, lighting, camera, color, music, editing. Such overkill can result in a redundancy that actually weakens the tone. Contrast, juxtaposition, dissonance—these are the terms the director should keep in mind. They might choose to label some tones as *major key* tones and others as *minor key* tones, the former affirmative, the latter darker and often unsettling. It's vital, on the other hand, that the director does not flinch from the demands of the story. If the tone is angry, bitter, violent, cruel, or harrowing they need to know it and capture it. The director's task is not to make a film with which they feel, or the audience feels, comfortable; their imperative is to make a film that works on its own terms. Audiences rarely forgive kindness a movie does not earn.

8 Structure

To describe the *structure* of a screenplay is to say how it is put together, both in whole and in part, the architectural and the granular. The different sections of a film are usually described as *acts*, after their counterparts in theatre plays. They might equally be called *sections*, but this word lacks the specificity of *act*, which the Shorter Oxford English Dictionary describes as "one of the main divisions of a play" and Merriam-Webster defines as "one of the principal divisions of a theatrical work (such as a play or opera)." The *acts* of a film can be sub-divided into *sequences*, and further into *scenes* (as can the acts of a play), but may also incorporate *montages* or *vignettes*, while such *vignettes* may be the components of a *montage*. A *sequence* might also consist of more than a single narrative thread—usually two—in which *parallel action* plays out, separate elements of story alternating that are connected plot-wise but are perhaps tonally and/or rhythmically dissonant. (A split screen might offer the *simultaneous* telling of two or more such stories, or show the same story told from contrasting points of view, including the angle from a surveillance camera, for example.) One term that might be of value in describing each of these varieties of sections is the *narrative unit*.

So much for the bare bones of *structure* and some terminology useful in considering it. Structure, however, demands more comprehensive anatomical insight on the part of filmmakers—most specifically screenwriters, directors, and editors—the broader picture afforded by the concept deserving more than a mere glossary. Jean-Luc Godard famously said that every film has a beginning, middle, and end, although not necessarily in that order. Krzysztof Kieślowski commented that the beginning should be at the beginning, the middle in the middle, the end at the end. Setting aside Godard's mischievous prestidigitation—wouldn't a middle at the beginning or end become a beginning or end and no longer be a middle?—the opposing views of these two great directors might in part be seen to relate to notions of linear and non-linear storytelling. In the first case the chronological sequence of the events of a story gives rise to the progression of a film's narrative, and therefore its structure. In the second instance it is the *rearrangement* of the sequence of events in the story that forms the progression of the narrative, which follows neither the sequence nor the structure of that story but in its story*telling* takes on its own order and form. (Although any story, or more precisely the raw passage of time that underlies it—its *fabula*, as a narratologist might call it—unless it is told in the entirety of its minutiae and takes the same time in the telling as in its action, will be structurally modulated.) There are indeed films in which the audience is led to believe it's faithfully following the sequence of events in the story only to learn it's been tracing a re-ordered narrative. At this point in the film the members of the audience have to reconstruct the original story in their own minds. (Chapter 1 referred to *Pulp Fiction* and *Memento*.)

Whether the storytelling is linear or non-linear, however, the overarching form championed by mainstream Hollywood, not to mention by many screenwriting teachers, is the *three-act structure*. Some claim this as the essence of, and even the magical key to, the construction and writing of a successful screenplay, an orthodoxy from which screenwriters deviate at their peril, an absolute and the correct way in which screenplay and movie are to be constructed. It is sometimes vested with an arcane air, its precise formulation deemed worthy of years of study, although its founding assumption is hardly complex, reflecting the inescapable beginning, middle, and end.

Broadly speaking, these are its elements. The First Act consists of the *set-up* and *inciting incident* when something changes, goes wrong, and needs to be put right. The Second Act follows the action that results. The Third Act leads to the climax and resolution that yield some manner of restoration of order.

The end of the First Act establishes the beginning of the protagonist's dramatic journey. The end of the Second Act leads ultimately to a nadir in the protagonist's circumstances. In the Third Act the protagonist is forced to take the action that leads to final victory over their circumstances and/or antagonist, or in cases more rare, to their defeat in the face of them.

The three-act structure might be thought of as a baseball diamond (with second base the mid-point of Act Two)—but with one exception: the third base, unlike its baseball counterpart, appears to be not nearer but *further* from the home base than its predecessors, although it transpires that it brings the protagonist *closer* to victory or defeat. The structure can thus also be seen as one of *four acts*, its long middle act divided into two by some event, revelation, or reversal that takes place at its mid-point to boost the energy of the narrative drive by shifting the vector of its story and raising the stakes of the drama.

There are innumerable books and articles on three-act structure, most geared towards teaching the student how to become a true screenwriter by observing the recipe's firm tenets. This book does not pretend to be a manual for the budding screenwriter, and whether the formula is valid or not (surely it's not in all cases), the director needs to understand it should they be making a movie thus constructed, and take a look at its math—as math it is. (Some, fearing once they know this they may never escape its clutches, may prefer to avoid it, although, should they be making a movie constructed in this fashion, this might handicap their approach).

ACT ONE: It is here that the main character/characters (often a single protagonist) is/are introduced and their traits made apparent—although there may be crucial contradictions revealed later. It's in this act that the audience learns of the protagonist's conscious desire and it's here that the central dramatic question is made apparent. The first sentence of the *three-sentence premise* is dramatized here.

ACT TWO: The longest act. The protagonist's actions in the face of the forces of antagonism, and the decisions they have to make, reveal contradictions in their character and point to the unconscious desires motivating them and ultimately leading them to their destiny. (See chapter 10.) The forces of antagonism grow more powerful and are manifested in unexpected ways, while mid-way through there's a reversal of some kind that provides an energy boost to the narrative—a surprising discovery, a reversal of fortune, a shift in the protagonist's understanding of what is going on, of their perspective, a realization of some betrayal, a new force of antagonism and greater jeopardy for the main character, a change in the protagonist's vector of action or a switch in their tactics and in their goal—a turning point, a point of no return, an alteration in the world of the movie, or a combination of two or more of the above. The dramatic stakes are raised and the protagonist is forced to move from reaction to action and to engage with the true or core conflict of the story.

ACT THREE: Often slightly shorter than Act One, this leads, invariably by way of new revelations, to the climax of the film. The stakes are at their highest, the peril at its greatest. The protagonist's inner contradiction, which they've been refusing to recognize until now, is exposed, and the character is forced to know and confront it—either it will defeat them or they will defeat it and in the process gain a new and greater strength through which to vanquish the main force of antagonism. This weakness may be transformed into a strength so that what was a problem in a dysfunctional character becomes a solution in a newly functional one. Then comes the final conflict, related to the theme or thematic question of the film, in which the antagonist is defeated (or wins out). At the very end of the film comes the denouement, the final tying up of loose ends, a completing release of tension, and the beginning of a new status quo based on some new order.

As stated earlier, the French word *dénouement* in fact means an *untying*, and this true translation perhaps points not to those films which come to a stop when they end in the movie theatre, every element put neatly to rest, but to those that continue after, resonating in the hearts and minds of the audience. A way of looking at this is to understand that, although audiences may yearn for a character's victory and its consequent celebration, while fearing their defeat and its resulting disappointment, through the best endings they gain a sense of resonance and meaning that renders either almost irrelevant. It's the paradox inherent in truth that the audience takes away to perplex and haunt it—an *antinomy* to use the precise term for two laws each in themselves reasonable but when seen side by side found to be mutually contradictory. (See chapter 16.)

The danger with three-/four-act structure is that it can hamstring new or less capable writers in the development of their story, that it can become predictable and consequently boring to audiences even if their members are largely unaware of the concept. There are, however, many great films in three (or four) acts. Most "Hollywood" movies have worked this way over the decades—*Rear Window*, one example, its initial act culminating in Mrs. Thorwald's scream of "Don't!," its mid-way point the introduction of Doyle, the detective, and the beginning of its third act Lisa Fremont's delivery of "Jeff's" note to Thorwald. Many films made outside of America, however, and some made inside, do not. Quentin Tarantino, as mentioned above, creates his own structures, organizing his films more like a novelist who utilizes chapters of indeterminate number rather than three acts, his movies usually longer than the 90–120 minute duration favored until recently. Damián Szifron's *Wild Tales*, an anthology of standalone shorts, quite obviously eschews the three-act paradigm, its form as much mischievously moral in construction as it is dramatic.

How do screenwriters and directors work with structure? Structure functions more effectively when evolving *from* story rather than imposing its template *onto* story. When structure becomes paramount, when it becomes a fetish, story serves structure and not the other way around. Films can become dull and predictable as the skeleton predominates over the flesh and blood of character and emotion, causality and drama—as though a clock is being held up to the progression of the narrative. (The strength of so much TV drama over recent years might in substantial part be attributed to its freedom from the structural constraints of so much mainstream cinema.)

It will be useful at this stage, rather than accepting it as a given, to understand where three-act structure with its clearly defined form (and its predominantly individual protagonist who battles against some force of evil) has come from. Screenwriters, like any other artists, do not work in a cultural vacuum, nor do their teachers or mentors. All of us soak in and subsequently project, invariably without reflection, the generally accepted tenets and collective myths of our own communities, societies, and cultures. To ignore the boundaries of this terrain and fail to stand outside them is to blinker us to the fundamental questions and mysteries our particular environments may have buried and to see life solely through the eyes of our specific collective unconscious. The nation pre-eminent in the development of cinema from around 1893 to the present day has been the United States. American cinema grew up as America itself matured and grew into modernity. Nation and art form have thus been inextricably linked, national consciousness, myth, and mindset informing the stories Americans have chosen to tell and the way in which they have chosen to tell them. What then, might be the broad cultural precepts behind American dramaturgy, and what might be the nature of the impact they've had?

There are four predominant areas of American culture that can be seen to have a bearing on the mantra of three-act structure. The first is the importance of structure in a nation founded on eighteenth-century neoclassicism in which the concept was understood as the seminal foundation. As the United States evolved, this central notion of structure yielded the essence of national models: in politics (the checks and balances of executive, legislature, and judiciary—presidency, congress, the courts), in sport (the structured order of play in baseball, basketball, and football), and later in film (the three-act structure). In respect of these domains, the neoclassical eighteenth century lives on in the United States as it does not in the rest of the western world, still less in other parts of the globe where cultures and myths are often more ancient, more deeply rooted, and less readily defined.

The second formative influence that survives in so much of the collective consciousness of the United States is the Manichaean world-view held by the Puritans fleeing persecution in England, a vision of life as a conflict between the forces of good and evil that must result in the defeat of the latter. Such is the central conflict of many American movies. The good guys are good and the bad guys are bad in much of mainstream cinema (not so much maybe in the less morally assured terrain of contemporary TV). This clarity of conflict serves the dynamic of three-act structure and its tussle of good and evil, the latter asserting itself in Act One, the former in increasing danger of defeat at its hands in Act Two, yet, when all seems lost, finally succeeding in winning at the end of Act Three.

The third area of importance is the *individualism* seminal to the American consciousness. The combination of eighteenth-century mercantilism and the nineteenth/early-twentieth-century influx of immigrants fleeing poverty and oppression to strive for a better life the other side of Ellis Island has vested a heroic agency in the individual, whose imperative is to take action and in doing so overcome their adverse circumstances. In movies that utilize the three-act structure, power, for the individual, is there for the taking, while for the universe it is there for the losing. Indeed, it is the individual who *is* the universe.

The fourth area springs also from America's influx of immigrants, a phenomenon occurring alongside the development of *silent* cinema. Early filmmakers were tasked with telling stories that would engage audiences who lived in different communities, spoke different languages, followed different cultural precepts, and worshipped different gods, so they needed to tell those stories in ways that would most effectively reach into the hearts and minds of those diverse audiences. A cinema of image and musical accompaniment was an ideal starting place. Characters, protagonists, heroes, and villains had to be created, genres, forms, and structures developed whose appeal would be universal. The particular belief systems of any individual culture were stripped away so that an *essence* of humanity's collective precepts was left behind, to be incorporated into stories and storytelling—with all their elements, including the most basic structure of beginning, middle, and end—that would connect with any immigrant from any country or background. (As the main period of immigration came to a close and as English became the standard language spoken by everyone, so "talkies" came into being and dialogue made its way into cinema.) So effective were the storytelling crafts that resulted that American movies succeeded in engaging not only audiences from New York to Los Angeles but others the world over. A central element of that universality was, and still is, the three-act structure. What came out of a peculiarly American set of circumstances thus became a global currency—and it became that because it works.

But is it the only currency?

Aside from, and not mutually exclusive of, what is also known as *classical* structure is the imperative that a screenplay should be constructed in such a way as to engender a film that will engage its audience throughout its duration. Through tension, mystery, suspense—"anticipation mixed with uncertainty" (the words of director Alexander Mackendrick)—surprise, action, and story in each section or act, either the audience's engagement needs to deepen and intensify (the movie "grips") or, as in Stanley Kubrick's stately *Barry Lyndon*, for example, it needs to cumulatively lay the foundations for the ultimately emotional reward the film delivers. Thus the concept aired at the beginning of this section, of the *narrative unit*, comes into its own. The director might benefit more from the navigation of these smaller sections and their connectivity, or the grouping of such units without unconditional obeisance to the carapace of three acts—Martin Scorsese has said "A narrative film can be one long take for three hours, you know? It doesn't have to be a conventional beginning, middle, and end." He also asked why the terms first, second, and third act should be used when they come from the theatre and this "belittles the medium."

Indeed, the current flourishing of the TV season is an indication of how flexible structure can be. An eight- or ten-part drama gives the opportunity to explore different narrative threads, to digress (*Breaking Bad's* episode *The Fly* is an example), to peel away layers, to dwell on aspects of character, to play with tone, with expectation, and with a slaloming of story in ways the tighter three-act approach prohibits. It's often commented that the consecutive seasons of a TV show are more like a novel than a movie. Perhaps shows such as *The Sopranos* and *The Wire* marked an escape from that triptych of acts. That said, there has to be a first and last episode, and there have to be episodes in between. A beginning, middle, and end. But isn't this true of anything? Of life itself? We are born. We live. We die. There's no escaping that structure. In the words of the Swiss writer Robert Walser, "There is nothing truly good in this world where something bad hasn't had to have been overcome." Doesn't this, in essence, describe the path of three-act structure? Something bad. The struggle to overcome. Something good (or maybe only understood).

Structure in short films merits its own consideration. There exists a plethora of short-film advice, although much if it, it seems, applies just as much to the feature form. A simple idea, simple story, novel question, and surprising answer are as important as any consideration of abstract structure. This might be almost anything just so long as it works. A short film might work with a three-act structure. It might work with a two-act structure, an act of tension in which the set-up is revealed, and the briefest act of resolution that follows. A middle with no beginning, then an end. One might think of this as a single act, which begins *in medias res*, topped off by a rapid denouement. A short might have what is known as a *joke structure*—a set-up and a pay-off, or, to put it another way, an expectation and a surprise. Directors should be wary of this approach, however. Shorts which involve no more than an informational ploy—a misleading situation ultimately revealing its misdirection—may be popular, but what they are doing is simply describing a circumstance in a deceptive fashion, then revealing this, rather than telling a story. A situation mistakenly interpreted then finally suddenly understood may be an aspect of the storyteller's craft but by itself, without serving a story, is little but a trick.

An example of an excellent short film is Bálint Kenyeres' *Before Dawn*, a simple, structured narrative told in a single shot of stunning virtuosity that remains wide until the end of the film. The short begins as the camera pans over an empty field just before dawn (the Prologue). A truck draws up and two men climb out, waiting a few seconds before people emerge from an adjacent field of wheat. They climb into the back of this truck, which then heads towards the main road. This section could be described as Act One. In Act Two, the truck is stopped by unspecified forces (at the mid-point), has to retreat and returns to the spot at which it took on its load. Its manifest is subsequently arrested in an Act Three that appears to complete the story—but doesn't. It's the final revelation, maybe a *coda*, which brings the film to its conclusion, a solitary man emerging from the field of wheat (a survivor or a betrayer?) after the forces of authority and those it has apprehended have left the scene. *Before Dawn* is a film of a single shot of nine and a half minutes whose structure can be broken into three acts (Act One: Escape; Act Two: Escape thwarted; Act Three: Consequence) plus a preceding Prologue and final Coda, but can also be seen as a sequence of *narrative units*, each a step in the story: 1. An empty landscape—the Prologue shows the status quo. 2. A truck draws up, reverses, and two men climb out—the status quo disrupted. 3. After a brief while, one toots the truck's horn and people emerge from the field to climb aboard—the true meaning of the status quo is revealed. 4. The truck is driven to the main road, then sets off on its journey—a "character" en route to a goal. 5. The truck reverses and heads back into the fields followed by police vehicles—the force of antagonism making its appearance, the conflict introduced. 6. Followed by these adversaries, the truck returns to the spot at which it took on the people—the reversal of the narrative. 7. The people try to escape but the police round them up as a helicopter hovers overhead—disaster! 8. The police take away their captives and the truck—the false denouement. 9. The empty landscape—the return to the status quo, as it was originally understood. 10. A single man emerges from the wheat—the final narrative reversal. 11. The man exits the frame leaving the shot empty—the film ends with the emptiness of its beginning, now a true emptiness and understood as such by the audience.

This incremental or *episodic* approach to structure provides a focus on the connective tissue of cause and effect that the director must understand in order to articulate their plot and tell their story effectively. The director needs to know where the division between each narrative unit and the next falls. They may then punctuate them through a shift of rhythm and pace, mood or tone, energy and movement, light, space, place, or the picking up of some new narrative thread whose connection to the story told thus far is yet to be revealed.

A strong sense of structure provides the director with a *map* of their film, an overview that informs the nature of its filmic discourse and the flow, modulation, and progression of this as its story develops. It is here that the value of the director's engagement with structure lies, rather than in the reassurance that a template might be seen to offer. As the novelist Ursula K. Le Guin wrote: "There are no recipes." True for the novel, not always so true for films, some of which rely on a recipe, but perhaps true for the TV show.

Finally, whatever its format, *story is about myth—not math.*

9 Passage of time

According to Aristotle's *Poetics*, the earliest surviving treatise on dramatic theory, three unities are to be observed in the construction of a tragedy—*time*, *place*, and *action*. Theatre plays may adhere to such decorum successfully. Films, however, rarely do. The passage of time in a film tends to proceed from one selected event to the next, missing out what Hitchcock described as the "dull bits" in between. *Real time*—the uninterrupted flow of the passing minutes throughout an entire film's duration, a movie of two hours in length portraying events lasting two hours in length—is rare. Richard Linklater's *Before* trilogy is a notable exception. In these films there is unity of time and, consequentially, action, their two characters leading the audience from one place to the next as they walk and converse. Stephen Knight's *Locke* clearly demonstrates an Aristotelian unity of time, its story that of a man on the one-and-a-half-hour drive from Birmingham to London while on the phone. Alexander Sokurov's *Russian Ark* and Alejandro Iñárritu's *Birdman* are other significant examples, while Sam Mendes' *1917* consists of a single shot lasting over one hour as (almost) does Bi Gan's *Long Day's Journey into Night*. Some movies, Francis Ford Coppola's crime thriller *The Conversation* for instance, or Alfonso Cuarón's *Children of Men*, may include long scenes in real time that take up a considerable proportion of their duration. Tarantino is an example of a director unafraid of immersing audiences in lengthy scenes staged in one place, eking out suspense and dramatic tension with such aplomb they are helpless in the face of his precise control. Most filmmakers, however, tend to avoid lengthy scenes, opting instead for the narrative energy afforded by the relentless progression of shorter ones.

Considering, managing, modulating, and articulating the passage of time across the duration of a movie is a fundamental aspect of the director's storytelling craft, a task that begins with an understanding of how the screenwriter has incorporated it into their storytelling, both architecturally and in the granular sense. Does the story take place over several hours, a day, a week, or a month, over years, over a lifetime, or even longer? How does this correlate with the pace and rhythm of the film, the journeys of the characters, the ramping up of tension and drama, and the probable acceleration of events as the film nears its end? Are the individual scenes long or short? Does time flow or does it jump forward, even back? Is it, broadly speaking, continuous, or is it fragmentary? Where does it speed up, where does it slow down? How does the duration of the story compare with the duration of the film? How do shifts in the flow of time relate to shifts in the flow of story?

Most films utilize sequences, what might be called *narrative units*, which occur across a span of time and in different places to convey if not a *unity*, then a connectivity, or what director Billie Wilder described as "a clean line of action." Such narrative units are invariably instances of conflict, shift, or change or the rebalancing of power that move the story forward. They may, on the other hand, in the manner of Tarantino's work, slowly and stealthily ramp up tension. Delineated as individual components of the narrative by their function and flow, and particular energy, narrative units need to work both on their own terms and in the context of the film. A montage, for example, might usefully be thought of as a narrative unit, telling a single story or conveying a single idea through a sequence of shots or vignettes occurring at different times in different places. The *grand guignol* bloodbath towards the end of *The Godfather* is an instance of this. The usual form of such a narrative unit, however, is the *scene*. Although editing may truncate the flow of time within a scene (and even within a shot if fragmented by jump-cuts), audiences will usually be largely unaware of this, perceiving the events as passing in *real time* rather than the *compressed time* afforded by editing.

The director should keep in mind Tarkovsky's observation, expressed in his book *Sculpting in Time*, that a film works not so much through the montage of shots, as by shots within which time is seen to pass—an aesthetic that has come into its own since the invention of the steadicam and, with the digital revolution, the increasing portability of cameras along with the technology to conjoin two shots in ways that give the appearance of a single shot. The increasing use of the *sequence shot* and its cutting within the camera, a filmic equivalent of a run-on sentence, has brought units of real time to the fore. (*Real space* need not go hand in hand with *real time*—the re-situating of scenic "flats" during the long take in Martin Scorsese's gangster movie *Goodfellas*, in which Henry Hill takes Karen into the labyrinth that leads to a night club, a moral maze as much as a physical one, created a purely fictional setting. The real time of the shot gives credibility to what in actuality is an impossible route.)

Further consideration of passage of time should be given to the *organization* of time within the narrative. Is the film's storytelling linear or non-linear? If it's non-linear, what is gained and what is lost? Going on a journey with a protagonist in linear fashion may well yield greater emotional involvement on the part of the audience than the more distanced connection that tends to come of non-linear storytelling. In Polanski's *Chinatown* the audience shares in private investigator Jake Gittes' emotional voyage while sharing in his cognitive one. (This is related to narrative point of view—see chapter

11). A non-linear approach, on the other hand, may allow the audience agency in appreciating the narrative by connecting the dots in a storytelling game set up by the screenwriter and director. Tarantino's *Pulp Fiction*, Denis Villeneuve's *Arrival*, Joe Wright's *Atonement*, David Lynch's *Inland Empire*, and Chan-wook Park's *Oldboy* are examples of this. Time may even run backwards—as in Christopher Nolan's *Memento* and David Fincher's *The Curious Case of Benjamin Button*. (A novel in which time moves backwards is the appropriately named *Time's Arrow* by Martin Amis, in which the author reverses morality as well as chronology, with Nazi killers rendered as physicians bringing life into the world rather than ending it.)

Film narrative is capable of contracting, expanding, rearranging, and duplicating or repeating the passage of time through editing. If the screenplay is the initial step in the fabrication of a film's storytelling, and the shooting is the second, editing is the third. Although a story may remain the same throughout these processes, its telling will change and develop, not because the screenwriter has failed in their job, far from it, but because what becomes apparent on set, with actors and camera, and in the cutting room with the palette of options that the footage from the shoot provides, can supersede earlier preconceptions and articulations. It's not that new telling need change the story, but that it may improve it. Filmmaking, like any artistic pursuit, is a process that renders options apparent along the way. Just as a first draft may prompt general story development while a second can offer the writer more specific ways forward, the shooting of a scene can reveal to the director facets of the passing of time not immediately evident in the screenplay, while its editing will further hone its address to the audience. Thus, even if a well-written screenplay can, through the rhythm of its description and specified action, through its idiom, syntax, and punctuation, yield a precise sense of how the passage of time is to be modulated in the film, such modulation will itself be adjusted and refined during the subsequent filmmaking process. Terrence Malick, in his *A Hidden Life*, for example, cuts scenes together from disjointed vignettes, paying little attention to any "realistic" flow of time within a scene, by contrast fragmenting it. Martin Scorsese and his editor Thelma Schoonmaker are filmmakers with consummate skills in the manipulation of the passage of time, articulating it in filmic ways words on the page cannot emulate. A notable example of this is the repeated action employed in *The Wolf of Wall Street*, when the Quaalude-laden Jordan Belfort collapses mid-phone call and his topple is shown from different angles, including that of his own POV, over and again. Traditional wisdom as to repeated action might prohibit such bold discourse. The editing of this scene reveals that, in film, time and story do *not* always need to move on. The scenes that follow provide further cinematic invention, as Belfort's heavily drugged drive home is shown to be accident-free, a trip repeated in a flashback to reveal the multiple collisions inflicted along the way—what appears to be third-person objective storytelling in the first version transpires in the second to have been subjective. Again a passage of time is repeated, again successfully so.

Time may also be repeated within instants of intense action or violence, although the editing will tend to make this invisible to the audience. Were such abrupt moments depicted in real time, they would pass too suddenly for the audience to register them and feel the appropriate visceral and emotional reaction. Cutting together different angles to extend a brief moment allows the audience to register its power—a phrase in a screenplay may become a plethora of shots in the movie.

When time moves on between scenes, as it usually does, the director should ensure that the screenplay isn't using that *ellipsis* to avoid something unpleasant, hard to confront, or inadequately conceived—pain, for example, a shift in a character's outlook (unless that is to be explained later), a hole in the plot, or a scene too difficult for the screenwriter to dramatize or perhaps conceive. On the other hand, the director should beware of permitting the audience to get ahead of the film. A deft leap forward can be invigorating, prompting an alert audience to piece together the intervening action. The passage of time *within the story* and the passage of time *within the film* require separate but symbiotic consideration. It's a fundamental skill of the storyteller to understand when to speed through events, accelerating or slowing down and stretching time, when to elide them—perhaps having a character relate them later or perhaps leaving the audience to deduce what has happened—when to convey them in real or apparently real time, and when to expand, duplicate, or repeat them. With the TV season this can become an elaborate, sometimes labyrinthine process as the writers take the viewer into a maze of multiple narratives, times, and places—the very opposite approach to that of Aristotle's three unities.

One well-used technique in relation to transitions, especially when it comes to breaks between major sections of the story—*act breaks* as they are often described, and often stated in the screenplay—is the caption that states ONE DAY/MONTH/YEAR/FIVE YEARS LATER. This can be a lazy way of storytelling, especially if events within an act seem to have come to a conclusion or run out of dramatic steam, but, should the energy of the story not have died but promised to continue, the technique might be used knowingly and boldly to surprise the audience, pushing the story forward and making it work to catch up. In Richard Linklater's *Boyhood*, by contrast, the director eschews captions while employing the deftest of transitions to keep his audience guessing as his protagonist passes from one period of childhood and adolescence to the next. Linklater selects an angle from which protagonist Mason Evans Jr.'s face can't be seen as he enters shot. That considerable time has passed becomes apparent only moments later, the director allowing his audience the opportunity to work things out for itself. These contrasting approaches perfectly illustrate a central question the storyteller faces: when to make information clear and when to allow the audience to piece together the elements in order to reveal it. Sometimes, what the screenwriter has felt needed to be clear, the director finds can be left to the audience to deduce. Sometimes, what the screenwriter felt could be left to the audience to deduce, the director finds needs to be made clear. The screenwriter does not have the gift of hindsight; the director does.

In a TV show, major periods of time can conveniently vanish between episodes and between seasons. Whether the viewer watches from week to week, from day to day, or "binge watches" a web series or box set, they will take these progressions in their stride, often indeed expecting them. Such major transitions seem integral to a form that in many ways echoes the long novel with its archetypal episodic narrative. The director, whether of a single episode or of an entire season, needs to grasp the nature of such profound punctuation in the passage of time and plan how best to articulate it. There may or may not be a "house style" to which to adhere. Such transitions may, or may not, be the norm. The jump may be of major consequence or a regular aspect of the show's episodic progression. Whichever way it works, the passage of time in a TV show affords a narrative reach, one of the virtues of the form, which needs to be understood and embraced by the director in order that they register its effects on energy, tone, and the pitch of the drama and performance. A long TV show can explore a narrative versatility movies can rarely afford to indulge. The passage of time in a story can slow down, take a rest, stand aside in order that the storytellers mine diverting situations and threads denied the director of the two-hour movie. The seasons of *24* were a notable exception, each episode covering one hour in real time, each of the seasons, twenty-four hours.

In short films, by contrast to most TV, real time comes into its own. The real time of *Before Dawn* (mentioned in chapter 8) is a case in point, going hand in hand with the film's dramatic tension, indeed creating and sustaining it. The film is a perfect example of Aristotelian unity. In the standalone shorts comprising the feature *Wild Tales*, moreover, only one of the six stories is not told in real time. Fragmented time in a short of up to twenty minutes often has the effect of fragmenting tension. With real time, by contrast, there is no escape for the audience, which finds itself trapped in the story.

The director can, of course, modulate the passing of time by the use of slow or fast motion, or by "ramping"—the acceleration or deceleration—of the shot. Such manipulation, however, is usually not mentioned in the screenplay. Some directors might wish to see shots, camera moves, and more details of visual discourse specified on the page. Others prefer such elements omitted, the drama or emotion of an event prompting the use of such visual language. One of the most memorable examples of slow-motion is the dream sequence in Luis Buñuel's *Los olvidados*, which was shot both over-cranked (in slo-mo) and in reverse, a double manipulation of time that conveys a chilling oneiric terror impossible to describe. Directors such as Akira Kurosawa and Sam Peckinpah by contrast, would use slo-mo as a means of heightening the impact of violence. The slightest, practically unnoticeable slo-mo on a facial expression, meanwhile, can intensify the emotion it conveys and is a technique few in an audience will notice. In Stanley Kubrick's *A Clockwork Orange*, the director emphasizes the absurd mechanical antics of Alex the Droog's sex act with comedic *under-cranking* (fast-motion), an approach that gels with the director's thematic fascination throughout his career and specifically in this film for the blurred boundaries—sometimes comical, sometimes unsettling—between the human and the mechanical.

Passage of time in fiction relates to tense. In a novel or short story, as in languages that incorporate tense into grammar (Mandarin, for example, does not), events may be portrayed as having taken place in the past, in the past of the past, in the present, even in the future or some possible future, or, in the case of conditional forms, a different past, present, or future that would have been the case were other eventualities to have occurred. In film and TV, however, the tense is (almost) always the present. The action in a flashback, whatever the treatment of the image—whether black and white, desaturated, sepia-toned, bleach-bypassed, pixilated, or whatever—is conveyed in the present tense, and the audience's connection is immediate and experiential. An atypical means by which a story is told in the past tense can be seen in the short film *In Sound We Live Forever*, written and directed by Joshua Giuliano, in which the camera dollies over the remnants of a picnic while two lovers are heard talking. The audience soon realizes that what it is seeing is the detritus left behind after what happened to the couple. The horror of the past plays out in sound as the camera reveals the present, the camera then tilting up to reveal an empty field, a woman rising from the long grass. From this point the movie tells the story of her escape attempt in the present tense.

The management of the passage of time is a prime duty and challenge of the screenwriter, director, and editor. It affects the flow of emotion, energy, and tone. It affects the audience's relationship with a film's story and characters. Seconds may pass in a story, centuries may pass, but a story rarely takes only seconds to tell and surely can never take centuries. It's that magical transformation from the story to its telling that falls to the filmmakers to achieve.

10 Character

What is a character?

Before examining how a director might understand the individual characters in a screenplay along with their collective configuration, and before considering the *character breakdown* a director needs to draw up, it's important to ask a question rarely considered: what might the entity known as a *character* actually be? Different kinds of character work in different ways, fulfilling different functions both within a single film and within and across different genres. Before examining that rich spectrum, however, it is worth considering what might lie behind the concept of character itself. Audiences have a working idea of what these fictitious individuals might be or what they might signify or represent, through their traits, appearances, and behavior, and, if they are not blatantly repugnant, strange, or evil (although even that may prove no barrier), generally have little problem in engaging with them, sympathizing, empathizing, even *identifying* with them. They would be hard pressed however, to explain what a character might actually be or in what way they relate to one.

This deceptively simple word has several other meanings, as in the terms *strength of character* (referring to some inner, central core of personality that relates to integrity or morality, courage or resilience) or *such a character* (implying that a person is in some way quirky, eccentric, odd, or noticeable)—two meanings which would seem to be polar opposites, although both correlate in their own way with what the Oxford Shorter Dictionary describes as "A person portrayed in a novel, a drama, etc.; a part played by an actor." The same dictionary adds the definition of a *dissembler*, suggesting that those conjured inhabitants of novels, plays, movies, and TV shows may not be so straightforward as they can at first seem, that they might have concealed depths and contradictions. In particular, it suggests those characters that might be called the shape-shifters, such as the shady Saul Goodman in TV's *Breaking Bad* and its *Better Call Saul* prequel.

The word *character* can also refer to a letter of the alphabet, a symbol, token, or emblem that *signifies* something—again an invaluable clue as to the way a character in fiction or drama may work, embodying and radiating emotional and psychological resonance for the reader or audience that renders fictional figures apparently as real, as human as living people.

Another use of the word comes with the term *character actor*, an actor who plays secondary supporting roles, who does not play the protagonist, even the antagonist, and whose idiosyncrasies, of appearance maybe, and manner suggest particular human dimensions and traits that set them apart from *leading actors*.

Just as audiences maintain an instinctive understanding of what character in fiction is, for actors who, like anyone else, might struggle to explain the concept, bringing characters to life is the core of their vocation. When an actor gives a strong performance, they may be said to *inhabit* a character, while they themselves may feel they are *possessed* by a character, as if to imply that characters are abstractions that actually exist in some sense, even before the actor has come to play them, and would continue to exist even without an actor's performance, inhabiting some fictive cosmos concurrent with our own, call it a *character universe* perhaps. A novelist or screenwriter might feel the same when discovering how a character "speaks" to them in the process of their creation, and how they determine their own decisions, as if they are not being invented by the writer but are imposing their own agency upon them. (The novelist E. M. Forster once described "that wonderful thing, a character running away with you—which happens to everyone"). Directors also may feel a palpable presence on the part of a character, their voice somehow speaking for itself from the screenplay, then in rehearsal, during the shoot, and later in the cutting room.

What then, are characters? Representations of people, as in portraits and sculptures? Vivid figures in games of make-believe? Imitations of individuals? Personifications of conflicting forces? Mimeses of all of us—mirrors into ourselves, our needs, fears, and desires? Or are they no more than dramatic constructs, the building blocks of story pieced together with other components of dramatic narrative? Indeed, the elements of a character are themselves often interlocked in calculated fashion in order to serve the action and motility of plot, to echo and embellish or subvert certain models of type or archetype, to satisfy the audience's expectations (or subvert them) and maximize its engagement. On the surface many characters will seem not so fabricated, although this may be because of "the art that conceals art." (The apparently naturalistic character of the eleven-year-old delinquent Cyril Catoul in the Dardenne Brothers' *The Kid with a Bike* betrays a truculence towards those who care about him and a gullibility in the face of those who seek to exploit him, and commits acts of violence along the way that form the precursor to a redemption as orchestrated as that in any mainstream movie.) Other characters, such as *Rear Window*'s L. B. Jefferies, on the one hand drawn to physical danger, on the other to the elegant Lisa Fremont of Manhattan society, embody inner contradictions that provide dramatic narrative with one of its most potent arenas of contrast and conflict, perhaps its *most* potent of all. In *Three Colors: Blue* Julie seeks freedom from the past while unable to deny her desire to resolve its unfinished business. Audiences, sensing that such paradoxical impulses, wants, and needs of a character may take them in one direction or its opposite—the one they hope for, the other they fear although perhaps secretly desire—find themselves caught between two compelling possibilities and thus connect more intensely with the film. Not least potent in such a bond is the unconscious recognition on the part of an audience that it shares with a character impulses and desires it would prefer not to reveal in the light of day—scruples that vary according to shifts in cultural and collective sensibilities.

Another source of suspense through character is the conflict of duty and need. In Andrea Arnold's *Wasp*, for example, Zoë, tasked with the care of her children while desperate for Dave's love, finds she can't have it both ways—until the note of tentative hope at the film's end, that is, when the sight of the wasp crawling into her baby's mouth reveals to her that her duty of childcare is rooted not in obligation but in love.

Some characters may be less conflicted, their function in a story more as force for good or evil in the struggle against its polar opposite. Villains may work in this way, as may a hero in a Genre 1 movie, but then so might a character in a social realist drama—Daniel Blake in Ken Loach's *I, Daniel Blake*, for example, who enshrines a benevolent humanity in the face of a callously indifferent bureaucracy, or Lazzaro in Alice Rohrwacher's magical realist *Happy as Lazzaro*, in which the singular central figure embodies a selfless innocence at painful odds with the scheming individuals of both the upper and lower classes who either reject him or seek to exploit him.

Any comprehensive understanding of the concept is further complicated by the consideration of characters based on real-life people. Historical movies and TV shows such as Steven Spielberg's *Lincoln* or TV's *Wolf Hall*, others dramatizing recent or contemporary events such as Kathryn Bigelow's *Zero Dark Thirty* or TV's *The Loudest Voice*, bio-pics such as Danny Boyle's *Steve Jobs* or Mick Jackson's TV movie *Temple Grandin*, or an alternative history such as Quentin Tarantino's *Once upon a Time in Hollywood* bring representations of actual people to the screen with varying degrees of accuracy. (How "accurate," though, can such creations be? When particular events are selected for their dramatic impact and function within the narrative, when scenes and dialogue are invented, when secondary characters might be combinations of two figures from actuality, or be invented, when main characters known from history or contemporary events are played by movie stars or known actors with their own auras, afforded the expert skills of a costume designer and a make-up artist, any considerations of "accuracy" would seem moot.) The nature of the original personage will have been mined by the screenwriter for those facets that most effectively inform the story, which are then distilled, exaggerated, supplemented, and vested with the impulses, flaws, strengths, and vulnerabilities that inform the construction of any other fully dimensioned protagonist. In addition, although a screenwriter might be studiously observant of facts and take care not to err too far from reality (or they might not), for their characters to come to life (or to fiction!), they cannot avoid using elements of themselves, as the writer of purely fictional characters inevitably does.

The filmmaker, whether screenwriter or director or both, has to find a balance between fact and fiction in such characters, adjusted according to the intended genre and tone of the film. Perhaps the fictional version of the historical figure will take on its own life yet maintain the spirit of the original, but if such a character fails to come to life, a filmmaker's blind adherence to facts will not save them. Faithful reconstruction does not necessarily make for good drama—better to acknowledge the ready-made authenticity of a known historical figure, such as the artist J. M. W. Turner in Mike Leigh's *Mr Turner*, and move on into the realm of the creative process, as Leigh does, aided by actor Timothy Spall. The casting of such roles indeed, whether conforming to or militating against an audience's preconceptions, is a further element in the complex process of creating or *recreating* such characters.

A *meta* approach to historical characters such as that found in Robert Altman's revisionist western *Buffalo Bill and the Indians, or Sitting Bull's History Lesson* poses further questions. William Frederick "Buffalo Bill" Cody existed, as did his Buffalo Bill's Wild West show, as did Chief Sitting Bull, who took part in that show, as did other characters in the movie, while the events the film portrays are invented. Its characters take on both the historical and the mythical mantles of their predecessors while serving Altman's individual vision and purpose—the revisiting and revising of widely accepted preconceptions about the Wild West. Here, there would appear to be three universes at work: the universe of historical actuality, the *character universe* drawn from it, and the movie's universe the characters inhabit. Miloš Forman's *Ragtime* mixes figures from history with purely fictional incident and characters, the invented and the actual being equally compelling. John Madden's *Shakespeare in Love* explores supposed amatory episodes in the bard's life, making use of material from his plays and poems, a meta-mix conjured by screenwriter Tom Stoppard, previously adept at creating the dramatic chemistry afforded by the interplay of disparate historical characters in his stage play *Travesties*, which features James Joyce, Vladimir Ilyich Lenin, and Dada founder Tristan Tzara.

Further into the spectrum of *meta* is the character of nineteenth-century poet Emily Dickinson in TV's *Dickinson*, an irreverent contrast of subversive meta-modern comedy to the wrenching power of the character of the same poet in Terence Davies' *A Quiet Passion*, a vehicle for the filmmaker's elegant aesthetic consummately realized to capture Dickinson's inner life.

In films based on or inspired by the filmmakers' own lives, a main character will provide their proxy in the story. Truffaut's Antoine Doinel, Fellini's Guido Anselmi, and Almodóvar's Salvador Mallo are examples, each a blend of *auto-fiction* and fictitious invention.

To return to the nature of characters in general, it would seem that for a character, at least a main character, and certainly a shape-shifter, to be effective, there needs to be an element of mystery at their core. Whereas some teachers of screenwriting insist the writer should have a god-like view of their characters and know everything there is to know about them, just as they need to understand how every element of their story fits together, how each serves the others, the Iranian master Abbas Kiarostami said there should be something *impenetrable* about a character. Certainly those who maintain an element of mystery throughout a film, even when the audience is "in their shoes," in their *narrative point of view* (see the next chapter), tend to be the most charismatic, the most resonant, perhaps the most haunting— they stay with an audience after the movie has finished, tempting it to see the film again or return for a sequel or the entirety of a TV season. How, then, taking this notion of a character's central mystery into consideration, should the director approach the realization of characters in a film or TV show? As in other areas of the creative process, they should embrace the enigma, accepting it as an aspect of the exploration and discovery necessary to the most effective of approaches. It enriches the process of the actor, who will work from intuition far more than reason, and it provides the director with the crucial if unsettling element of uncertainty without which their task is rendered moribund. The author Henry Miller said that "understanding is not a piercing of the mystery, but an acceptance of it, a living blissfully with it, in it, through and by it." The mystery of character is indeed one of drama's greatest gifts to screenwriter, director, actor, and audience.

That said, however, the director needs to understand how *character* functions in the context of *dramatic narrative*.

Character in dramatic narrative

When F. Scott Fitzgerald wrote that "action is character," he was providing the filmmaker, whether screenwriter or director or both, with a fundamental resource in creating compelling characters. A short-story writer or novelist can conjure the consciousness of a character who might do absolutely nothing—the inner world of Samuel Beckett's immobile and anonymous protagonist in his *The Unnameable* is an example. A novelist's language, their form, and the length, idiom, and texture of their sentences might be echoic of trains of thought and emotion in a character. The processes of consciousness are mirrored in the prose, a task not generally possible for the director, who requires a character to take action in order to reveal their nature. (Camera moves, fast or slow, the rhythm of the shot or the cutting, the tone adopted by the director might be thought to mirror the emotions of a character in the way that prose can, but would be challenged to sustain a narrative.) The word *drama* comes from the ancient Greek for *do, act, perform*, and it is through their action (or at times in their story, or in some stories, their failure to take action) that the *character* of a character is revealed. There are exceptions, of course, as there always are, but in film and TV consciousness is generally revealed through behavior and action.

If Fitzgerald's maxim "action is character" is fundamental to the understanding of how that relationship is manifested in dramaturgy, so are the words attributed to the philosopher Heraclitus—namely that "character is destiny." Aristotle in his *Poetics* wrote that it is the flaw of the tragic hero that leads them to their fate, and indeed in classical tragedy, that of ancient Greece such as Sophocles' *Oedipus Rex*, or of Shakespeare such as *Hamlet*, the character flaw of the tragic hero is what draws them to their inevitable nemesis, their tragic fate. The tragic flaw, or *hamartia*, of Oedipus is his pride and impulsiveness, this *hubris* (and it is through his actions that this is revealed) the failing that blinds him to the path he takes towards his prophesied fate and literal blindness. Hamlet's tragic flaw is by contrast his *inability* to act—he fails to take control of his circumstances, allowing his circumstances to take control of him. In other words, in the Prince of Denmark's case *inaction is character*. Hamlet is the archetypal *passive protagonist*, rejected as a valid element in dramatic narrative by many proponents of "Hollywood" screenwriting pedagogy, yet the play has survived for over four centuries and is still going strong—there are few absolutes in story and drama. What works for the tragic hero works also for other characters; a compelling protagonist often has a trait, flaw, or failing that leads them to their fate. The obsessive Scottie Ferguson in Alfred Hitchcock's *Vertigo*, terrified of heights, ends up atop a tower staring down at the body of the woman he loves after she's fallen to her death. Protagonist Star in Andrea Arnold's *American Honey*, who has needed to escape her "family" in order to find a family, discovers ultimately that she has to escape the "family" she's joined too, if only for a moment. The trait can also be an element of a character's nature that, although seen by others as a flaw, leads them eventually to a victorious destiny—Chiron in Barry Jenkins' *Moonlight*, for example, persecuted for being gay as a youth and veering into the machismo trappings of criminal drug-dealing as a young man, eventually finds personal fulfillment in his relationship with his former friend Kevin. The very aspect of himself that had led to his problems, saves him from them.

The writer Anaïs Nin said that "In this apparently chaotic world of the unconscious there is an inevitability as logical, as coherent, as final as any to be found in classical drama." One might equally suggest that classical tragedy is the dramatization of the unconscious and its impact on the individual. A *character*'s unconscious is their predominant force and the inescapable foundation of their *character*. It might be said, then, that *character* in a story represents the battle between the conscious and the unconscious, which the latter, for good or bad, must always win. The director therefore needs to understand the unconscious dimensions of their protagonist while the protagonist remains unaware of them, ultimately realizing their nature as a result of their journey through the story—a phenomenon Aristotle called the *anagnorisis*. In that sense the director *does* need to understand the mystery within a character, or at least intuit it.

A third maxim that might be applied to character, and to the protagonist in particular, has already been suggested, namely that *character is contradiction*. Barry Jenkins' Chiron, in *Moonlight*, is both sensitive and brutal, needy and independent, comprehending and uncomprehending, a dramatization of his inner paradox that keeps the film's audience guessing about his journey until its end.

Further consideration is often given as to whether, as Lajos Egri suggested, character should drive plot or, as Aristotle maintained, plot should drive character, free will being perhaps the philosophy underlying the former, fatalism the latter. (Again—character as human mystery as opposed to character as dramaturgical function maybe.) Plot-driven genres may be seen to follow that first dictum, character-driven dramas the second, while some screenplays might have been written observing the symbiosis of both. In a movie of two hours or so, particularly in the Genre 1 category, the constraints of form suggest the determinism of plot, whereas in TV shows of successive seasons there is more time to afford character the agency to develop, following the path it suggests or perhaps subverting it. These alternative possibilities also relate to the nature of endings, and the journey stories take to reach them, and whether that journey or that ending are what most informs the film, a topic covered in chapter 16.

The character breakdown

How then should the director approach the *character breakdown*, the listing and categorizing, that, when clear and comprehensive, proves invaluable to all aspects of storytelling and provides a vital perspective on casting, itself an important element in telling the story? (The contrast or affinity of looks, the variety and contrasts or otherwise of a film's milieu relate to the bigger picture presented by the character breakdown. The casting of secondary and minor roles in particular may be rooted not solely in the nature of a part itself, or the merits of a particular actor, but in its relationship to, and comparison with, other roles.)

The director can usefully set down the main, principal, or primary characters, then the secondary, then the minor characters, each individual part followed by a description of who the character is, their characteristics, their wants and goals, their place and function in the *character configuration* of the film, and their function in the dynamics of the story.

Main, principal, or primary characters are the protagonist(s), hero(es), antagonist(s), and villain(s). Central to the story, their journeys are followed by the audience above all others, whether eagerly and enthusiastically, or with a degree of trepidation, even protest. The audience will often be taken into the narrative points of view of one or more such figures. Some screenwriters and directors will restrict the narrative point of view to that of a single main character who becomes the audience's conduit into the story, its members sharing in and experiencing their emotions, thoughts, cognition, and understanding throughout (in large part) to the exclusion of those of other characters.

Secondary characters are those who interact with the main characters in ways that drive the narrative forward, functioning as catalysts for their decisions, shifts, and reversals of understanding and action. The audience may be taken into their narrative points of view, but will tend not to be while a main character is present, unless the director adopts a *third-person omniscient* approach, rendering the audience privy to the thoughts and emotions of *all*, or almost all, of the characters.

Minor, or tertiary, characters appear on relatively few occasions, maybe no more than once perhaps, and in general have a particular function within a scene or sequence rather than an indispensable purpose throughout longer episodes, acts, or the entire movie. They may on occasion, however, precipitate a major reversal—the putative assassin of *Gangs of New York* who prompts Amsterdam to save Bill the Butcher, the antagonist he's sworn to kill, is such a case. He appears briefly, coming from nowhere, and, having performed his function in the story if not carried out his intention, is swiftly dispatched by the hapless protagonist. Minor characters perform specific functions within the narrative, as heralds or messengers perhaps, or arbiters, or they may present a momentary obstacle to a main or secondary character, or provide them with assistance, or be present to add texture to the milieu of a scene or sequence. The audience will rarely, if ever, be taken into the narrative point of view of a minor character, unless this creates a moment of suspense (a guard spotting some sign of an intruder perhaps), or again the director adopts a third-person omniscient approach.

Generally speaking, the audience will have feelings most of all for the main characters, less so for the secondary characters, and less still for the minor characters.

The main characters

A *character breakdown* begins with the main characters, their "type" (should they have one), and their function in the story. Is there a single *protagonist*? Are there more? Is there a *hero*, as such? Is there a *villain*? Is there a *monster* to be slain? Is the *protagonist* battling an external *antagonist*, inner demons, or both—is a protagonist confronting an opponent who will force them to face their own personal devils? Then again, might there be other configurations of character within which the tension or conflict is not simply between good and evil, hero(es) and villain(s), but lies in some other conflict?

Any director needs to understand the meanings of the terms *protagonist* and *antagonist*. The Shorter Oxford Dictionary gives this definition for the former: "The chief person in a drama; the principal character or (usu. in pl.) any of the leading characters in a play, novel, etc." The same dictionary gives the following definition for antagonist: "An opponent, an adversary; an opposing force."

What might be the nature of the protagonist in a specific screenplay? (There may be one or there may be an ensemble—the eight *Inglourious Basterds* or the lone Jack Reacher, the five orphaned sisters of Deniz Gamze Ergüven's *Mustang* or *Orange Is the New Black*'s Piper Chapman). Is the protagonist a hard-pressed and fallible person such as Chapman or a hero such as Jason Bourne, a vulnerable mortal or a kind of god? Are they willing or hesitant, resentful even, in the face of the journey they take? Do they attempt to rise above their circumstances, are they trying only to survive, or are they merely getting by as best they can? If they are a hero, are they perfect or do they have flaws? Are they singularly obsessed or conflicted, or both? Is their nature challenging to an audience but compelling all the same? Are they self-aware or do their decisions and actions reveal aspects of themselves of which they remain ignorant, perhaps in denial? In short, will they engage an audience and, if so, how?

What are the qualities that constitute a *hero*? When inviting votes for its 100 Greatest Heroes & Villains, the American Film Institute defined a "'hero' as a character(s) who prevails in extreme circumstances and dramatizes a sense of morality, courage and purpose. Though they may be ambiguous or flawed, they often sacrifice themselves to show humanity at its best." Those words "ambiguous or flawed," "sacrifice," and "humanity" are seminal in the construction of heroes from Achilles to James Bond, from Wonder Woman to Carrie Mathison of *Homeland*.

What, by contrast, constitutes a villain? The American Film Institute defined a villain as "a character(s) whose wickedness of mind, selfishness of character and will to power are sometimes masked by beauty and nobility, while others may rage unmasked. They can be horribly evil or grandiosely funny, but are ultimately tragic." Darth Vader, Voldemort, Hannibal Lecter, and The Joker (at least in manifestations prior to Joaquin Phoenix's haunting and humane iteration) are universally known examples from mainstream genre movies, engaging, compelling, seductive even for their apparent freedom from conscience, empathy, obligation, or ethics—an independence that unleashes their intelligence and cunning to do their best or worst in the exercise of power. Who, in the audience, although they may not admit it, might not secretly envy such heady traits? Not that empathy is a requirement for an audience's fascination; serial killers as villains are a staple of popular entertainment, offering successive murders—the more brutal the more compelling—to sustain prolonged episodic narratives. There are villains in less commercial films, too, of course. The Nazi commander in Elem Klimov's war film *Come and See*, who takes merciless pleasure in the immolation of Ukrainian villagers, is a case in point—his fondness for his pet marmoset is a character tick worthy of any Hollywood bad guy, although few would find anything remotely sympathetic in such an evil character, one based on real war criminal Oskar Dirlewanger.

A common wisdom observed by many filmmakers and teachers in connection to the creation of a villain is that they should always be in some way humanized—the Nazi's affection for his marmoset is an example, although it chills in contrast to his sadism towards humans. Does this dictum always withstand scrutiny though? Hasn't there been a significant place in myth, folklore, and story since time immemorial for the *monster*? The Gorgon Medusa, slain by the hero Perseus, Grendel, slain by Beowulf, the dragon slain by St George perhaps find their modern-day counterparts in the aforementioned serial killers and psychopaths of contemporary fare as well as the monstrous predator of the *Alien* franchise and the slasher figures of *Halloween*, *Nightmare on Elm Street*, or *Friday the 13th*. The increasing emphasis on our understanding of ourselves through the perspective of psychology may have enriched our insight into character, but has failed to render the monster obsolete, has maybe even deepened the need for such alien and nightmarish figures. The suggested imperative to humanize monstrous villains is well intended—the mustache-twirling figures of melodrama are rarely of interest, rarely believable—but without the power of the archetypal monster the culture of story bows to a universe without nightmare, lacking the primordial in deference to the dramatic aridity of reason and reductionism. Added to this is an increasing awareness of sociopathy and psychopathy as very real conditions affecting many in positions of power in contemporary society. Empathy, it seems, is *not* a universal human trait. Indeed, as Michael Haneke demonstrates, nor is it by any means always present in audiences.

In Jonathan Demme's *The Silence of the Lambs*, Hannibal Lecter is the monster who helps Clarice Starling track down a killer. Such a character needs no redeeming features (apart from his gruesome wit and charm perhaps), and indeed would not work so well were he rendered more psychologically realistic, complete with backstory to explain his cannibalism, to reveal traces of humanity in him and render his evil is some way comprehensible. (This, however, is explored by author Thomas Harris in his fourth Lecter novel, *Hannibal Rising*). Like Fritz Lang's earlier Dr. Mabuse from his *Dr. Mabuse the Gambler*, Lecter is the monster of myth, of fairy tale, incontrovertibly evil, opaque in intention, a taboo-breaking devil who fascinates audiences with his duplicity and control. (He is also a *shape-shifter*, largely malevolent but offering the protagonist wisdom.) Starling *needs* him more than he needs her, their relationship a tense, suspenseful, and dangerous interplay to keep the audience on the edge of its seats. Lecter is not so much a mirror to humanity as to *in*humanity, not a hissing melodramatic villain (although he hisses) but a demon who drives the narrative forward and compels Starling to defeat the killer and, in doing so, discover the truth about herself. As Roberto Calasso wrote in his novelization of Greek myth *The Marriage of Cadmus and Harmony*:

> The monster waits near the wellspring. The monster is the spring. He doesn't need the hero. It is the hero who needs him for his very existence,

because his power will be protected by and indeed must be snatched from the monster. When the hero confronts the monster, he has as yet neither power nor knowledge. The monster is his secret father, who will invest him with a power and knowledge that can belong to one man only, and that only the monster can give him.

Where the villain is the protagonist, and where the audience is put in their narrative point of view, the filmmaker has an *anti-hero*. Patricia Highsmith's Tom Ripley, the anti-hero of the adapted movies *Purple Noon* by René Clément and *The Talented Mr. Ripley* by Anthony Minghella, does not do battle on the side of good—he dissembles, manipulates, and murders in the most self-serving, expedient manner. TV's *Dexter* is a serial killer who derives gratification from the cruelest of murders although at the same time working in a police department to track down other killers—a neat, and, it might be suggested, disingenuous moral balancing act on the part of the writers. Decades before him, Fritz Lang's anti-hero Beckert in his *M* is a child killer with no redeeming features or actions, even if in his own moments of terror we cannot help but sympathize with him. In the previous century Dostoevsky had shown the way as regards anti-heroes with the murderer Raskolnikov in *Crime and Punishment*, although John Milton perhaps got there before him with the Satan of *Paradise Lost*, in which, as William Blake said, Milton was of the devil's party "without knowing it." The Patrick Bateman of Mary Harron's *American Psycho* and the Bret Easton Ellis novel on which the film is based is an example of the monster serial killer as anti-hero, his visceral murders of women punctuating the drama under the banner, maybe guise, of dark satire. Tony Soprano, the anti-hero of TV's *The Sopranos*, offers a more approachable anti-hero, a ruthless killer yes, but a family man too—a successful example of the humanized villain.

A protagonist may be neither a hero nor an anti-hero but simply a character in the throes of adverse circumstances over which they have limited or no control. The conflict and/or tension of such a story may be more compelling than a simple duel between the good and the bad. In Asaph Polonsky's drama *One Week and a Day*, the protagonist Eyal Spivak has to cope with and ultimately overcome his grief over his son's death, a challenge as formidable as any presented by a vindictive opponent, and one that has universal resonance in the common human experience of grief. There is no willful antagonist, no struggle for power, no contest between any one side and another, only the painful situation with which Spivak finds himself, in which the configuration of the characters is less one of offense and defense, to be reversed from act to act, than of a faltering struggle against the emotional agonies inflicted by devastating loss shared with other characters.

Secondary and minor characters

These characters also come in many shapes and forms. They may exemplify the cultural, social, and moral canvas of the story, acting in accordance with the codes of their milieu—the screenwriter's means of illustrating those codes dramatically rather than have a character merely explain them. (Star's fellow delinquents in Andrea Arnold's *American Honey*, each distinctive but each a member of the gang, provide such a compelling group.) As "heralds" of one kind or another, they may announce the challenges or quests a protagonist needs to accept. They might be catalysts for the shifts and reversals of a main character's journey or relationships with other central figures—lovers, for example, buddies, fellow travelers. They may offer triangulation, a third force that precipitates the resolution of a central conflict, perhaps by uniting two enemies who must join forces to defeat them. They might be parental or mentor figures teaching or guiding a protagonist, or giving them a force to react against. They might externalize and dramatize some element of conflict. They might be characters that meet fates a main character must subsequently be careful to avoid, or they may follow the conventional path a protagonist must seek to break away from. They might be secondary bad characters that will eventually kill the main bad character when, as a consequence of the hero's victory, the screenwriter cannot afford to leave the dirty work of disposing of the antagonist to the hero and so evil turns on evil. In all of these later cases such characters are not introduced as mere texture for the story and world but as instruments integral to the narrative.

In Hitchcock's *Notorious*, written by Ben Hecht, there are several of these examples at work. Secondary character, intelligence chief Prescott is a kind of strict parent to agent and protagonist Devlin, sending him out into the lethal world of espionage and insisting he put Alicia in danger. The minor character of a tedious English commodore meanwhile, by inviting Alicia on a cruise, prompts her to accept Devlin's assignment instead, the triangulation the Englishman provides thus ending, if only temporarily, the central couple's quarrel. The Nazi co-conspirators of antagonist Alex Sebastian's, a motley crew of secondary and tertiary characters, ultimately prove his nemesis—bad characters to vanquish the central bad character. In another Hitchcock film, *The Wrong Man*, Miss Dennerly, an insurance office clerk and minor character, becomes convinced that Henry Fonda's Ballestrero is the man who's previously held up her colleagues, thus setting the film's story in motion. (Note Dennerly's penetrating eyes, all the better for seeing into Ballestrero's soul, or at least appearing to—a measure of the director's meticulous casting.)

Minor characters often become cannon fodder for the screenwriter. Loudmouths, ne'er-do-wells, fools, heartbreaking unfortunates, and many more hapless figures meet some unpleasant fate once they've fulfilled their dramaturgical purpose and need to be excluded from a developing story. They may find themselves hurt, humiliated, wounded, punished, murdered in the course of a narrative that requires their misfortune in order for it to progress. They provide the collateral damage of the story, the injustice that needs to be redressed, the victims of a crime the detective needs to solve. They may be innocent, they may be guilty—and to a calculated extent.

In thriller and action movies, for example, there is often a kind of balance sheet of guilt on the one hand and the fate meted out on the other, as if the badder guys are, morally speaking, more expendable. (Steve McQueen's *Widows* follows this formula assiduously.)

Filmmakers should be wary of having two secondary characters performing the same duty in the same area of the story so that one gets in the way of the other. Say there is a troubled young boy who is rejected by the secondary character of the estranged father he loves. A young woman takes a liking to the youngster and introduces him to her boyfriend, another secondary character. Were the boyfriend to remain in the story, the boy might bond with him and so no longer need his absent father, making the young woman's bid to tame his behavior easier. The boyfriend thus becomes a dramaturgical problem and needs to disappear from the story. Such is the configuration of characters in the Dardenne Brothers' *The Kid with a Bike* and such is the filmmakers' solution—they have boyfriend Gilles, angered by her attempts to care for the young Cyril, dump Samantha. Once Gilles has left to go his own way, the drama of Cyril and Samantha can continue. (The functional nature of minor characters begs the question as to how fully dimensioned they should be—Gilles is less dimensioned than Cyril's father, for example. Tertiary characters may need only the minimum of brushstrokes, although they always need to be believable if the film as a whole is to "ring true.")

The configuration of characters

After delineating the line-up of characters in the *breakdown*, the director can map their *configuration*, the groups into which they fall, their placement in respect to other groups and the conflict of the story, their composition and possible mirroring between one group and another, and the spectrum of their functions.

In considering the configuration of characters in their screenplay, one might usefully reflect upon the theory of tragedy proposed by the German philosopher Arthur Schopenhauer (1788–1860), in his *The World as Will and Representation*, which posits three categories of "tragedy" (a word that in this context can be taken to mean "drama"):

1. It can take place through *extraordinary evil*, an evil that reaches the limits of the possible and is attributable to the one character who is responsible for the misfortune …
2. It can also take place through *blind fate, i.e. chance and error* …
3. Finally, the misfortune can be introduced *by means of people's positioning with respect to each other*, through their relationships, so that there is no need for a terrible mistake or unheard of accident or even for a character whose evilness extends to the limits of human possibility; instead, morally ordinary characters in everyday circumstances are positioned with

respect to each other in such a way that their situation forces them knowingly and clear-sightedly to cause each other the greatest harm without the injustice falling on one side or the other.

He goes on to adjudge that:

This last type seems much preferable to the other two because it shows misfortune not as an exception, not as something brought about by rare circumstances or monstrous characters, but rather as something that develops effortlessly and spontaneously out of people's deeds and characters, almost as if it were essential, thereby bringing it terrifyingly close to us.

Polonsky's *One Week and a Day* is an example of this dynamic, as is Hirokazu Kore-eda's *Shoplifters*, in which an assortment of characters, none of them evil, although most are far from innocent either—forced by their circumstances into forming and maintaining a "family" of thieves—encounter the tensions that undo them through the conditions of their co-existence. In Lulu Wang's *The Farewell*, both Billi and her family want to act out of the best of moral intentions, the conflict between them providing the drama of the story. In Jean Renoir's farce *The Rules of the Game* the characters' relationships form a web of love and deception that leads to tragedy. There is no hero in the film, nor even a central protagonist. Robert Altman's movies from *Nashville* to *Gosford Park* also tend to make use of an ensemble of main characters in imperfect relationships.

(An example of category 1 would be a story in which a hero is pitted against an evil mastermind, one of category 2 a film such as Polanski's *Tess*, in which a crucial letter, when delivered under a door, slips under a mat and is not seen, the cause of subsequent tragedy.)

Characters in broad comedy

A particular rigor needs to be applied to the understanding of character in broad comedies. Writing at the beginning of the seventeenth century, the English playwright Ben Jonson described the characters in his satirical plays as "humors"—not fully fleshed-out characters as such but constructs embodying maybe a single *humor* or trait, mercilessly lampooned. Today, movies in the genre of broad comedy make use of similarly limited but effectively calculated figures. The Farrelly Brothers' *Dumb and Dumber* and *There's Something about Mary*, to take two examples, may not be vehicles for profound psychological or emotional depth, but then nor are revered classics such as Jacques Tati's *Mon Oncle*. They don't need to be. They work with other mischief. Through their galleries of characters precisely conceived and presented to meet their purpose, they reveal instantly recognizable human traits ripe for comedic effect. Comedy is often regarded as the most difficult of the genres for the screenwriter and director, maybe because the challenges of getting such minimal character construction right are considerable, and because it isn't so easy to make an audience laugh. Paradoxically, although clearly defined character and structure are central to the execution of comedy, anarchic energy is also vital. A comedy star or known clownish figure in the central role, a Charlie Chaplin, Buster Keaton, Jacques Tati, Steve Martin, Jim Carrey, or Jack Black exudes chaotic abandon, and in such cases a comic protagonist will often have been written as a vehicle for a specific performer who will bring their persona and style of comedy to the character. A director needs to support and facilitate that performance, in itself a comedic vision that informs the energy and tone of the film while contrasting to the "straight" acting of other main and secondary characters.

Characters in TV and franchises

A TV show offering multiple seasons facilitates a prolonged, exhaustive journey of exploration into every nook and cranny of a fictional psyche and soul that may never reach a conclusion. An audience both gets to know a character intimately yet never gets to known them entirely, and so there come about both familiarity and mystery, perhaps the fundamental precepts of the compelling protagonist, one who is known and at the same time never completely known. Such characterization amounts to an excavation that can never be completed. Shape-shifters, such as the aforementioned Saul Goodman in *Breaking Bad*, are thus a staple of successful long-running TV shows.

A similar phenomenon occurs in franchise movies, in which heroes and superheroes, invariably drawn from counterparts in novels or comics, undergo successive adventures, never aging and played by one different star after another. With each outing the screenwriters bring some element of backstory and/or character not only as yet unrevealed but in many instances previously *not even conceived*, the ever more complex constructs of such figures taking them further into a mythology that stands outside the specific confines of individual films while according them added richness. Aside from these enduring protagonists, there are those who come with pre-established credentials that render them almost as "real" as actual historical figures. Sherlock Holmes, played by different actors, has been gracing movie and TV screens in contrasting manifestations for generations, reappearing in worlds and circumstances ever more remote from his home at 221B Baker Street (the number never existed) and stepping out of his character universe as and when producers, screenwriters, and directors find an opportunity to employ him.

Final notes on character

The director needs to look at how their screenplay treats its characters and needs to beware of the screenwriter—it may be themselves—who pulls their punches by being too kind to them, sparing them the ordeals and fates a story demands. The logic of story and character is ruthless and neither screenwriter nor director should flinch from enforcing it. It is, after all, only that engaging abstraction known as a *character* that will suffer the consequences—no actual person will be hurt in the process, apart maybe from those in the audience, who, if the movie or TV show compels, may accept such pain gladly. Another failing of the timid filmmaker is the denial or avoidance of the potential flaws and unpleasant traits of a character and the failure to make use of them in the intensity of the drama. It is through these shortcomings indeed that a character's true depth and dimension might be exposed—as Saul Bellow wrote in his novel *The Adventures of Augie March*: "You can know a man by his devils and the way he gives hurts."

An effective character, much like an effective story, embodies both specificity and universality. They may not be any particular member of the audience, but they are at the same time *all* members of the audience, in some respect *all* of humanity. Dramatic narrative and fictional storytelling in movies and TV are among the mimetic arts. Mimesis is one means of knowing ourselves, recognizing the nature of our existence and finding some sense of meaning. Characters are mimeses, reflections of us. They may be courageous, they may be cowardly, they may be noble, they may be despicable, but if they fail to ring true to some aspect of human nature, its essence and mystery, they will not come across as credible or compelling in either screenplay or film. Both the screenwriter and the director need to be acute judges of that quality, and it is instinct as much as analysis that has to lie at the heart of their judgment.

It is through the fruits of that instinct that the director connects with the actor, for whom the analytical current of this chapter is not intended. Just as an actor's task is to capture the moment and not tell the entire story, so their charge is to realize their character, not to understand its dramaturgical purpose. The director will guide, coax, nudge, conspire with the actor, facilitating their performance without getting in their way, a process outside the scope of this book and amply covered elsewhere in filmmaking literature. Character and performance need to be understood by the director as integral rather than standalone elements of filmmaking, however, a concept to inform the casting process, which might more helpfully be seen as the assembling of the interactive community of characters rather than the selection of isolated parts. That achieved, the director can work with the actor and their emotional intelligence to bring to life their performance.

11 Narrative point of view

What is narrative point of view?

Filmmakers, and indeed informed filmgoers, understand the nature of a *point of view* (POV) shot: the camera lens is located in the same position as a character's eyes, pointing in the direction of their look and shooting what they see. The term *narrative point of view*, or *NPOV* as it will be referred to here, is, however, less widely understood and often confused, even by filmmakers, with that specific shot. Narrative point of view refers not to any particular type of shot—although POV shots may contribute to its articulation—but to a concept both in literature and in film that is a seminal aspect of storytelling, namely the nature of the narrator and the relationship of the reader or audience to them. A narrator of one kind or another is necessary in order for a story to be told—in literature this may be the writer, who may make themselves evident or remain hidden, or may be a character, usually the protagonist. In film and TV it may appear on first consideration that there is no narrator, unless there is a voice-over, for example the one in Stanley Kubrick's *Barry Lyndon*, the identity of its sardonic storyteller never revealed, or as in many of Martin Scorsese's films, in which the narrator tends to be the protagonist. Yet, even without any voice-over, moments, scenes, and even whole movies can indeed be told from one or another character's NPOV. An important aspect of the director's job, in telling the story, is their approach to NPOV, which has an impact on the audience's relationship to the characters, the main character(s) especially, and their feelings for them, by rendering it observer of, companion to, or sharer in their experience.

While the concept and execution of NPOV is often explored in relation to literature, it is less often touched upon in relation to film and TV, and, even if frequently referred to by experienced screenwriters and directors, is rarely analyzed by filmmaking educators. Yet directors have been putting the audience "in the shoes" of one character or another, in one sense or another, to one degree or another, for decades. For all that, there are no manuals of the language or techniques they employ. Instead, the means by which a director connects the audience to one or more characters more closely than others would seem to comprise knowledge that has remained "tacit"—known but not articulated—and taken as a "given," in little need of explanation. This is surprising when one considers that the most powerful engagement an audience has with a movie is through the channel of emotion; when the audience *feels* the emotion a character feels, a protagonist especially, and shares in their emotional journey throughout the duration of a film, that involvement can be at its strongest. How is it, though, that an audience *observing* a character in film or TV can enter their emotions and thoughts, understand and feel what they understand and feel, when it can't read descriptions of this as the reader of a short story or novel can? And how is it that an audience's experience can as a result be as intense, more intense even, than a reader's?

 The human capacity for empathy and the nature of story as a mimesis of life play fundamental roles in this phenomenon. As discussed in the previous chapter on character, people have since time immemorial been drawn to gods and monsters, to heroes and villains, and whether such fictive beings make their journeys in myths or folklore passed down orally, in epic poems, stage plays, short stories, novels, movies, TV shows, or graphic novels, readers and audiences follow their escapades eagerly and to a greater or lesser degree care about what might happen to them. Audiences meanwhile may feel closer to, even *identify with*, a character played by a familiar actor or star, while in a TV show the viewer will come to know the main characters intimately over successive episodes and seasons. (Even secondary characters may begin to seem like old friends.) It's also the case that for those equipped with an adequate facility for empathy, the simple act of watching an event play out on the screen will spark, as well as pity or sympathy, "mirror" emotions. (After all, this is how theatre has worked for centuries, although in stage plays there may also be the soliloquy, a device to lock an audience into the thoughts and emotions of a character, while the aside offers a passing glance into some observation or insight otherwise inaccessible—Martin Scorsese achieves this latter with voice-over asides that connect the audience to a character's observations and reflections, a technique used in original noirs.) It is true as well that when one looks at any group of unknown people simply sitting or standing still, whether in a photograph, on a screen, or in any other context, there will be individuals who catch the eye, who prompt more interest than others. Such magnetism might be physical and sexual but can often be less readily explained—something in the eyes, a demeanor, an ambience hard to describe, perhaps welcoming, perhaps not. The mere act of gazing at someone or some event then—and the love of gazing is very much a part of human nature, as Hitchcock's *Rear Window*, in which a character spies on his neighbors, illustrates—can be enough to prompt empathy. In film and TV, however, and in the address these make to the audience and the viewer, the organization of visual and editorial elements can be put to use in order to accentuate and intensify the connection the audience forges with one or more characters, indeed to determine which character(s) will lead it through the film. When a movie's narrative is told through a character's

NPOV, that character becomes the audience's conduit into the story, doing exactly that—leading it through the film. Narrative point of view is one of the foundations of storytelling, and the director will be at a considerable advantage when aware of how it can be articulated on the screen through the language of film.

Narrative point of view in literature

In a short story or novel it's not so difficult for the reader to understand which character(s) they feel closest too, perhaps even feel they are "with." When the author chooses the *first person*, an *I*, as the narrator, they are involving the reader in a *subjective* point of view, prompting them to share directly in the character's thoughts and emotions, imagining taking their actions with them. When the author describes a character as a *she* or a *he*, the story is said to be told in the *third person*, and it's the author who is the narrator, observing and maybe *commenting on* a character's experiences. (In actuality, of course, the author is always the narrator.) Compared with the reader of a *first-person narrative*, the reader of a *third-person narrative* is one step or more further removed from the character.

These basic concepts are not as simple as they may at first seem: a *first-person* narrator cannot always be trusted—the *unreliable narrator* has become a mainstay of both literary and popular fiction. The reader may think they know their character intimately, but it may transpire that they are being fooled—the character has been hiding information and dissembling.

Third-person POV is not simple either and has variations: 1. *Third-person omniscient*. The author tells the reader what every character is thinking and feeling while also describing what is going on around them, whether the characters themselves perceive or understand this or not. The author's view is god-like, the word *omniscient* meaning *all-seeing*. 2. *Third-person objective*. The author *observes* the characters purely from the outside. A character may speak, gesture, act, but there is no description of their inner thoughts or emotions. The nature of their interior world may be deduced by the reader, but the writer does not presume to directly enter their psyche or describe it. 3. *Third-person limited* or *intimate*. These two terms for much the same approach give another sense of how the different forms of third-person POV can result in different relationships to story and character on the part of the reader. When an author tells a story from the POV of a particular character without stepping outside their frame of reference but does not use the subjective narrator, the *I*, employing instead the *she* or *he*, this is said to be the *third-person limited* or *intimate POV*. The reader knows what the character knows, feels what they feel, knows how they think, and is not privileged with any wider, god-like vision. On the one hand, this can be restrictive, since events outside the experience or comprehension of the character cannot, strictly speaking, be communicated. (Although the reader may, of course, glean an understanding that eludes the character. An adult reader, for example, following a child in a story, may comprehend events the child fails to fully or correctly interpret.) On the other hand, this approach privileges the reader with a closer connection to the character. They will share more deeply and *intimately* in their experience. Another term for this literary method is *free indirect discourse*—Jane Austen was one of the first writers to adopt this technique, one that in time, as it focused more and more into the interior lives of characters, led to the stream of consciousness style of writers such as James Joyce and Virginia Woolf.

Why this concern for NPOV in literature though? What is the relevance of NPOV to the director of a movie or a TV show? Why is it so important for a director to understand it and, even if they do, by what means can they articulate it? Here there are two areas to be considered: the nature of NPOV in visual storytelling—what are the *types* of NPOV employed in film?—and the nature of the visual and auditory language used to express and modulate it.

Third-person intimate, or something very close to it, would seem the predominant form of NPOV in visual storytelling, although the objective and omniscient variants also come into play. The audience *observes* a character, is situated on the outside of them, but can be led by the director, through the visual and aural resources of filmic language, to sympathize, even *empathize* with them, sharing in their perception, comprehension, action, and, most importantly, emotion and visceral sensation. This has to be founded in the director's understanding of the screenplay and of the screenwriter's intentions regarding the relative positioning of their characters within the hierarchy of audience engagement.

Narrative point of view in the screenplay

A screenplay is not like a novel. Written in a form derived from the script of a theatre play, it has no *I, she,* or *he* as narrator. (It may be an adaptation of a short story or novel, however, which will indicate which character(s) have the NPOV—so long as the screenwriter has not switched this.) How, then, can the director know "in the shoes" of which character the screenwriter wishes to put the audience? A voice-over spoken by the protagonist will, of course, provide the answer, but many, maybe most, scripts lack this. If the screenplay draws a reader into its narrative and emotional flow, though, and if the filmmaker-reader has the instincts of a storyteller—essential to the director—the character(s) who have the NPOV should be apparent. (If it isn't, maybe the screenplay is not working, maybe the screenwriter has not thought about it sufficiently and has given it to arbitrary characters simply in order to get through the story, or maybe they have adopted a colder, more distanced approach to their protagonist, for example as in a satire or a dystopian allegory, or maybe it's a comedy which in classical fashion invites its audience to *laugh at* its protagonist rather than *feel with* them.) In a story about a detective investigating a crime, for example, and encountering a number of suspects, none of whose thoughts the detective or the audience are privy to, it stands to reason that the NPOV has to be that of the detective as there is *parity of knowledge* between character and audience. There is also, presumably, a shared desire for the culprit to be found and justice to be done. Equally, when one character can see something others cannot, a ghost say—as in the scene from Kurosawa's *Throne of Blood* (based on Shakespeare's *Macbeth*), in which Lord Washizu alone sees the specter of the man he's just had murdered—it's evident the NPOV must lie predominantly with Washizu and not with any of the other characters who remain unaware of the ghost. (In this case there will need to be an element of third-person omniscient NPOV also, so the audience may understand that others do not see the ghost. The director's duty to convey necessary information, in other words, is ever obligatory.)

Note: a screenplay may suggest a single character's NPOV, a dual NPOV, or a multiple/ensemble NPOV. A romance or buddy movie will make use of a dual NPOV, a film with a team of protagonists an ensemble NPOV.

Once the director understands whose the story is, who the protagonist is (or who the protagonists are), generally speaking they will know who should have the predominant NPOV throughout the movie. Sometimes, however, the main story might be told through the eyes of another character—think of F. Scott Fitzgerald's novel *The Great Gatsby* and of Baz Luhrman's adaptation in which Nick Caraway tells the story of Jay Gatsby, the reader of the book and the audience of the film perceiving and understanding the events of Gatsby's life through his eyes. Gatsby's story is thus related from Nick's *narrative perspective*. Usually, however, the narrative perspective is that of the character whose story is being told.

(There is a difference between the terms *narrative POV* and *narrative perspective*. In literature, the former refers to the nature of the reader or audience's connection to the character, whether they are an *I*, a *she*, or a *he*, while the second refers to the relationship of that character to the central story. Fitzgerald presents Nick Caraway in the *first person* but might feasibly, if less effectively, accord him a *third-person* narrative. Either way, Gatsby's story is told from Caraway's *perspective*. Filmmakers often refer to narrative POV and narrative perspective as if they were the same concept, but strictly speaking they are not.)

Another factor in the working of third-person intimate NPOV, and how the director chooses to articulate it, is the different aspects of the audience–character relationship it involves. These might be described as the cognitive, the perceptual, the visceral, and the emotional:

1. The cognitive. Here, the audience knows what the character knows, no more and no less. In other words there's *parity of knowledge*. In detective movies, *Chinatown*, for example, the audience embarks on a journey of discovery together with the protagonist—private investigator Jake Gittes in this case—learning the details of the Mulwray family's intrigue

as and when he learns them. The director Roman Polanski had screenwriter Robert Towne include Gittes in every scene so that the audience knows no more than he does. (There is one exception—when, early in the film, Gittes fails to be aware of the presence of Mrs. Mulwray, whom the audience sees, as he tells colleagues a blue joke.) This makes it harder for screenwriter and director to set up suspense since the audience can never know information of which the protagonist remains ignorant, such as that described by Alfred Hitchcock as "the bomb under the table." Threats that remain unknown to a character create suspense—a banana skin on the sidewalk, a bucket of water over a door, a lurking killer, a ticking bomb. By letting the audience know something the character does not, a screenwriter or director would be breaking the third-person intimate NPOV. This is not to say the filmmaker should not do this, only to point out that it changes the audience's relationship to the character. *Cognitive third-person intimate NPOV* closely ties the audience to the mind of the character as they ask questions, as they interpret or misinterpret, and as they draw conclusions. How the character and the audience *feel* about that epistemic journey may not always equate. The latter may not get to know the former's true emotions until these are revealed later. Such is the case in Alfonso Cuarón's *Roma* in the scene in which Cleo gives birth after an agonizing journey to the hospital. Here, because the audience knows exactly what Cleo knows—that her child has been stillborn—it assumes it shares in her emotions. Later, however, it discovers this assumption to have been misplaced—it was in her *cognitive NPOV* only, not in her *emotional NPOV*, her emotions being entirely at odds with how it imagined them.

2. The perceptual. At first glance the *perceptual* and *cognitive third-person intimate NPOVs* might appear to be the same, and often they are. What a character sees becomes what a character knows, but this is not always the case. In *perceptual NPOV* the audience *sees* or *hears*, or *becomes aware of*, what the character *sees* or *hears* or *becomes aware of*, but may not grasp how the character *understands* that perception. In other words, it does not necessarily share in their cognition. Think of how Sherlock Holmes and James Bond, to give two examples, keep one or more steps ahead of reader and audience, interpreting what they perceive in ways the latter, having shared in their perception but lacking in their powers of deduction and insight, fail to comprehend. (This is not to deny that acute members of the audience may put two and two together and keep up with sleuth or spy.)

3. The visceral. Emotional feeling and visceral sensation are often thought to be one and the same. They are not. Visceral sensation is more primordial than emotion. Lust is not the same as love, "kick" not joy, the gut not the heart. The category of *visceral NPOV* concerns the adrenal, sexual, and gut-based sensations of a character an audience might come to share. The bond can be strong indeed, eliciting, in the darkness of a movie theatre especially, primordial, animal sensations constrained in

everyday life. A film watched in a movie theatre on a large screen with substantial sound system offers an experiential engagement, and when this locks the audience into the visceral sensations of, say, an "action hero," the result can be all-consuming. *Visceral third-person intimate NPOV*, amoral and deeply potent, forms an indisputably compelling currency of film. (The audience may also experience events in a film in a visceral way that characters do not—for example when shocked by a sudden action a character takes in their stride or when made anxious by a danger of which a character remains unaware. There again, the resulting effect can be profound.)

4. The emotional. *Emotional third-person intimate NPOV* is the category that sustains and deepens an audience's relationship with a character throughout a film or TV episode(s) most effectively. The experience of sharing in a character's emotional journey is what most directors, in most films, seek to bring to their audience. (With comedy and satire this may not apply, nor when a protagonist is insufficiently self-aware or deliberately conceived as alienating to the audience, as in the case of Don Diego de Zama in Lucrecia Martel's *Zama*.)

Further to this list, there are three terms pertinent to emotional third-person intimate NPOV that indicate how the audience might relate to a character, or indeed how in life one person might relate to another. Often seen as interchangeable, they are not.

The first is *sympathy*. Here, the ancient Greek word for "with" is combined with the word *pathos*, which meant feeling, sickness, or suffering. The audience watches a character endure physical or emotional discomfort and feels sorry for them. It pities them, but does not *share* in their pain.

The second is *empathy*. Here, the Greek for "in" is combined with *pathos*. The audience *experiences* the emotions of the character, feeling their joy, pain, longing, sadness. Empathy provides the second closest of bonds between audience and character. When the filmmaker elicits empathy for a character, they take the audience on their emotional journey whether or not it agrees with their decisions and actions, because the emotional connection is so strong.

The third term is *identification*. This word has Latin roots—*idem* or "the same" and *entitas* or "thing." When an adult male watches Guillermo del Toro's *Pan's Labyrinth*, he may soon *empathize* with Ofelia, the protagonist, but as she's a young girl and he is not, nor ever was, he does not yet *identify* with her. Later in the film, however, he may find her emotions so recognizable, so universal, that he can indeed begin to *identify* with her. This is the very closest connection of audience to character.

The director's articulation of narrative point of view

Having understood the intentions of the screenwriter as regards NPOV and what might be its shifts and flow both throughout individual scenes and during the film as a whole, the director can employ resources and visual language in order to articulate it that will include casting, mise-en-scène, camera (lensing, placement, movement), sound, music, and editing. When taking into account NPOV, the director does not merely "cover" a scene, shooting whatever angles and footage are required as raw material for its editing ("hosing it down," as journeymen put it), but selects what shots, what angles are needed in order to capture and convey the perception and experience of a particular character or characters.

A director might begin their preparation for the shoot by considering how to introduce their protagonist's NPOV. In Krzysztof Kieślowski's *Three Colors: Blue*, for example, while the NPOV of the protagonist Julie is not ushered in until almost five minutes into the film, it coincides, when it is, with the first time Kieślowski allows the audience to see her—not her face yet, but her eye in huge close-up, a doctor reflected in its pupil. The doctor delivers news of her family after its car accident as, *together with Julie*, the audience awaits the most important information of all—the question that like her it's desperate to have answered: whether or not her young daughter Anna has survived. As Julie asks that crucial question, and like her, the audience awaits the answer, Kieślowski cuts from the close-up of her eye to Julie herself in a big close-up, so that the audience sees her face for the first time, and *feels* what she feels as she waits for and then receives the doctor's devastating answer. This is consummate filmmaking set up in a screenplay that has given the audience only one innocuous line from Julie, spoken off camera, beforehand. The NPOV of Julie established at this moment is both rigorously *cognitive* and heartbreakingly *emotional*, so that from now on the audience keeps with her as she proceeds on her odyssey of painful enlightenment. (In a screenplay without any specific shot descriptions—as indeed is the case with this scene in the script of this film—which some screenwriters and directors prefer, such visual storytelling and articulation of NPOV is left to the director.)

Three Colors: Blue. The doctor, reflected in Julie's eye, delivers news of her husband's death ...

Julie asks for news of her daughter Anna—the first time in the film the audience sees her face.

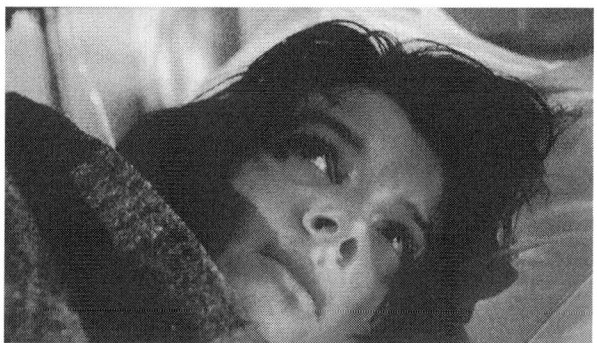

Another movie that keeps the audience waiting for the introduction of the protagonist's NPOV is Cuarón's *Roma*. At the beginning of the film, Cleo is observed from a third-person objective NPOV—the audience observes her as she moves through the shots. Later, in the first scene with her boyfriend Fermin, he's shown through her eyes as the audience is introduced to her NPOV. He's shown in long shot, what's more, while she's seen in a closer shot, an example of the use of *proximity* to bring the audience physically closer to a character. From this intimate and playful moment onwards—when *exactly like Cleo*, the audience misunderstands the nature of Fermin's character (he's not so innocently mischievous, it transpires)—the film's NPOV remains, on the whole, with Cleo. (Although see the earlier note on the subject of Cuarón's deft misdirection as regards cognitive third-person intimate NPOV).

Looking at how NPOV can be modulated, the director will benefit from understanding the various approaches at their disposal, from the most basic to the most sophisticated. The difference between a POV shot and NPOV was explained at the start of this chapter—in its most immediate form, however, NPOV can indeed be articulated through a continuous POV shot in which the camera is the eyes of the character. Such is the case in Chris Milk's Kanye West music video for *All Falls Down*, in which the audience sees events exactly as does the singer.

94   *The approach*

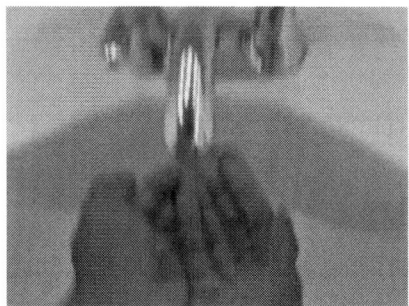
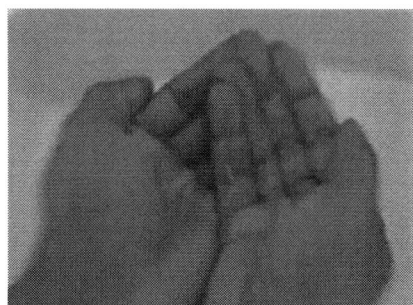

The audience shares Kanye West's view of himself as he raps in a mirror, then splashes his face, in Chris Milk's first-person NPOV music video for *All Falls Down*.

By utilizing third-person intimate NPOV, though, the director can bring more resources into play. In Michael Mann's *The Insider*, Al Pacino's Lowell Bergman, from TV's *60 Minutes*, meets Russell Crowe's Jeffrey Wigand in a hotel room to have him explain key technical documents. Once the two are seated, the NPOV remains with Bergman, who wants information from Wigand just as the audience does—an example of parity of knowledge. Mann uses a tighter lens to bring the audience closer to Bergman and to accentuate him in contrast to his "soft" background while using a wider lens to keep Wigand further away. When Bergman leans in, and is himself closer to Wigand, he motivates a cut to a closer shot on a tighter lens of him so that the experience of the audience is the same as Bergman's. In this instance, the scene's cross-cutting is not "matched" but edited to Bergman's NPOV.

Bergman in close-up, on a tight lens faces Wigand, in long-shot on a wide lens, in Michael Mann's *The Insider*.

When Bergman leans in to a big close-up, he motivates the cut to Wigand, now also in big close-up on a tighter lens. Put simply, Bergman's NPOV is the audience's conduit into the scene.

The looks a character gives—or "shoots," in the language of the screen-writer—provide a crucial motivation for cutting in such a scene too. When cuts are prompted by the look or glance of one character but not another, the NPOV is with that character. It is Bergman's looks to Wigand, not Wigand's to Bergman, that bring about the cuts.

Another means of conveying a particular character's NPOV is to cut at the instant a character moves out of shot to a wider shot so they remain in the frame. In Michael Apted's *The Coal Miner's Daughter*, when Sissy Spacek's Loretta Lynn moves, there's such a cut.

96 *The approach*

Had the NPOV been that of Tommy Lee Jones' Doolittle Lynn, the cut would have been not to the wider shot of the two characters but to a close-up of him. It would have been necessary to show a turn and look from him in order to motivate a cut back to Loretta.

It's important to understand that a scene may be cut to NPOV, rather than to dialogue. When the audience watches a character say nothing but instead listens to someone else speaking, it feels closer to that character, listens with them, and perhaps picks up from their nuances of expression a sense of their inner thoughts and feelings. The director thus gives the character that has the NPOV the most screen time. (This touches on the effectiveness of scenes in which the character with the NPOV is alone, either carrying out some action or in repose—opportunities to deepen audience intimacy with them. This will be evident in a screenplay in which the screenwriter has written such moments.)

As already stated, NPOV need not be restricted to a single character. The director may need their audience to enter another NPOV in order to tell the story. In Hitchcock's *Notorious*, for example, early in the second act, the director selects the NPOV of Nazi antagonist Alex Sebastian. Here, Hitchcock is familiarizing his audience with this in order to set up Alex's own story, but also to prepare for his later glimpse of a sudden kiss between the protagonists Devlin and Alicia—by that point in the film the Nazi's wife. The jealous Alex perceives this in exactly the way Devlin intends, believing they are merely secret lovers and not secret agents snooping for clues to his activities. The NPOV switches from Devlin's to Alex's in that moment so that the audience can share in his sight of the kiss and know he's been fooled.

On hearing Alex coming down the stairs, Devlin and Alicia, having found a Nazi supply of uranium ore in his wine cellar, kiss each other lovingly in order to fool him into believing they are secret lovers and allay any suspicion he might harbor that they're engaged in espionage. Alex appears on the stairs and, as he sees them, the NPOV switches from Devlin's to his:

Alex's POV shot is followed by a closer shot on him that shows his reaction and affirms the NPOV as his.

While a film of course need not be restricted to a single character's NPOV, the director might consider that the more NPOVs they utilize, and the more omniscient the approach they adopt, the more they dilute the audience's emotional connection to their film. This equation is especially pertinent when it comes to shorts. With only twenty, fifteen, ten, or five minutes even, the director needs every precious second to tauten the audience's emotional engagement—by way of a single character's NPOV if possible. There are no firm rules, however, especially for features and TV shows. In Robert Altman's movies, for example, the NPOV weaves constantly among ensembles of characters. In TV the richness of the long novel comes into play, and the suspense created by shifting from one story strand to another, from one character's NPOV to another, can be cumulatively compelling, holding an audience through a season of episodes, then through several years' worth of seasons.

Finally, a note that individual shots, as in the case of the POV shot, may suggest a specific connection between the audience and the film. It may be helpful, then, to list the following terms:

1. *Third-person voyeur.* The audience sees through or past foreground elements as if spying. The director may reveal the character whose POV this is, or they may reveal that it is no one's, but the tension and suspense such shots create can be highly effective.
2. *Third-person obscured.* Similar to third-person voyeur except that the audience sees crucial information in part only.
3. *Third-person ignorant.* The audience sees nothing. Something important is concealed.
4. *Hyper POV.* The camera is placed at the most dramatic place in the action, regardless of any safe or even plausible human perspective, to shoot the most dynamic aspects of an event in the most dynamic fashion. Often used in action movies, but first seen in the famous

Lumière Brothers short in which a train barrels towards the camera. Unused to the experience of watching a film, audiences flinched at the approach of the locomotive.

Another articulation of NPOV might be described as *Third-person "follow and accompany."* Andrea Arnold does this in *American Honey*. The camera tends to show the protagonist Star from behind as it follows her, then settles to show her in profile rather than from the front, whereas it shoots what she sees in the way she sees it, so that of course the audience shares in her perception. This creates both a distance and a closeness to the character, according her a touching respect.

In Andrea Arnold's *American Honey*, the director does not allow the camera to get ahead of protagonist Star, but shows whom she is confronting from her angle.

Sound design is also an important element of the articulation of NPOV. Sounds significant to a character are exaggerated so that the audience hears them as the character does, or so that it shares with them an image or event previously connected to that sound. Music also can be effective; stings or themes replayed can evoke memories of previous scenes and emotions significant to a character.

12 Introduction of the protagonist and main characters

The director needs to take scrupulous care in noting precisely when and how in the screenplay the main characters are introduced, and must consider how these moments are to be executed in their film. Because the nature of these introductions and the preconceptions they might convey will have a crucial impact on how the audience feels about these characters going forward, the director, on "meeting" their screenplay, needs to ask certain essential questions. At what point, in what context, and how, do the protagonist and other main character(s) first appear? Will the audience understand they are central to the story? Or will it be led to discover this? What is revealed and what concealed about these central characters before they begin their journey? How will the audience feel about them? Do they seem likable, or neutral, or are they problematic? What will the audience know about them? What will it *want* to know and what *questions* will it ask? How much is it supposed to understand and how much misunderstand them and any action they are taking or predicament they are in? Will it observe them initially from a distance or will it be closer to them, perhaps even be taken directly and immediately into their narrative point of view? Are they taking action? Are they in jeopardy? Are they trying to do something or looking for something? Or are they simply going about their daily business?

Will the protagonist be alone? Will they be alone in a shot apart from other characters that are present, or will they be seen among other characters, one of a group or a crowd. Will they be in the back of the shot, or prominent in it, in the foreground perhaps, or in a strong position in the frame—maybe on the third, "the golden mean"? Will they be large in the frame or small? On the left or right? How much will the audience see of them? Will they be masked at first, then revealed? Will they be in shadow or light? How long will the audience have to wait before it sees their face, their eyes? What will distinguish them from other characters? Placement in the frame? Costume? Movement or stasis? How long is it before they speak? Will they speak before they are seen or be seen before they speak? Will they motivate camera movement and/or a cut, either by moving or by "shooting" a look somewhere or to someone?

Is the protagonist present in the first scene or brought into the story later? If later, how much of the world of the film and how much of its tensions and conflicts does the screenplay reveal before they are introduced? How much of the story has already taken place? When the protagonist appears, is their connection with what has already been shown evident, or will the audience be made to wait before it discovers that link? How much will a character's introduction lead the audience to be invested in them? Will it be invested in them to begin with or will that deeper connection follow, once it has become familiar with the character?

Then there are questions related to what kind of a film or TV show the screenplay has been written for. For example, will this be the first time the audience has met the main character or has it met them before—in previous movies within the same franchise maybe, or in previous episodes of a TV show? How, at the start of a further season of a TV show, are the main characters to be introduced—as the audience has previously known them, or in different circumstances? Do such circumstances prompt questions as to what has taken place since the previous season ended? Does a familiar protagonist enter the action early on, or does the screenplay make the audience wait before its hero or anti-hero enters the fray, perhaps for most of a first episode (a means of creating powerful suspense)?

Is the protagonist a child when first seen, becoming an adult sooner or later? Is there anything in the screenplay to indicate how the audience is to recognize the character when the shift to a different actor is to be made? In Richard Linklater's *Boyhood*, protagonist Mason Evans Jr. goes through several transformations as he passes through the stages of boyhood and adolescence, and the deft and inventive variations the director employs in order to introduce each one—the way the character enters shot, his changes of appearance, the change from one actor to another—are an indication of a filmmaker not only in control of the elements of directing craft but fully aware of how they can be used in relation to the specific film he is making.

Above all, the director should consider how the crucial elements of dramaturgy and storytelling in their screenplay inform *how* they might choose to introduce the main characters in their film. Are there specific intentions that might determine the ways in which the moment is to be staged and shot? A character is talking on the phone, or working on a computer perhaps and a chat exchange is shown, which sparks the story, lets the audience know the character's name, introduces other characters, so there's no need to reveal the face of the character present until the very last moment, or at a point of dramatic significance. When a character is preparing for some task, getting dressed, assembling equipment, there's a story to be told in that without showing their face immediately, the nature of their costume or equipment provides clues to attributes of the character, so that when they are finally revealed the audience already knows important aspects of them. When a character is going about their business and something untoward is to occur, the director might want the audience to see the character beforehand in order that they register their shift of demeanor when circumstances change. When an apparently innocent character transpires to be devious, their introduction might be made to seem innocuous so that, when their intentions are revealed, they have greater impact (Firmin in *Roma*).

A protagonist may be "announced" in their predicament, as in Lucrecia Martel's *Zama*, in the first shot of which Don Diego stands on the shoreline regarding the ocean, while in the background a group of indigenous children walk from the sea carrying pots. Here the shot, presumably described in Martel's screenplay, gives an immediate sense of the film's period and place, shows Don Diego's somewhat pompous demeanor, thus suggesting his unsympathetic nature, and reveals through its setting and composition his situation as a character eager to return home while also giving visual representation to a thematic concern of the film—European colonization. (Don Diego looks from right to left, which perhaps seems to suggest a look to home—a look from left to right might seem to suggest a look *out* from home.) Although this character introduction, also the prelude to the film, might be described as expository, it is far from being merely descriptive. Don Diego, seen in long shot in western attire complete with tricorn hat, makes a bold contrast to the indigenous naked children and the untouched environment around him. The audience asks who this man is, where he is, and what he's doing here, away from home. Both the shot's formal composition and Don Diego's posture are static and striking, conveying the sense of an immobile, inflexible world from which the audience, as much as the character, is eager to escape—a purposeful introduction to the film's protagonist that informs the audience's sense of him as the story progresses.

A protagonist may equally be concealed throughout initial scenes and sequences until a key dramatic moment, as is the case with Julie in *Three Colors: Blue* (see the previous chapter). Kieślowski has ample opportunity to reveal her to the audience beforehand, as she travels with her husband and daughter in their car, but chooses not to—while her husband is shown from behind, his face hidden. Only their daughter is seen, whom the audience will lose from the film just as Julie loses her from her life. Julie is, however, allowed to speak off camera at one point, thus making the audience aware of her presence. (Were it not aware, her eventual introduction would be confusing.) There's a further aspect to the manner of this introduction too, related to the casting of Julie. Audiences are almost certain to know that Juliette Binoche plays the main character in the film, and will be keen to see her at the earliest opportunity. Kieślowski teases them by allowing them to hear her but makes them wait until they see her face. Having a known actor or star playing the central role affects how the director chooses to announce a character, adding an element of additional suspense to their storytelling that lesser-known actors and non-actors cannot elicit.

A screenplay may indicate that a main character need not be announced in such a bold fashion, that the communication of their importance should be delayed—the reverse approach to Kieślowski's in *Three Colors: Blue*.

In Alfonso Cuarón's *Roma*, housekeeper Cleo, played by non-actor Yalitza Aparicio, is seen moving through the large house of an affluent family as she goes about her business. There is nothing to suggest the central story of the film is to be hers. It isn't until the later scene with her boyfriend Fermin (see the previous chapter) that the audience, in entering her NPOV, comes to know her as the central character. Had the director chosen to connect the audience more directly with her from the beginning, its involvement might not develop so effectively. By introducing her as he does, he gives a strong sense of her modest status, avoids aggrandizing or romanticizing her, and provides both a surprise and a boost to narrative energy when he comes to grant her the spotlight. He also gives himself time to introduce the world of the family for whom she works, its home, and its individual members. In contrast to Juliette Binoche, Yalitza Aparicio, at least at the time of the film's release, was not known and when cast wasn't even an actor. Cleo's introduction, then, could not be less conspicuous. She is an ordinary person going about her ordinary life. The depths of her emotions and the honesty of her insights and self-awareness, as they come to be revealed, gain in resonance as she becomes more and more the soul of the film.

A screenplay may place its protagonist in a situation of danger in order to bring a sense of drama into a film early on, when the tension in the main story itself will take time to develop. Such is the case with Michael Mann's *The Insider*, which begins with Al Pacino's Lowell Bergman on a mission to secure an interview for *60 Minutes* in a war-torn Middle-Eastern country. Here, Mann makes great use of Pacino's stardom by having the character's face obscured by a blindfold. As with Binoche in *Three Colors: Blue*, so with Pacino here—the audience wants to see the star, but the director makes them wait. Pacino's tell-tale locks of black hair, splayed out over his blindfold, make his identity obvious—but it isn't until the end of the second scene that he takes off the blindfold, and even then Mann does not show his face, shooting him in silhouette from the back.

There are two main characters in the movie, the other being Russell Crowe's Jeffrey Wigand, and in introducing them one after the other, Mann demonstrates another aspect worth consideration in the introduction of main characters—the importance of announcing them separately and striking a contrast between them. Whereas Bergman is introduced on a mission, in an environment outside of his own, in a war-torn Middle East, Wigand is seen taking papers from his office while colleagues are in the throes of a birthday party. As he drives home—a substantial residence indicating a considerable degree of affluence—to his wife and two daughters, the tension of the Bergman introduction echoes, helped by an ominous score. The contrasts between the two characters are pronounced. The casually clad Bergman is introduced blindfolded among potentially hostile people, his sole companion the electrician scouting the location for an interview, the purpose of his mission revealed during the sequence. The besuited Wigand, introduced in a close profile in his office, walks out of the building with documents he evidently shouldn't be taking, and is then seen at home with his family, his purpose still not revealed. One character is at ease in a hostile environment, the other uncomfortable in a familiar one.

Rear Window offers an especially ingenious introduction of protagonist L. B. "Jeff" Jefferies. The audience is privileged with an initial voyeuristic survey of his neighbors' activities, out of his eponymous rear window, only to discover the camera settling on the sleeping Jeff, who soon after adopts the same "peeping Tom" gaze. The audience, having itself enjoyed the diversion of snooping, can hardly complain about Jeff's habit, to the contrary, empathizing with him. Absent that first foray, it might have a quiet different attitude!

The director should ensure that the introduction of each main character in the screenplay is clearly marked, that they are distinct, and that one does not get in the way of another. It will help if each has their separate scene or sequence, perhaps in different locations. Hitchcock re-shot the opening scene of *Notorious* so that it introduced Alicia only, leaving the introduction of Devlin until the next sequence. That such a master should have accepted Devlin's presence in the screenplay in the opening scene shows not only how any director can make mistakes, but also how attention to the detail of the screenplay is paramount. The director is neither a parrot, blindly translating the page to the screen, nor a wrecker, sweeping away the screenwriter's complex connective tissue merely in order to "make the film their own." If directing is a "job of work," as John Ford described it, it is also the job of making the film work. When a problem in the screenplay is not fixed in the screenplay, it invariably has to be fixed at much greater expense in production, re-shoots, or post-production.

The director should consider what the screenplay reveals about the mindset of a major character through any action in which they're engaged as they are introduced, and how *economically* and *visually* such information is imparted. Sofia Coppola begins her story of a washed-up movie star in *Somewhere* with a scene depicting a car driving around in three circles, going out of shot each time in a dreary, flat, arid, nondescript landscape, until it pulls up. In the continuing wide shot Stephen Dorff's Johnny Marco climbs out to stand and gaze absently into the distance. Nothing could illustrate the ennui of the character more clearly—through emptiness, action repeated, setting, and the lack of satisfactory outcome. Barry Jenkins' coming-of-age film *Moonlight* starts with Chiron running from bullies and hiding in a crack house—his flight from open to enclosed space the prelude to the retreats he makes throughout the film until his final meeting with Kevin, at which point, eschewing defensiveness and fear, he accepts his love.

The introduction of what seems to be a main character, but who will vanish from the story at an early stage, requires particular attention on the part of the director. Janet Leigh's Marion Crane in Alfred Hitchcock's

Psycho fails to survive the film's infamous shower sequence. Were the director to have implied that Crane was destined for an early demise, her death, for all of the calculated skill of the montage that depicts it, would not be so shocking. It is because the audience has come to know her, know her NPOV, and despite its qualms come to be invested in her and her actions, that it is so shaken by her murder. Julie's daughter Anna is lost to *Three Colors: Blue* when the family's car runs into a tree early in the film. Until her mother, she is the only character to whom the audience is granted access. Kieślowski shows Julie's husband from behind as he stands outside their car, stretching his arms, but his face remains hidden—an example of how important it can be for the director *not* to announce a character in the film, although they may be introduced in the screenplay. The youth who witnesses the crash is seen in profile looking right, looking down, then in profile looking left, but never looking anywhere remotely close to the axis of the camera, so the audience, quite deliberately, is denied connection to him. The daughter is thus the audience's sole "entry point" into the film (made all the stronger as the film's opening shot, under the chassis of the car as it speeds along the freeway, is so *un*-human as a POV).

As a screenplay will not often describe the exact visual language of a character's introduction, it will be up to the director to understand the screenwriter's intentions and to translate them into the language of the screen as an address to the audience. When a director makes the audience have to wait, have to work to see a character's face, when they conceal then reveal it, the audience, already more interested in the character, will become more invested in them. When that reveal finally comes, the director might do well to afford it one clear beat to heighten it, providing the audience with the answer to the question for which it has been waiting, namely "Who is this?" Showing a character firstly from the back before showing their face, as Hitchcock does with Devlin, and Ari Aster does with Florence Pugh's Dani in his *Midsommar*, may be a detail, but is an important stratagem in the process of character introduction. Showing a minor character talking but delaying the reverse shot on whom they are talking to, as at the start of Mike Leigh's *Another Year* or Quentin Tarantino's *Once upon a Time in Hollywood*, is a similar device to keep the audience waiting, thus creating suspense through simple visual storytelling.

Whether a director storyboards their entire movie (as would be the case with an "action" or superhero movie probably, or any film dependent on complex stunts, special effects, and visual effects), storyboards certain scenes, or does not storyboard at all, the introduction of a main character is better storyboarded in order to make clear the connection of intention and execution. The director's shot list then needs to indicate the coverage that will ensure this initial appearance is realized to greatest effect—from screenplay to screen, few elements are more important.

Note: following a story, and watching a movie, are processes of cumulative memory, and there may be a moment later in a film when the audience might need to be subliminally reminded of a character's introduction and of the impressions it left. The angle and composition of the original shot might then be mirrored, in which case the scene in which this occurs should also be storyboarded.

13 Key images, objects, and motifs

Because screenwriters *write*—they use words on the page to describe the action and provide the dialogue of the film—many people assume that the means of their discourse defines the limits of their currency. The screenwriter writes the words, the director and cinematographer add the images, the actors the emotions, each cumulative step in the creation of a film discrete and inviolable by the others. This is a misperception, in the first instance because filmmaking is a collaborative process, each craft serving and served by each other craft, and in the second because a good screenwriter writes so much more than words and dialogue. In the latter case, for instance, they write *subtext*—currents of meaning that lie beneath the surface of speech contradicting what is actually being said: "You don't love me!" = "I need you to tell me you love me!" Moreover, the actions they write have a *visual* component—their words are used to describe not ideas or other words but the *events*, *images*, and *world* of the film. The dialogue, subtext, description, and action, what's more, convey the *thoughts* and *emotions* of the characters. The language of the screenplay may be functional—the polar opposite of the prose of, say, Marcel Proust or Vladimir Nabokov—but can nevertheless convey the narrative, image-rich, and emotional universe of a film.

A screenplay may not be a storyboard but, while the screenwriter does not draw the panels of a graphic novel, they *do* describe and define individual images. The action they write will involve props, objects handled and used in one way or another by the characters. The descriptions they write will specify concrete things too—a character's possessions maybe, that convey a sense of their *character*—or objects significant to the plot and/or the story. They may describe a place, as landscape or a cityscape, and they may describe a thing that is a part of something larger—what is known in literary terms as a *synecdoche*—a cart wheel for a cart, a foot in a gleaming shoe stepping out of a car for a besuited man, a staring eye for a corpse. The specificity of such an image can carry far more resonance than a shot of the entire thing itself because it is an image that prompts a second image on the *screen of the mind*. (The visual language of film is not merely the portrayal of something on a physical screen but the conjuring in the minds of the audience of something else that first entity suggests.)

An object or image may also be a *metaphor* (a thing representative of another thing) or *symbol* (usually taken to mean a material thing that represents an abstract thing or quality). In an early scene in Alfred Hitchcock's *Vertigo*, for instance, James Stewart's injured Scottie Ferguson tries to balance a walking stick on his desk, only to have it topple over. Like the tower of the church in which the movie's finale takes place, the walking stick is a phallic symbol. There's a fear of impotence in the protagonist, and the film exudes both his male insecurity and perhaps that of its director. Both metaphor and symbol, the image of the toppling stick, its implication of limpness watched by Scottie's female friend Midge, encapsulates the movie's thematic paradox: male sexual obsession derives from male fear of impotence. In the same director's *Notorious*, the white drink Devlin has given the hung-over Alicia early in the story and the black coffee Alex gives her towards the end, the one an elixir, the other a poison, form a *motif*—a *repeated image*—of life and death that counterpoints the narrative bookending: Alicia heads into mortal peril/Alicia heads out of mortal peril. There is also the motif of the wine bottle in the film: a champagne bottle, which suggests romance, and a burgundy bottle filled with the Nazi's uranium ore, which suggests death. (In the director's *Rear Window*, Jeff's camera, with its telephoto lens, is a potent image that encapsulates both his voyeurism and, with its phallic shape, his lust.)

Such images and motifs are integral to the story. The screenwriter writes them. The director shoots them. But the director might also check to see that, where there's a significant image or object, it has been set up earlier so it might become a motif, with all of the resonance that can carry. Alfonso Cuarón wrote the screenplay to his film *Roma*, but at what point in his writing process did he arrive at the decision to make the first image of the film the waves of soapy water from Cleo's mop flowing over tiles? Might he have found this only once he had his ending—when Cleo enters the waves of the ocean to rescue the children? Both kinds of waves here form a symbol of cleansing, Cleo cleaning the house, the ocean cleansing Cleo of her guilt over her desire to see her baby stillborn. The poetry of the image here is neither decorative nor descriptive, not poetry separate from story or character but, to the contrary, integral to both. This is the type of imagery, maybe "image system," a proficient screenwriter will set up in their screenplay.

In Andrea Arnold's short film *Wasp*, the climax to the story occurs when Zoë discovers a wasp crawling into her baby's mouth. Earlier, she opens a window to release a wasp from her kitchen. A motif, then, and as with those in *Notorious* and *Roma*, one that suggests a narrative and thematic symmetry. A wasp set free while Zoë remains trapped. A wasp set free again, but on this second occasion also freeing Zoë from her obsession for David and clearing the air, maybe, for a realistic relationship between them. (The image of a wasp in a child's mouth was Arnold's inspiration for her film, her screenplay constructed around it.)

Some directors repeat certain images in successive films, a phenomenon possible usually either when they are also the screenwriter, or when they are working closely with a writer on their screenplays. Or it may be that such imagery is not specified in the screenplay but comes about through the collaboration of director and production designer on the texture and detail of set dressing. Wong Kar-wai, for example, favors fans and clocks. What might this mean? Are these images just as integral to story and character as Arnold's wasp? Maybe not, and maybe Wong Kar-wai himself does not fully understand their significance. Is such poetry of time and motion superfluous? Is it the icing on the story and character cake? Or is it a breath of the director's unifying sensibility and vision, the agent that binds the cake's ingredients? Perhaps it can be helpful sometimes for the screenwriter and director *not* to understand an image entirely? The same goes for the audience. As with character and Kiarostami's insight into it, there perhaps needs to be an element of mystery at the heart of key images. Cinema after all, at its best, expresses what cannot be understood consciously or analytically, and the image takes pride of place in that deep and enigmatic communication.

Some objects or images are included because they are dissonant—to an event or a tone maybe. Bank robbers in balaclavas or ski-masks might prove frightening, but a gang posing in the masks of US presidents, such as the one in Kathryn Bigelow's crime thriller *Point Break*, offers more ambiguous fare. Playful, sinister, satirical, and dehumanizing at one and the same time, the masks bring tonal suspense to a scene already suspenseful by its very nature. Such an image is all the more powerful because the audience will have in its mind the expected picture of ski-masked miscreants so that the clash between what it would have expected and what it sees produces a *meta* drama, one that lies beyond the portrayed event—a useful instance of how a film "happens" in three places: within the world of the film, across the planarity of the screen (the vehicle for visual language), and, perhaps most importantly of all, in the hearts, minds, and guts of the audience. (There's a fourth region too: in the memories—emotional, cognitive, and visceral—of the audience after watching the film.)

While on the subject of images and dissonance, it's worth considering how an image, a presence, may be used to convey an absence. There are few better examples of this than the shots of the empty mats in Akira Kurosawa's *Throne of Blood*. After Washizu has had Miki and his son murdered, he is confronted by the sight of two empty mats at court, an image contrasted with a row of occupied mats on the opposite side of the room, and that is repeated and reduced to a single mat before Miki's ghost appears. This image of absence evokes powerfully the protagonist's crime in a way that no line of dialogue, no action even, could. It is an example of purely cinematic language. It has no need of dialogue or subtitles and speaks across cultures and verbal languages. There is something quintessential and primordial in its eloquence, its embodiment of meaning simple, uninflected, and chilling.

The word *motif* may be applied to visual elements, such as the stripes and bars so frequent in classic film noir, manifested by venetian blinds and the shadows they cast. Line, shape, depth, contrast and affinity, color are some of these elements—one might usefully refer to them as *ikones* after the Greek word for image (a parallel with *phonemes*, elements of spoken sound, from the Greek for sound). Such *ikones* are often referred to as an aspect of the *image system* of a film. In *Notorious* there is a contrast of angles and curves manifested in locations and set design—the curving shoreline seen in the distance beyond the curving facade of Alicia's balcony and the angular design of the panels in the front door of Alex's mansion, for example. Image systems such as this are perhaps unlikely to be specified in a screenplay, although they may be implicit in the story it tells. In *Notorious*, for instance, Devlin is the masculine, the inflexible, the selfish, the weak, Alicia the feminine, the flexible, the selfless in the face of the demands made upon her, and ultimately the more resilient. Doesn't the film's dual geometry reflect this? Would it work with such subliminal force of it didn't? Doesn't it have its foundations in Ben Hecht's screenplay and in his masterly construction of Devlin and Alicia as characters, even though he may not have explicitly described such geometry in his screenplay? If so, isn't this an illustration of the deep level at which a director needs to understand their screenplay? Themes, tones, characters, conflicts—the director, with their production designer and cinematographer, needs to render the narrative and dramaturgical visual. Such a task is far from the additive process often imagined that is described at the beginning of this chapter. It's both extractive and transformative, taking the abstract notions the screenwriter has made dramatic to render them an indispensable aspect of a film's visual language.

In past decades in the UK, one would talk about going to the movies as "going to the pictures." While movement may invariably be a vital element of cinema, pictures *always* are, whether up on the physical screen or in the screen of the mind.

14 Opening image, frame, shot

When students of filmmaking discuss the merits of their favorite opening shots, they tend to focus on those of technique, of grandeur, or of bravura conception rather than purpose or function—not that these are by any means mutually exclusive. While an effective final shot may resonate and remain in conscious memory, the first, so often lost in the accumulation of everything that follows, tends to lack that staying power and, unless it's spectacular or markedly unusual, can be passed over without a second thought as the movie begins. Yet when one returns to the first image or shot of a great film, a good film even, a day later, a year, maybe years later, one often discovers that, spectacular or not, it has remained filed away in one's memory. The initial step in a director's storytelling, it can be deceptive in its simplicity or bold in its complexity, but when deftly conceptualized and effectively designed may grab attention, pose a question, set a tone or tones, reveal character, usher in the narrative point of view, establish a world, incorporate theme, initiate rhythm, affirm a genre, play with a trope, place the audience *in medias res* of an action, inaugurate the register of the drama or introduce the opposite in order to lay a trap, prompt in the minds of the audience a particular desire or need to know, simply mesmerize it, proclaim the director's voice and style, or achieve a combination of several of the above.

This understood, what are the fundamental questions the director needs to ask as they look for their opening image and shot (which may incorporate many images), irrespective of whether the clues come from the screenplay or whether they will need to be designed. There are of course many issues to be considered. How should the film announce itself and what might the audience see? A person, people, an object, a setting—whether a room, a place, a vista, or what? Should the director start their film with a wide shot or a big close up? Should the frame be empty or full? Should the image be shown immediately or should it be discovered? And what of the choice of framing? Might something be shown in its entirety or only in part? How will the *aspect ratio*, the proportions of the frame, affect these decisions? 1.33:1 / 1.66:1 / 1.85:1 / 2.40:1 will inform them in different ways—a close up in the first will leave little else in the frame while one in the last will leave most of the length of the frame free and need to be placed to the left, the center, or the right. Might the shot show *flat space* (a close view of a brick wall, a painting, patterned fabric as some examples)?—Michael Mann's *The Insider* begins with a shot of the blindfold as seen by Bergman, its wearer—or might it show *deep space* (a view down a hallway, a street, a valley perhaps)?— George Lucas' *Star Wars IV – A New Hope* begins with a spacecraft heading off into the deep universe, chased by the behemoth of a craft hunting it down. Or might the audience be faced with mid-space, something more neutral? Should the NPOV be from a human perspective, should it be god-like, or should it be striking in some way? What might the audience understand about this image/shot and what might it not understand? Should the shot pose a question? If so, what? Should it be contextualized? Uncontextualized? Familiar or not? Mysterious, ambiguous, or definitive?

Does sound precede this nascent visual moment, does the image precede the sound, or are they simultaneous? Is the shot static or does it move? Does the shot develop to explain itself, its meaning, or does it lead to something very different, a different object or depiction of space or depth, or is it self-contained but perhaps with a significance that will become apparent only later? (The act of following a story, whether on the page, on the screen, or from the lips of a storyteller, tribal bard, or everyday friend—if their storytelling is any good—is not so much the constant search for *knowledge* as it is the unremitting, ongoing hunt for *meaning*.) Does this image comply with the audience's expectations of the movie they're about to watch, its genre, its tone, its precursors should it have any, or is it incongruous, dissonant, in short unexpected, or is it perhaps innocuous—deceptively so, perhaps? Does it soothe or does it startle? Does it lull or does it shock? Is something happening or is nothing happening? Is something starting to happen or does the camera capture an action *in medias res*? Does it show an object to be pondered or does it immediately engage the audience in the process of following a story?

In the screenplay to *Looper*, writer-director Rian Johnson begins thus:

```
EXT, EDGE OF CORNFIELDS - DAY
A pocket watch. Open. Ticking. Swinging from a Chain
```

And in *Beasts of the Southern Wild* writers Lucy Alibar and Benh Zeitlin start with this:

```
EXT. HUSHPUPPY'S HOUSE - DAWN
An abandoned looking trailer sits on top of two
15-foot-tall oil drums. Distant thunder trembles
through the peeling metal panels. The structure is
in such disrepair, that surely no one lives here.
But then, a light goes on.
```

112   *The approach*

Each example offers a precise description of an *image*. Each hints at *motion*, whether "swinging" or "trembling" (the latter a deft link between the auditory and the visual). The first poses the questions "What does this mean?" and "How is the concept of time to factor in to this story?," while the second establishes *a place*, a decaying trailer, and poses a question: "Who turned on the light?" (Note the judicious comma before "a light goes on"—the punctuation a nuance of nimble suspense.) Neither is spectacular, neither proclaims virtuosity or grandeur, but the writers of each are completely clear as to the function of their choice and, with a single, simple shot, begin to tell their story.

Other screenwriters may be less exact, describing a situation while leaving the choice of the precise opening image to the director, as is the case with Emily V. Gordon and Kumail Nanjiani's screenplay for *The Big Sick*, which, after an initial voice-over, begins thus:

```
A CREDIT SEQUENCE PLAYS.
Kumail drives an Uber around Chicago with VARIOUS
PASSENGERS in the backseat.
```

Nothing here to define an opening shot. The film begins *in medias res*, the audience invited to catch up with an ongoing story as Kumail's job and the world of Chicago are established without further ado.

Even an auteur as precise in his craft as Stanley Kubrick may not describe his exact opening shot in his screenplay, or such is the case with *A Clockwork Orange*:

```
INT. KOROVA MILKBAR - NIGHT
Tables, chairs made of nude fiberglass figures.
Hypnotic atmosphere.
Alex, Pete, Georgie and Dim, teenagers stoned on their
milk-plus, their feet resting on faces, crotches,
lips of the sculptured furniture.
```

Hardly precise. The shot that begins the film is by contrast meticulously crafted, beginning with a big close-up of Alex the Droog gazing into the lens with threatening mischief, his demonic stare motivating the camera to pull back and reveal, firstly, his three fellow Droogs, and then the clientele of the Korova Milkbar with its singular decor. This arresting opening shot with its images conjures characters, world, and an uneasy tone teetering between the comedic and the menacing.

Krzysztof Kieślowski's *Three Colors: Blue* begins with a black screen, opening titles over, accompanied by a rushing sound. "What," the audience wonders, "is that sound?" The first traces of any image on the screen are faint, vertical stripes, black on black. "What," the audience wonders, "are those stripes? What is their black background"—in short "What are we seeing? How do the stripes connect to the sound? And when will it know what that sound is?" As the camera pulls back, to reveal more stripes and more blackness (an example of what Bruce Block, in his book *The Visual Story*, describes as *ambiguous space*), the audience wonders "What might be the scale of what we are seeing, large or small?" As Kieślowski's camera continues to pull back to reveal this to be a huge close up of a car's tire, the audience has its answer to the question of the meaning of the image and to its scale while also understanding the nature of the rushing sound—the tire on the road surface. It also gains knowledge of where the camera, and thus the audience, is placed—under the chassis of a car hurtling along the road and perilously close to its surface, a position that *feels* as well as looks dangerous. The rushing sound then breaks into a rhythm that matches the pillars and the light passing in the background—again a link of the auditory to the visual. "Who," the audience asks, "is in this car and where are they going?" (The audience does not reflect on these questions but asks them nevertheless, albeit passingly—one might say that it *experiences* them.) And, although this is probably not a conscious question: "When will I meet a character who can offer a conduit into the film?" It is, of course, also asking the most fundamental question, namely "What is this story to be?"

At this very moment Kieślowski cuts, giving a partial answer to who is in the car by showing a hand, a child's it seems, holding what appears to a flapping candy wrapper, reaching out of an open window. This new information begs the following questions: "Who is this child? Are they in danger, traveling in such a fast car?"

There's nothing spectacular in this, nothing out of the ordinary as regards the things or events shown (although the camera placement is striking), yet the audience's mindset of curiosity, questioning, and foreboding has been acculturated within the space of a few seconds. It's a notably effective way to begin the movie, conveying the visceral sense of danger that prefigures subsequent events with an adept economy. With its camera position it also eschews any human NPOV, so leaving the audience longing for a character to be "with"—and thus, after the second cut, causing it to invest in the girl revealed looking out of the car's rear windshield. Not a word is spoken during that initial shot, nor any character revealed, nor any narrative context or exposition offered, and yet it immediately engages the audience by involving them in the game of meaning central to story and storytelling. (The shot also prepares the audience for a similar camera position to be employed in an upcoming shot when Kieślowski reveals leaking brake fluid.)

114 *The approach*

An opening shot that contrasts with this simplicity is also a fine example of conception and *visual storytelling* craft. In Max Ophüls' period romance *The Earrings of Madame De ...* the long introductory shot, coming after a couple of initial captions describing the uneventful life of Madame De ... (the audience never discovers her full name), begins with the image of jewels in an open drawer as a woman's gloved hand points at, and hovers over, a pair of earrings before opening an adjacent case of jewelry and effects, again hovering, then reaching to open a closet opposite—in the mirror of which the audience does *not* see the woman herself—to reveal more drawers, closed but with an extrusion of ostrich feathers, after which—the camera pulling back to show the woman's shadow—she moves on to open a second mirrored door that, like the first, fails to reveal her reflection, disclosing a row of dresses and a top shelf of bric-a-brac before she continues to a third mirrored door that once again permits no view of her, inside of which are fur coats on hangers, one of which she takes down, fondles, then replaces before returning to the previous closet—the audience catching a fleeting glimpse of her partial profile now, and also of her other, ungloved hand—to reach for a hat on the top shelf, knocking over in the process a bible, which she retrieves (as again the audience catches sight of her profile), before taking the hat and returning to the dressing table—evidently where she was first situated—and in looking at herself in an ornately bedecked mirror provides the audience with its first view of her face, tries on the hat, lowers its veil, takes up and poses with a jeweled necklace, which she rejects in favor of a crucifix that in turn she discards for the earrings she originally hesitated over, tries them on, slips them into a pouch, rises, and, pushing shut one of the closet doors she passes, heads for a bed from which she picks up a handkerchief before crossing to the door of the room and exiting.

End of shot!

Such a falteringly elaborate sentence fails to do justice to either the elegance or the eloquence of Ophüls' shot, in itself a *visual sentence* of remarkable virtuosity that achieves the following: 1. The introduction and emphasis of the earrings of the film's title. 2. The introduction of a character, Madame De ..., searching for something but being indecisive in the process—a flaw that will have consequences for her as the story develops. 3. The use of a camera that has the audience *follow* and *accompany* her in that search. 4. The audience wants Madame De ... to achieve her goal even before it knows what this is. 5. The revelation, through her belongings and wardrobe, of her tastes and lifestyle. 6. The misdirection of the audience, who will later come to understand she is far from affluent and has financial problems—the reason she is trying to decide on what to pawn. 7. The teasing of the audience by the withholding of Madame De ...'s face. 8. The introduction of the notion of moral transgression, implied when she knocks the bible from the shelf and when she rejects the crucifix. 9. The revelation of her sensuality as she strokes the fur of her coat. 10. The eventual introduction of the protagonist as she looks at herself in the mirror, a moment when the audience *shares* and *invests in her* because it's been made to wait to see her face. This brings the audience into her NPOV, establishing her as its conduit into the film. 11. The showing of the environment of her bedroom and its decor—further insight into her world. 12. By not cutting but "editing" within a fluid camera and so utilizing real time, Ophüls places the audience in Madame De ...'s temporal experience and compels it to follow her story.

A similarly complex opening shot in an interior, but involving many more characters and lasting in this case all of nine minutes, can be seen in Hou Hsiao-hsien's *Flowers of Shanghai*, while few openings can be more spectacular than that of Orson Welles' *Touch of Evil* or Paul Thomas Anderson's *Boogie Nights*, both involving whole neighborhoods, the latter traveling from an exterior to an interior to give a comprehensive introduction to both world and milieu. Another approach can be seen at the start of Hitchcock's *Rear Window* as the camera pushes out of an open window to pan around the backs of the apartments beyond, spying at the matins of their residents, and coercing a willing audience into a voyeuristic POV so that it can hardly criticize protagonist L. B. Jefferies when, moments later, he chooses to spy on his neighbors himself.

While the virtuosity of such shots requires formidable resources in terms of budget, production design, location control, background action, and camera and lighting equipment, the example from the Ophüls film demonstrates how equivalent skill can be equally effective in more modest spatial and dramatic circumstances.

An opening shot might also work by giving the audience a jolt in one way or another, perhaps by abruptly shifting its perception as is the case in Ari Aster's family drama/horror *Hereditary*. From its view out of a window to some kind of tree house, the film's first shot slowly widens and pans to reveal a room filled with a congeries of ancient filing cabinets, assorted artwork, models of houses in various states of assembly, painting equipment, and model-making materials, before it tightens in, stealthily still, on one particular house, and one particular bedroom in which a figure lies in bed. Once the shot has settled, there's a knock on the door, which opens suddenly as a character walks in ... With no cut, the model room becomes real. If this doesn't exactly scare the audience, it startles it, and in so doing acculturates it to the film's discourse in which shock, delivered invariably with similar guile, is an important currency. This dramatic change of perception, accentuated by the slow camera move that lulls the audience while leading up to its *frisson*, alerts it also to the nature of Aster's storytelling as a game to be played, one that demands full attention. And there's more. Two main characters are introduced in the moments that follow—Peter, the youth lying in bed, and his father Steve, the character who enters, telling him to get up and asking whether his sister slept in her room the night before (thus introducing a third character).

In a little over two minutes the shot introduces a world, a model world, three characters (not that the sister is shown) and possibly four (who makes the models and what does the state of the room say about them?). It incorporates a richness of conflicting elements too. The model-making room is cluttered and devoid of characters or any event. The model bedroom is by contrast sparsely furnished and provides the setting in which Steve orders his son to get out of bed. Stasis, then movement, counterpointed by a roaming camera to explore, then a static one to observe. (The camera move is unmotivated, i.e. not prompted by the movement of any person or thing within the frame, and so gives the audience a sense of forces operating outside the control of the characters.) And there is a layering both within and without the fiction of the film: the room revealed within a room then yields the room of the film's first scene. The fiction enfolded within reality becomes reality, and all of this within the fiction of the film. The first frame of the shot looks out, the last frames look in, just as the film looks both at the world within it and at the game of fiction it itself plays, a self-aware filmmaking announced alongside the characters and their world.

Opening image, frame, shot 117

The model becomes the room, the fictional the "real" in Ari Aster's *Hereditary*.

But for all of the breathtaking ingenuity and craft involved in such work, or in the complex sequence shots described earlier, a simple, familiar image well chosen can be sufficient to carry considerable power through its iconic resonance while at the same time economically setting the scene, as is the case with David Lynch's *Blue Velvet*. Here the simple opening shot, in a few brief seconds, evokes a world, a milieu, and a cultural and moral canvas:

```
1. EXT. BEAUMONTS' FRONT LAWN - DAY
Blue skies. PAN SLOWLY DOWN to clean white picket
fence, with beautiful red roses in front of it.
```

A title sequence can similarly provide an economical but striking even haunting opening. As the titles to Martin Scorsese's *Raging Bull* play, the figure of Jake La Motta dances in slow motion in a boxing ring, wreathed in a smoky light and imprisoned within the foreground ropes that seem to entrap him. This image (*not* described in the screenplay) of both grace and captivity counterpointed by the title's declaration of anger—elements of the protagonist's character instrumental in the tragedy that will unfold—prefigures, as with so many successful opening images, the movie's closing image, the one the audience takes away as the credits roll.

It may indeed be the case that the screenwriter and the director will find their opening image only once they have settled on their final image—"In my end is my beginning," T. S. Eliot wrote in his *Four Quartets*. Perhaps this was the case with *Raging Bull*, at the conclusion of which La Motta is seen in very different circumstances, but ones that nevertheless echo the film's memorable opening titles frame.

15 Closing image, frame, shot

The closing scene of *Raging Bull* is both *a contrast to* and *an affinity with* the opening titles shot. The bloated La Motta, so much the physical opposite of his former self, faces himself in a mirror, attempting to recite Shakespeare, the ropes entrapping him from the outside in that first shot now stretched intractably on the inside. The entire journey of his character throughout the movie is captured in those two images of loneliness and the comparison of one with the other. And so the movie bids its farewell by reasserting its story and themes.

If the opening image or shot prompts the beginning of the director's storytelling, so the closing image can encapsulate all that the film has been, resonating in the hearts and minds of the audience after the credits have rolled. As in the case of *Raging Bull*, a final shot can offer a thematic symmetry but may also delineate a visual symmetry, as is famously the case in John Ford's western *The Searchers*. At the very start of the film, Martha Edwards opens a door to reveal a rider approaching from the far distance, her brother-in-law Ethan Edwards, while at the end of the film a door (an optical effect) closes as Ethan walks away—visual storytelling at its simplest, clearest, and most profound that embodies the film's theme and bookends the journey of its central character. Moreover, it leaves the audience with the film's unanswerable contradiction: the need for Ethan's brutality in rescuing his niece as opposed to its obsolescence once his task has been completed. The coming and going of Ethan Edwards, shown in two such simple, lucid compositions, present the unity of dramatic construction and filmic language that lies at the heart of cinema. No visual language could be more consummate.

120 *The approach*

A similarly precise mirroring of composition, although working in a different manner, can be seen in Stanley Kubrick's *2001*, its final image of an embryo within a spherical womb the echo of the film's opening shot in which the sun rises above the earth. What in the first instance is cosmic in a literal sense becomes in the second cosmic in a metaphorical sense. The geometry of the compositions unifies the opposites—the universe and the human, the vast and the tiny, the exterior and the interior, while emphasizing the affinities—the beginning of both a day and a life, the indifference of the universe and the insentience of the unborn child, the cycles of the days and the generations. The images straddle an epic of time and space that under its director's mastery evokes more emotion than many a tragic romance, perhaps because it is in a sense itself the romance of the two crew members and Hal, their ship's computer, humans and machine who work together in the setting of a vast and mysterious universe. Kubrick renders abstract concepts dramatic so that the last image prompts not only a mysterious and haunting wonder but also an emotional resonance that remains with audiences long after the film has finished.

 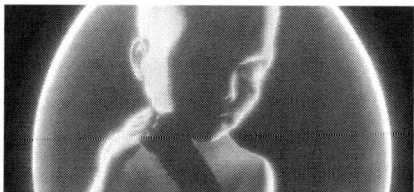

These two examples demonstrate how the choice of image and composition that conclude a film are at their most effective when rooted in that film, its story, its characters, and its themes. If there is no basis for the selection of imagery in the movie's dramaturgy, the images will fail to resonate. If, what's more, they wrap up a story too neatly and shut down the film without some element of echo or mystery—*2001* exudes mystery, while, if the story of *The Searchers* is wrapped up, the moral dilemma it dramatizes never can be—a film will invariably vanish from the minds of its audience. The spinning top seen at the end of Christopher Nolan's *Inception* illustrates how the most enigmatic of images can also be the most resonant. (He cuts to black *before* the camera has settled on the shot, and thus adroitly and almost imperceptibly delivers an image and a motion the audience craves to continue.)

Max Ophüls' *The Earrings of Madame De ...* ends with a shot of the earrings that began the film but now carry a wealth of resonance. Placed on the altar of a church by the respectably married Madame De ..., found by the camera after the death of both her and her lover, the framing teasingly omitting her last name (and playing to the film's in-joke), and illuminated by a flickering candle, they take on a poignant poetry. Seen first in the opening frame, the instrument of the plot, a symbol of the protagonist's transgression, the two earrings at the film's conclusion become a metaphor for the two lovers, the audience's realization of this delivering a final sense of meaning—Ophüls' thematic paradox: the love that saves, destroys; or, put another way—only the love that destroys us can save us.

The fateful story of Madame De ... and Baron Donati has finished by this point, so the final scene in which the camera pans around an empty church to find the earrings serves as a *coda*—a new and closing element of structure that embodies the entire film in a single frame. Martin Scorsese achieves this feat of poetic economy in his *Silence*, at the end of which the audience sees the crucifix clutched in the palm of Jesuit missionary Sebastião Rodrigues' hand in a big close-up as at his cremation his corpse approaches the flames, his faith held close until the very end despite all he's endured. The same director's coda to his *Gangs of New York* sees 150 years pass while the overgrown gravestones of Priest Vallon and Bill the Butcher fade and vanish in the undergrowth as the *history* of New York City supersedes the *myth* played out by Amsterdam and his two father figures—a *vista* as coda after an *epic movie*, in contrast to the *big close-up* at the end of *Silence*, an intense *interior drama*, genre and theme central to the director's selection of scale and scope for each of these final images.

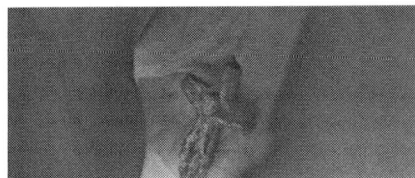 

The very opposite approach to the coda entails the use of the freeze frame, leaving an action unfinished and *in medias res*, often with an ambiguity that also resonates. François Truffaut's *The 400 Blows* utilizes this technique with masterly power, protagonist Antoine Doinel, having run away from playing football with other boys, having fetched up at the edge of the ocean he has always wanted to see, and having come of age in a classic *coming-of-age* film to begin the next stage of his life. The director chooses to end his film on a close-up of his protagonist, Antoine's emotions not defined but left in the audience's imagination to linger and haunt after the movie has finished. (By freezing the frame, then pushing in optically, he adds additional emphasis to the uncertainty.) In George Roy Hill's western *Butch Cassidy and the Sundance Kid*, the two protagonists are frozen as they charge towards the camera (and a firing squad), while in Ridley Scott's road movie *Thelma and Louise* the protagonists' car is freeze-framed high in the air as it takes its duo hurtling off a cliff (while by contrast in Darren Aronofsky's drama *The Wrestler*, Randy "The Ram" Robinson leaves an empty frame as he leaps to what is surely certain death). In each of those three instances the moment is one of both an affirmation of what brings meaning to the characters' lives and a foretelling of the doom that will end them—life and death, whether literal or metaphorical, essential ingredients of story, together in a single frame.

Claire Denis, in her *Beau travail*, does the exact opposite, not freezing a frame but showing in a final vignette the manic dance of protagonist Sergeant Galoup that echoes the gentler dancing at the crowded disco seen at the film's start, while in contrast isolating the character as he does all that is left for him to do once he's accepted his moral bankruptcy. The surprising shot is prolonged, returning after a cut to the actors' credits, Galoup's movements growing increasing wild as though only his physical energy remains, unstoppable in the face of the devastation he has brought upon himself.

A film may end with a character(s) heading away from camera, perhaps into the sunset (or, in the case of Ethan in *The Searchers*, making for some less lyrical fate), or heading towards camera, as in the case of *Butch Cassidy and the Sundance Kid*, or like in Abderrahmane Sissako's *Timbuktu*, at the conclusion of which the young Toya flees her murderous pursuers. It may end with an ambiguous expression on the part of the protagonist or it may end with a more clearly understood expression, such as Dani Ardor's smile at the end of Ari Aster's *Midsommar*—although this also points to the ambiguity of the sense of belonging to her new "family," the cult in which she's found herself, that she seems to have discovered. It may end with a group of characters, as in Kurosawa's *Seven Samurai*, when the surviving samurai pay their respects to their dead comrades, whose swords, seen as the camera tilts up, mark the mounds at the top of the frame (an example of ending as lament). It may end on a single character, as is the case in Lucrecia Martel's *Zama*, in which the severely incapacitated Don Diego lies in the boat that will take him to his final destination. It may end with a character facing the demons they confronted at the film's start, as in Hitchcock's *Vertigo*, or facing a new beginning as in *The 400 Blows*.

Ideally, the director will find the closing shot and image set out in their screenplay. Sometimes, however, it will be found in the course of production and post-production. If writing, as often stated, is *re-writing*, filmmaking is an ongoing creative process too—not in the sense that it should undermine the screenwriter's work but in the process by which it should seek to capture and tell their story in the most effective manner, one to be revised and honed in the shooting and editing. The director should leave nothing to chance but should at the same time be perceptive to the unanticipated opportunities chance may offer. They may sometimes discover that the screenplay contains a closing image obscured by a subsequent scene at first apparently necessary but turning out to be superfluous. In such an instance it's the image—placed in the screenplay by the writer's subconscious and rising to the surface only when what follows cannot be made to work—that dictates the point at which the film ends. Such was the case with Hitchcock's *Notorious*, which ends in much darker fashion than either Hitchcock or screenwriter Ben Hecht originally intended, an example that invites a broader consideration of the nature of endings themselves and how they work …

16 Endings

After Devlin has rescued Alicia from the murderous clutches of Alex Sebastian and his mother in *Notorious* and the couple have driven away, Alex's fellow Nazis, aware of his error in marrying American agent Alicia, invite him back up the steps into his home. As the door closes on him he knows, as the audience knows, that he is going to his death … and at this point the film ends. There's no cutting back to the happy couple in the car, or in Alicia's apartment, or weeks later on honeymoon maybe, no final celebration of their victory, but only the ominous image of that dark door shutting on the defeated antagonist, then the closing title THE END—which indeed it is, not only for the film but for Alex Sebastian and his mother. Such was not the original intention of the filmmakers, however. Versions of scenes of the lovers in their newly happy circumstances written to provide a coda did not work. The movie had come to its natural end, and, with all tension and suspense gone, any additional scene was found to be superfluous. The film *demanded* it finish with the tragedy of Alex, not with the triumph of Devlin and Alicia. The image of the closed door, a coda in itself but portentous rather than celebratory, insisted on taking pride of place and pushing away further narrative development or tonal shift. As Billy Wilder said in his interview with Cameron Crowe, when listing his ten rules for screenwriters: "The third act must build, build, build in tempo and action until the last event, and then—that's it. Don't hang around." Hitchcock discovered precisely that. He could no nothing but leave Alex to his fate.

(On the other hand, Martin Scorsese's *The Irishman* lingers with enormous power as the lives of its characters, along with the film itself, wind down—the thrill of violence overridden by a pervasive melancholy and the sense of the main character's intractable isolation. The hard and fast rules so beloved by teachers are, it seems, ever to prove inadequate.)

In *On Film-making*, Paul Cronin's compilation of Alexander Mackendrick's writings, the master director is quoted as saying that "If you've got a Beginning, but you don't yet have an end, then you're mistaken. You don't have the right Beginning." This raises the issue of the nature of the screenwriter's screenplay and the director's understanding it. Once at the end, they need to work back through the story to the beginning.

At some point, obviously, they will have to find both a beginning and an end, so Mackendrick's maxim is in danger of leading to an impasse unless they select one and then re-conceive the other to work in tandem with it. Nevertheless, Mackendrick's maxim is well taken—an ending that in the process of writing informs an opening invariably trumps an opening that informs an ending.

Ben Hecht, his subconscious genius seminal in his writing process, had written the ending to *Notorious* without knowing it, but not until the film had spoken to its filmmakers did this become apparent. The door that *closes* on the Nazi Alex at the end mirrors the door to the court room which, in the first scene of the film, *opens* to reveal Alicia's Nazi father as he's sentenced by a judge. The first event unleashes the story, the second shuts it down, although not without a sobering resonance that lingers long after the credits have rolled. The director, then, without destroying the mystery at the core of any good story, will do well to excavate the subconscious elements of a screenwriter's work, disguised by their rational processes, and bring them to the fore.

Writer and director David Mamet has commented that endings should be *surprising* but also *inevitable*, and the *Notorious* ending meets this dictum. The parent–child relationship of childhood has to yield to the romantic relationships of adulthood, so that when Alex fails to move on from the former to the latter, he is inevitably doomed. Looked at as a whole, then, there is in the film's closing scene both a victory (Devlin and Alicia's romance matures) and a defeat (Alex's romance with his mother collapses), the latter given a dark emphasis, visually, by that closed door. An ending that offers complete and total victory may prompt the audience's momentary gratification but tends to leave little lasting impact. The put-upon character who wins the court case, wins the money, wins the lover, and generally triumphs against all odds can come across as a figure of juvenile wish fulfillment. The investigative journalists who bring down an organized child-abuse ring and put the world back to rights as the audience cheers them on, thoroughly approving of the film, may offer temporary moral reassurance but provide nugatory drama and little emotion apart from the easy complacency of moral righteousness. With story, victory needs to come at a price. In Lynne Ramsay's *You Were Never Really Here*, Joe vanquishes the child abusers, but only at the cost of passing on his penchant for violence, employed along the way, to the child it has enabled him to rescue. In David Mackenzie's heist movie *Hell or High Water*, Toby Howard succeeds in providing for his family but will be forever morally compromised by the lives taken in the course of his robberies. In Barry Jenkins' drama *If Beale Street Could Talk*, Tish Rivers and her son have dinner with Fonny Hunt and their loving family is reunited, but the setting is Fonny's prison, in which he will spend the next years for a crime he hasn't committed.

In a story, life must go wrong. A. S. Byatt wrote in her novel *Ragnarok*: "It was a good story, a story with meaning, fear and danger were in it, and things out of control." When these elements are not merely brushed aside by a triumphant hero but instead have consequences, or when the actions the hero takes in order to overcome those forces themselves come at a cost and when that cost becomes evident at the story's ending, a film stays with its audience. In short, when the irreconcilable opposites that inform dramatic construction and thematic paradox are incorporated into a film's ending firstly by the screenwriter, then by the director, that film finds its voice.

Comedy obeys different imperatives. In classical comedy, the restoration of harmony at the story's end is an imperative a screenwriter ignores at their peril. Chaplin's *City Lights* finishes with the Flower-Seller's sight restored, her recognition of Chaplin's Tramp as her benefactor earlier in the film, and their romance set to thrive. At the end of Paul Feig's *Bridesmaids*, Annie not only makes up with her former friend Helen but rides away with Officer Rhodes to commence the romance the film promised since they first met and he excused her a ticket for broken tail lights. Another happy end all round. Such endings in comedy are achieved through, and justified by, the mastery of the film's plot construction, a knowingness on the part of the filmmakers that is enjoyed by the audience, whose acceptance of total victory is founded in an appreciation of the clever and playful game the story plays in bringing about ultimate harmony. (In a dark comedy, however, endings may well prove twisted, macabre—even if at the same time wistful, as in Bong Joon-ho's *Parasite*).

But if in broad or romantic comedy all's well that ends well, in a drama, can all that's bad end badly—and in all respects? Do audiences need to take away some ray of hope? Shouldn't fiction, even tragedy, offer some *catharsis*? Before considering this question, it's important to reflect that here is a word customarily employed with scarce regard for its original nuances. Aristotle, in his *Poetics*, uses the term *katharsis* once only as a metaphor for what he seems to suggest are the *purification* and *purgation* that tragedy offers an audience. Today this is the general understanding of the word. What such interpretation omits, however, is the further sense of the term as it was used in Aristotle's time, when it was also understood to mean a *clarification*—a clearing of obstacles along the route to *understanding*. In that sense of the term the films of Andrey Zvyagintsev, his dramas *Leviathan* and *Loveless*, both of which inflict endings of unremitting hopelessness on the audience, can be seen to offer, with a clarity of hellish dimension, their own manner of *catharsis*. George Sluizer's thriller *The Vanishing* concludes with the interment of its protagonist, from which it's hard to imagine an audience experiencing *purification*—rage the more likely reaction—although upon reflection it might realize that Rex, in seeking to learn the fate of his girlfriend, has discovered it, and so his story must come to an end. Sluizer's US version, released five years later, has a different ending in which Rex, now Jeff, kills his would-be killer to win not only total victory but a publishing deal to boot. (The film was a failure critically and commercially.) Another film with an ending that's unlikely to purify audiences or purge them of unsalutary emotion is Michael Haneke's *Funny Games*, in which two young home invaders torment and kill a family with impunity, smirking to camera while about to continue their "games" at the end. This movie offers clarification too, in the *meta* domain of audiences' engagement with the thriller genre, which makes use of tropes and moral sleight of hand in order to permit the entertainment derived from violence and cruelty. The final scenes, during which the killers drown the sole surviving family member and look to continue their mayhem elsewhere, confound audience expectations but encapsulate with terrifying force the vision of the director. It may be argued that this *meta* arena betrays the immersive imperative many see as fundamental to storytelling, but, in the sense that film and TV, like any form of storytelling, is an address to the audience (whether calculated, as with most American mainstream cinema, or less defined, though no less expert, as in the work of a director such as Abbas Kiarostami), the ending to *Funny Games* can be seen as an acknowledgement of, and comment upon, this symbiotic relationship. (Haneke remade his film in the United States ten years later, but in contrast to Sluizer did not pull his punches. It was a box-office failure too, however.)

An indication of how audiences can accept and indeed warm to endings of narrative and moral ambiguity can be seen in the inventive conclusions to long-running TV shows such as David Chase's *The Sopranos* and Vince Gilligan's *Breaking Bad*. At the end of the former, after six twelve-episode seasons, Tony Soprano sits with his family in a diner, and when the door opens the picture cuts to an interference pattern, the show's end. Has the audience been put in the anti-hero's NPOV? (There's little in the shooting or cutting of the scene to indicate this.) Has he been killed? In short, has there, or hasn't there, been poetic justice? Or was this a meta device on the part of show-runner David Chase, a way of concluding a long-running saga so long-running it could have no easy, comprehensive, satisfying conclusion? Walter White, at the end of the final episode of *Breaking Bad*, machine guns the neo-Nazis—villains ever acceptable as cannon-fodder—and saves the life of his sidekick Jesse Pinkman, smiling as he dies at the thought that he's finally achieved a measure of redemption. But has he? His family is left devastated by the path he's taken, which, far from providing for them as he planned, has destroyed their lives.

These are two examples of TV shows allowed to run their course. Many more are canceled before coming to their desired completion so that endings planned as season endings become show endings. Such conclusions can seem, as they invariably are, arbitrary, but often appear not to spoil the viewer's experience of the show in retrospect. (Zal Batmanglij and Brit Marling's *The OA* is a case in point, although its ending, as the characters seem to step out of the fiction into meta-fiction, might be thought to offer a fitting conclusion to a show of agile invention.) In the case of TV it's the show-runner who decides on the ending, but the nature of a story that runs in episodic form for many hours in comparison with that of a feature film that runs for ninety minutes to a couple of hours or so, or a short that may run between, say, five minutes and half-an-hour, reflects on the nature and function of their endings. With the multi-episodic, multi-season TV show, the *journey* is all (not unlike long literary novels, with which some TV shows bear comparison). For the commercial movie and the genre novel, on the other hand, the journey serves the destination, and, even with less popular fare, the destination is frequently at least as significant as the route traveled, if not more so. With the short film, the ending invariably needs to be even more integral to the narrative and visual design. Bálint Kenyeres' *Before Dawn* ends where it begins, on a wheat field, one now not merely deceptively but truly empty of people.

There is a similarity, however, between the nature of the ending to a TV season and that of a movie within a franchise in that each employs an open element to both suggest the beginning of a new story to be followed up in a subsequent film or season and tempt the audience to see it. In a TV show an unexpected element of a known character might be unveiled that promises new consequences in the next set of episodes. In a movie from a spy franchise, the hero might have defeated their adversary but not yet have learned all there is to know about them, as is the case when, in the final moments of *Casino Royale*, James Bond, having shot but not killed Mr. White, confronts him, proclaiming his renowned catchphrase "The name's Bond, James Bond," and thus heralding his next outing *Quantum of Solace*, which opens with Bond transporting the captive Mr. White in the trunk of his car.

The suggestion of a new story need not be limited to the TV season or franchise movie. At the end of any coming-of-age film, the protagonist faces the journey of adulthood, whereas at the end of a romantic comedy the lovers might look to the challenge of a settled relationship. Other endings might indicate that a story is to play out over again, a trope used to chilling effect in Roman Polanski's *The Tenant*, which ends with protagonist Trelkovsky discovering himself in the same hospital bed in which he found Simone Choule (the previous tenant of his apartment seen at the beginning of the film), in plaster and bandages and unable to talk. This last scene is the same as the first scene except that now Trelkovsky experiences the event from Choule's NPOV, seeing himself through her eyes, his story, the director seems to be saying, to be repeated ad infinitum. Endings that proclaim their stories will *never* have an ending are particularly suited to psychological horror such as this. It's also an example of the *twist ending*. Most endings come with a twist—the element of surprise that comes with that of inevitability—and twist endings are common in Genre 1 movies. In one of the most famous and chilling of twist endings, the murderous mother of Hitchcock's *Psycho* is finally revealed to be Norman Bates, who, it turns out, has murdered her and taken on her personality.

Such a twist in an audience's understanding is not limited to Genre 1, however. Pedro Almodóvar's *Pain and Glory* ends with a revelation of an astonishing meta nature as one of the narrative threads is revealed to be not what it's been perceived as being, not a part of the fiction of the film, but a fiction *within* the fiction of the film.

Endings may, of course, by contrast be left open, the audience uncertain as to the subsequent final step in the story. Such is the case with Yorgos Lanthimos' *The Lobster*, at the end of which there is what is known as a *fulcrum* scene—in which a character has to choose between opposite courses of action—when protagonist David, seeking commonality with the blind woman with whom he's formed a relationship, stands before a restroom mirror holding a steak knife. Will he blind himself? The audience is left wondering, and so the film resonates beyond its ending … (Note how the director eschews the god-like perspective championed by some teachers of filmmaking, embracing instead Kiarostami's impenetrability of character.)

As can be seen from these various examples, there are many ways, often contradictory, for an ending to succeed, so the director needs to be clear in their mind not only that the ending of their screenplay works, but *how* it works. They need also to consider how it functions within its specific genre(s). A psychological horror movie that ends with an action movie shoot-out, for example, might be thought to betray itself, the suspicion being that its filmmakers were unable to come up with an ending organic to their film—unless, of course, that film were an amalgam of the two genres. A genre romance that ends with a couple *not* getting together, perhaps culminating in a scene similar to the final moments of Michelangelo Antonioni's *L'Eclisse*, when neither of the couple turns up at the arranged place on the arranged evening, risks disappointing an audience that has been led to expect at least a measure of *rapprochement* if not a total meeting of hearts and minds. Expectations—the way in which they are fulfilled, the *unexpected* route a story takes to meet them, their subversion or confounding when they are met or not met—are a fundamental consideration in the search for and understanding of the nature and appropriateness of a film's ending.

Finally, consistency of narrative point of view is crucial. In *The Tenant*, Trelkovsky assumes Simone Choale's NPOV at the end of the film, but, while he has morphed into her, seeing himself as she saw him earlier, one's sense is that he is now trapped within her body. The NPOV has not shifted so much as has the location of his identity. Alex, at the end of *Notorious*, takes the NPOV, but this has been meticulously set up throughout the film. In Carol Reed's *The Third Man*, a movie widely perceived as a classic, and with a screenplay by major twentieth-century author Graham Greene too, there is by contrast a shift in the NPOV at its end that violates the integrity adhered to until that point. When protagonist Holly Martins chases antagonist Harry Lime, his NPOV, held throughout the movie, switches to Lime's in order to dramatize the villain's terror. Thus is Martins' own emotional journey jettisoned in favor of his adversary's. His final decision to kill Lime is not shown, the instant of the murder not witnessed, only heard. (Compare this with the scene from Karyn Kusama's *Destroyer* in which Erin Bell kills Silas, or the Coen Brothers' *Miller's Crossing* when Tom shoots Bernie.) The result is an avoidance of Martins' uncomfortable emotional path and the moral quandary to which it gives rise. Reed's ending allows only an oblique final punctuation, but *final punctuation*, if it's to work, whether as completion, coda, pointer to new story or question as to what will happen after the film has finished, needs, in an emotional as well as a cognitive sense, also to be *encapsulation*.

17 The 5-step creative analysis of the screenplay

This is a suggested approach to their screenplay, scene by scene, for the director.

17.1 A brief summary of the scene

A concise synopsis. One sentence. Who does what, and what is it they do? Or maybe the scene works in another way. (See "The function of the scene" below.)

17.2 The journey of the protagonist

This can be expressed by a *beat-by-beat* analysis of the main character's journey through the scene, sequence, or *narrative unit*. The latter might consist of a succession of scenes tracing a single line of action or following one narrative thread. It might be intercut with a second sequence that traces a different narrative thread—a technique known as *parallel action*.

Where relevant, such analysis should include the three imperatives that form the engine of dramatic narrative: objective, obstacle, action. The *objective* is the character's goal, what they want. The *obstacle* is what stands in their way. The *action* is what the character does in order to overcome the obstacle.

Example: *Objective:* X wants to enter the inner chamber. *Obstacle:* Y, armed to the teeth, holds the keys. *Action:* X tricks Y into drinking a sleeping potion so that they can take the keys and access the inner chamber.

Or, in *Rear Window*: *Objective:* Jeff wants to send a note to Thorwald. *Obstacle:* He's wheelchair-bound. *Action:* He has Lisa take the note.

This may not apply to every scene. A character may have no goal, or there might be no obstacle—the action might be routine, not integral to narrative drive but revealing an element of a character's life, or the scene might be setting up something the audience may not understand until later. The protagonist may not have a goal so much as the antagonist does—even an *active protagonist* can be passive at times.

The director should note the importance of scenes depicting moments of resonance, reverberation, reflection, or of prolonged, perhaps unbearable tension. (Quentin Tarantino is a master of the latter.) Cutting to the chase, as is commonly advised, may not always create so much tension as *not* cutting to it.

Note: it can be particularly effective when an obstacle becomes the means of the action taken or even turns out to be the goal. An example of the latter can be found in *Notorious*, when Devlin, searching in his wine cellar for clues as to the nature of Alex's activities, knocks a bottle from a shelf. The bottle smashes on the floor loudly and it seems that the Nazis, alerted, will arrive before he has time to complete his search. What happens, however, is that the bottle's contents spill to reveal not red wine but dark sand—uranium ore. Devlin has stumbled upon the true nature of the Nazis' conspiracy: to gather the material for an atom bomb. An example of the first trope, obstacle as the means to action, can be seen in John Krasinski's horror movie *A Quiet Place*. Marcus and Regan have sought refuge from alien creatures by hiding atop a grain silo when the hatch on which they sit gives way. Marcus falls into the silo where, apprised by the sound, his adversary attacks. Marcus uses the hatch door that put him in peril as a shield against the creature. Thus the obstacle to his successful hiding becomes the means of his saving himself. The problem is rendered the solution.

The director should set out the journey of the protagonist(s) scene-by-scene, sequence-by-sequence, narrative unit by narrative unit throughout their film.

17.3 The journey of the audience

Why should it be helpful to trace the journey of the audience? Some might think this is "selling out" by engaging in cynical manipulation, but that is to deny that a film or TV show has to work in more than the fictive world beyond the screen. The art of storytelling comprises not only knowing what is a good story to tell; it also requires the storyteller to know how to tell it, and the storyteller can know that only if they have an idea of what it is they want the audience to think, feel, know, not know, want, fear, dread, need, hope for, understand or not understand, mistake, question, or deduce, connect or not connect. A movie, feature or short, a TV season or episode is an address to an audience or to viewers, and it is in them that the real emotion is evoked. Hitchcock talked of playing the audience like an orchestra. Abbas Kiarostami disagreed. For him it wasn't for the director to say how the audience should feel, and yet his own, rarely seen, *Shirin* appears to suggest the opposite. The film shows a fictional audience watching a fictional film about a legendary Persian romance that audiences of *Shirin* itself never see. Kiarostami shows the shifts of emotion, often intense, in the faces of the women watching their movie as the real audience watching *Shirin* hears its dialogue, effects, and music. There are two stories, then—the doomed romance of the film within the film, and the emotional journey of the audience within the film, revealed in its faces—all that the real *Shirin* audience sees on the screen (although the film's sound track of course conjures for audiences images on the screen of the mind).

The "journey" of the audience throughout their film is one the director will greatly benefit from by articulating. A sense of this intended emotional and cognitive journey will have profound effects on approaches to what is shown and what is not shown, on how it is shown, on what characters are shown at what point, on the audience's relationship to the characters (the choice of NPOV), on camera angle, movement, and lensing, on cutting, sound design, and score. The director should set down this journey scene-by-scene, sequence-by-sequence, narrative unit by narrative unit. It is the stream of consciousness of the audience both in its emotional and in its cognitive complexity—just as one character may know or understand more than another (the hierarchy of knowledge), so the audience may know or understand more or less than a character does. If it understands more, this may lead to suspense (Hitchcock's "bomb under the table"), or it may lead to dramatic irony (Jake Gittes tells a lewd joke to his colleagues unaware that Mrs. Mulwray is listening, in *Chinatown*).

Film and TV should, of course, elicit emotions difficult, perhaps impossible, to express in words, and are perhaps at their most powerful when they do so. They also depict action and events that may be too startling, shocking, weird, wonderful, mysterious, novel, sublime, mischievous, ironic, or revelatory for any adequate verbal delineation of the reactions they prompt. In setting down the journey of the audience, the director should recognize and acknowledge these moments without reducing them to easy description. They will be among the film's riches.

The danger in not acknowledging the flow of perception and emotion in the audience is that a film might convey unintended messages that prompt unintended reactions. Laughter in the wrong place, disapproval of a character's action when the audience needs to be kept "on side," unwanted questions of one kind or another—related to information, perhaps, or to a character's motivation—confusion, or the failure to understand some fundamental aspect of story, character, or world, will sever an audience's engagement, a precious connection it can be hard to re-establish.

17.4 The turning point of the scene

This term refers to the moment when a character chooses to take one decision or another, when circumstances or narrative direction change and cannot be reversed. The director should ask what it is that *changes* in the scene? What is different at the end from the beginning? Has anything changed? (If it hasn't, is it that the scene isn't necessary, or does it work in some other way, one of those listed below perhaps?)

17.5 The function of the scene

Scenes may drive the story forward or work in other ways. Most scenes involve a character taking an action, but sometimes there's no character and/or nothing happens. Maybe the scene offers a moment of resonance, reverberation, and reflection. Or perhaps the scene exists to increase tension and suspense or, to the contrary, lull the audience before a startling event occurs in the following scene. Maybe the scene sets up something that takes place later in the film. There might also be a moment of light or shadow, vista or detail or vignette, space or the lack of it, to set a mood, establish a place, or convey a passage of time, or to simply mesmerize, thrill, or chill the audience. Maybe the scene poses a question or answers one. Maybe it shows an action the audience understands. Maybe it shows one they don't. Perhaps it reveals a facet of character, of the film's world or social and moral canvas, shows some norm to be subverted. Perhaps it suggests a fate that the protagonist is in danger of meeting. Maybe it introduces a character or establishes their NPOV. Maybe it marks the end or beginning of an act or a sequence of scenes. Perhaps it dramatizes a major reversal in fortune or change in a character's understanding, or presents some apparently insuperable obstacle, or some unexpected key to overcoming it.

Note: scenes that merely offer an explanation, such as can often be the case with flashbacks, weaken storytelling. *Story is not explanation.* When an audience is allowed to put two and two together and tell itself the story, its active participation will intensify its emotional engagement. "Anything the reader can do for himself," said Ludwig Wittgenstein, "leave it to him."

18 The director's statement

In beginning collaboration with their team, the director would do well to set out a statement that addresses their own connection with, and commitment to, the material, one they might read to their co-filmmakers. In cases of the most passionate engagement, a director may not know exactly why they want to make the film. They may need to make the film in order to discover this. They may never discover it. Nevertheless, they might ask themselves the following questions.

What *excites* you about the story? What distinguishes the story as special? Why does it beg to be told? Why should you be the director to make it? As it stands, does its story engage? What issues, questions does the film explore (moral, social, cultural, behavioral, existential)? What is your connection to the story, world, and characters of this film? Personal? Cultural? Moral, Existential? Or otherwise? Have you or someone you have known shared in the experiences dramatized in the film? Is there something in the story you cannot articulate in words that only the film itself can express? Is there a heresy in the story that rings true—a new, transgressive, subversive way of seeing life—or is there "what oft was thought but ne'er so well express'd"?

In a contemporary culture in which "appropriation" has become an issue and there is a view among some that directors from one gender or ethnic group or socio-economic class or abled category should shy away from making movies with a main character of another, connection with, and grasp of, one's material would seem of prime importance. A strong story with fully realized characters should lie within any filmmaker's domain, however, although directors would do well to consider how they are positioned to make their specific movie. Emotional and psychological connection can be deeper than sociological commonality, while a link through personal experience, even if not in a similar cultural environment, can bring profound insight. Much of these considerations can be dependent on the nature of a film's genre. Genre 1 may be a less sensitive area than, say, an intimate coming-of-age movie. It's better always for the director to understand their connection to their material, to do thorough research, and to be respectful of sensibilities and people. On the other hand, as Elena says in Elena Ferrante's novel *The Story of the Lost Child*: "We must be careful not to become policemen of ourselves."

Part B

The case study—*Contrapelo* screenplay by Liska Ostojic and Gareth Dunnet-Alcocer

19 Screenplay

CONTRAPELO
(Against the Grain)

REV

15.4 8/26/13

Screenplay by Liska Ostojic and Gareth Dunnet-Alcocer

Based on the short story "LATHER AND NOTHING ELSE" by Hernando Tellez

1 INT. SUV - DAY

The droning RUMBLE of a CAR in motion. Then –

HANDS. Bound by hard plastic bindings. Fingers swollen from pressure, gripping a tattered, BLACK LEATHER SATCHEL.

We HOLD ON THE HANDS.

> BARBER (V.O.)
> Rasurar es un arte preciso. Un ritual sagrado. No se debe apresurar. *(Shaving is a precise art. A sacred ritual. It can't be rushed.)*

Slowly we begin to tilt up from the hands.

> BARBER (V.O.)
> Cada movimiento es importante. Cada paso tiene su próposito, su razón de ser. *(Every movement is important. Every step has a purpose.)*

We move up the buttons of a shirt, passing a GOLD CRUCIFIX around the sweaty neck …

                  BARBER (V.O.)
        Una rasurada es buena o mala, y
        no hay nada en medio. *(A shave is*
        either good or bad, and there is
        nothing in between.)

… to a man's head, a MASECA TORTILLA SACK covering it.

                  BARBER (V.O.)
        Todo depende del barbero.
        (It's all up to the barber.)

We are aware of the two HULKING MEN on either side of him.

CUT TO BLACK

TITLE: CONTRAPELO

2 INT. BARBERSHOP – DAY

The cutting edge of STRAIGHT RAZOR catches the light, sliding up and down a whetstone in effortless, calculated movements.

REVEAL the BARBER (40s), demonstrating the back and forth of sharpening a blade to his son, ARTURO (16), a painfully quiet, insecure boy.

                  BARBER
        Pa' fuera y pa' dentro, en
        movimientos circulares. Hay una
        especie de ritmo. ¿Te fijas?
        Levantando primero el filo.
        Nunca se le pone presión. Es
        algo delicado. ¿Sale?
        (Back and forth, back and
        forth. You see the rhythm? You
        see how I lift the edge first?
        You never put pressure on the
        edge. It's too sensitive.
        Yes?)

A CUSTOMER waits in the barber's chair with a HOT TOWEL over his face, DON CHAYO (80s) leafs through a newspaper by the front door, nodding his head to the distant Mexican music wafting in from outside. JUAN (19) sweeps the floor in the background.

The barbershop is small and dark, cluttered with a lifetime of collected photos, newspaper clippings, boxing match stubs. A cocoon of possessions and trapped, sweltering heat.

A coffee pot starts to beep.

>   BARBER
> Don Chayo, ya esta su cafecito.
> (to Juan) *(Don Chayo, your coffee is ready.)* Dale su café a Don Chayo. Con piloncillo. *(Get him the coffee, put cane sugar in it.)*

Juan eagerly gets the coffee. He brings it to DON CHAYO (87), a relic at the barbershop. The old man takes a sip of the scalding liquid, grimaces.

>   DON CHAYO
> ¿Le pusiste piloncillo? *(Did you put piloncillo in it?)*

Juan nods.

>   DON CHAYO
> (wiping his mouth)
> Sabe a verga. *(Tastes like dick.)*

The Barber smiles, finishes with the whetstone and dries the blade on his towel.

>   BARBER
> A ver hijo. *(Alright.)*

The Barber hands the blade to Arturo, a priest handing the sacrament to an altar boy.

                    BARBER
            Emparéjala. *(Strop it.)*

The Barber smiles, then removes the hot towel from his
customer, revealing MIGUEL.

                    MIGUEL
            No mames, pense que nunca me
            ibas a quitar la pinche toalla.
            Se me anda derritiendo la cara
            cabrón. *(Shit. I thought you
            were never taking that towel
            off. Felt like my face was
            going to melt off.)*

                    BARBER
            (to Miguel)
            No seas chillón. Los hombres de
            verdad aguantan la toalla
            caliente.
            *(Don't whine. Real men take the towel
            boiling hot.)*

He picks up a cup and whips up a lather. Arturo begins
stropping.

                    BARBER
            (to Arturo)
            Ojo, esto hay que hacerlo bien.
            La espuma hace que el pelo se
            levante, es donde se ve la
            diferencia. *(Now watch, you
            have to get this right. The
            lather lifts the hair from the
            skin. It makes all the
            difference.)*

The Barber looks at Arturo, stropping the blade with
the edge down, the wrong way.

                    BARBER
          (to Arturo)
          Contra el cuero, en diagonal.
          Hay que voltearla y luego bajar
          la navaja. ¡Como te enseñé
          ayer!
          (Against the leather,
          diagonally! You have to turn
          it, then bring it down. Like I
          showed you yesterday.)

Juan sweeping and leans towards Arturo.

                    JUAN
          Al revés – (The other way –)

The Barber shoots him a look.

                    BARBER
          (to Juan)
          Oye, el piso no les barre solo,
          eh? (These floors aren't cleaning
          themselves boy.)

Juan gets back to his floor. The Barber applies more lather to Miguel's face.

                    MIGUEL
          Mejor mándalo al salón de
          belleza. Al menos ahi si hay
          viejas, aqui anda entre puro
          tornillo. (You might as well send him
          to the beauty salon. At least he'll see
          women there. It's a sausage fest here.)

The barber smacks some lather onto Miguel's forehead.

                    BARBER
          Tu estate o te rasuro las
          orrejas cabrón.
          (You keep your mouth shut or you'll get your
          ears shaved off.)

MIGUEL
          Pérate guey. *(Stop that!)*

Arturo smiles at the interaction. Don Chayo leans in.

                    DON CHAYO
          Hazle caso a tu jefe, siempre
          ha tenido ese talento. Desde
          los 13 años rasuraba a su papa,
          y a los 15 se formaba la gente
          para que les diera una
          rasurada. Es el mejor que ha
          tenido Parral. *(Listen to your father,*
          he could shave his father when he was
          13, and by 15 there were people getting
          in line to get a shave from him. He is
          the best Parral has ever had.)

Arturo listens admiringly, hands the blade to his father.

                    BARBER
          Algunos barberos nomas llegan y
          pfft pfft pfft.
          (Some barbers just pfft, pfft …)

He waves his hand dismissively.

                    BARBER
          … dos minutos de principio a
          fin. Pero lleva tiempo. Si
          quieres encargarte del
          changarro un dia, tienes que
          respetar los pasos. *(… two*
          minutes in out. But it takes time. If
          you want to run this place someday you
          have to respect the way it's done.)

He frees his elbows from the shirt sleeves, and leans into Miguel.

                        BARBER
        ¿Te fijas cómo se balancea el
        peso? La navaja es una
        herramienta perfecta. Uno deja
        que corte solita. Sin
        empujarle. *(The blade is a perfect tool.
        It's already weighted to cut the hair.
        It does all the work. There's no muscle
        in it.)*

Suddenly he stops. Looks closely at the blade.

                        BARBER
        Sigue roñosa. *(This blade is still
        chipped.)*

Arturo looks down, defeated.

                        BARBER
        Mira, tienes que poner atención
        a lo que te estoy diciendo. En
        el filo de la navaja esta la
        reputación de uno. Si cortas al
        cliente, vales madres como
        peluquero. *(You have to listen to
        what I tell you. If you cut the
        customer, you are worthless as a
        barber.)*

He hands him the razor again.

                        BARBER
        Dale otra vez. Hasta que salga
        bien. *(Try it again. Do it until
        it's right.)*

Arturo fumbles with the strop. Juan takes it from his hand and expertly flicks the razor along the leather.

The Barber, momentarily surprised, quickly takes the opportunity.

                    BARBER
          Fíjate como le hace. En
          diagonal. Movimientos cortos y
          delicados.
          (You see how he's doing it?
          Diagonally. Short, smooth
          strokes.)

A2 INT. BARBER SHOP - CONTINUOUS

As Juan bends over the strop, a NECKLACE slips out from his shirt, the MEDALLION OF THE HOLY DEATH dangling on the end. The Barber zeroes in on it. He pushes his son aside and stops Juan. The boy straightens up.

                    BARBER
          Dame la navaja.
          (Give me the blade.)

Juan is surprised. Doesn't know what's going on. He hands over the blade sheepishly.

                    BARBER
          ¿Qué haces con esa porquería?
          Me dijiste que ya no ibas a
          jalar con esa gente. *(What is that garbage
          doing here? You told me you
          were staying away from those people.)*

Juan doesn't respond, wary, an animal suddenly sensing a predator. The shop is silent. It's just Juan and the Barber.

                    BARBER
          A mi tienda no metes esa
          mierda.
          *(You dare to bring that shit into
          my shop?)*

                    DON CHAYO
          Ta chavo. No pasa nada. *(He's
          a kid, no harm done.)*

                    BARBER
        No lo defiendan. Esto es
        importante. ¿Traes eso aqui?
        ¿En frente de mi hijo? Esos
        matones que dejan muertos en la
        calle para que los niños los
        vean? ¿Que envenenan nuestro pais?
        *(Don't defend him. This is
        important. You think I'm gonna
        let him bring that trash here?
        Into my shop? My home? In front
        of my son? Those butchers that
        leave their remains in the
        street for little children to
        find? That poison our country?)*

He turns back to Juan.

                    BARBER
        Quítatelo. *(Take it off.)*

Juan averts his eyes, tries to continue sweeping. The Barber reaches for the medallion.

Juan SLAPS HIS HAND AWAY.

It was a reflex, and he regrets it immediately. The Barber is taken aback. Almost embarrassed by the sudden violence.

                    BARBER
        ¿Te crees muy hombrecito porque
        traes esa porquería colgando
        del cuello? *(You think you're tough
        because you've got that thing around
        your neck?)*

                    MIGUEL
        Ta bien … ta bien … *(It's fine.)*

                    BARBER
        No esta bien. A todos esos los
        deberían de matar. A todos, y
        si pudiera, lo haria yo mismo.

>   (It's not fine. They should be killed.
>   Every one of them. If I could do it myself
>   I would.)
>
>   (to Juan) O te lo quitas, o te
>   largas. (Take it off or get out.)

Juan hesitates. The Barber doesn't flinch.

Finally, Juan backs up to the door, carefully leans the broom against the wall, his eyes never leaving the Barber's until he opens the door and walks out.

B2 INT. BARBER SHOP - CONTINUOUS

The door slowly swings shut behind him. The Barber picks up the strop, works at it with the blade.

>   DON CHAYO
>   ¿Y ahora quien te va a barrer
>   la tienda? Ese ya no
>   regresa. (Who's going to sweep
>   your shop now?)
>
>   BARBER
>   ¿Que quieres que haga? Es una
>   pinche manzana podrida. Palabra
>   que a esos los conozco. No
>   valen para nada, hay que
>   cortarlos de un jalon.
>   (What do you want me to do? Take my
>   word for it. I know his type. Kid's
>   a bad apple. You have to cut guys like
>   that out. Like dead skin.)

The door is an inch from closing when a HAND from the outside stops it, pushes it back open.

The Barber doesn't look up when the BELL over the door DINGS.

>   BARBER
>   Arturo, traeme una toalla.
>   (Arturo, get me a towel.)

No movement from Arturo.

                        BARBER
            Arturo …

The Barber turns around irritated, angry words springing to his lips, but is stopped short when he sees the look on his son's face …

White-faced and stiff, Arturo stares at the door. The Barber sees his customers staring in the same direction. He follows their gaze …

A BIG MAN in a polo shirt stands in the doorway. He is smooth-shaven. Even his head is smooth. Two more men follow, their shadows stretching through the barber shop.

3 INT. SAFE HOUSE – DAY

A hand roughly pulls the hood off of the Barber's head. He blinks and squints in the sudden light. OCTAVIO, the Big Man from the barber shop, grabs the Barber's tied hands and snaps open a blade.

                        OCTAVIO
            ¿Sabes quien somos?
            (You know who we are?)

The Barber nods. With quick movements, Octavio cuts through the rope around his wrists.

                        OCTAVIO
            Nosotros tambien sabemos quien
            eres. Prepara tus cosas.
            *(We know who you are too. Get ready
            to work.)*

The Barber reaches into his case and quickly withdraws his hand, his fingers wet. A slight tremor.

                        BARBER
            No puedo empezar.
            (I can't start.)

                    OCTAVIO
        ¿Por qué?
        (Why not?)

The Barber pulls out a broken bottle of aftershave.

                    BARBER
        No tengo loción. Se rompió la
        botella. *(There's no lotion. The
        bottle has broken.)*

                    OCTAVIO
        El otro barbero no la necesitaba.
        (The other barber didn't use it.)

                    BARBER
        Sin la loción se le va a
        irritar la cara.
        *(His face will rash if I don't
        apply lotion.)*

Octavio gets in the Barber's face. The Barber can smell his breath.

                    OCTAVIO
        Te la pelas.
        (Tough luck.)

                    BENJAMIN (O.S.)
        Dice la gente de Parral que
        usted es muy bueno.
        (The people from Parral say you're good.)

4 INT. SAFE HOUSE – CONTINUOUS

Octavio reacts at the sound of his master's voice. He and the Barber look to the door.

BENJAMIN, a short, wiry man (late 40s) stands in the doorway in dirty jeans and an undershirt, unscrewing the bottom of a toy police car. Thick stubble covers his chin.

                        BARBER
            Es mi trabajo.
            (It's my job.)

                        BENJAMIN
            La modestidad no deja.
            Enséñeme. (Modesty
            doesn't pay. Show me.)

                        BARBER
            No puedo empezar.
            (I can't start.)

                        BENJAMIN
            Ah cabrón, y ¿Porqué no? (Really?
            And why not?)

                        BARBER
            No hay loción. No puedo
            afeitarlo, porque al final se
            le va a irritar. Perdón, pero
            sin loción no lo hago.
            (There is no lotion. I can't shave you
            because your face will rash. I'm sorry,
            but without lotion I won't do it.)

Octavio is about to lose it with this little shit.

                        OCTAVIO
            Mira pendejo –
            (Look, asshole –)

                        BENJAMIN
            Esperate cabron.
            (Take it easy.)

Octavio immediately backs off. Benjamin studies the Barber.

                        BENJAMIN
            ¡Hasta que nos conseguiste un
            barbero con huevos! Muy
            diferente al anterior.

(Well, it looks like we have a barber with
                    balls. Very different from the last one.)

                    (to Octavio)
                    Ve y comprate un aftershave. Y
                    llévate a estos cabrones que ya
                    me engenté.
                    (Go and get the aftershave. Take these
                    two with you, it's crowded in here.)

Octavio and his buddies leave. Benjamin points to the Barber's traveling case.

                              BENJAMIN
                    Empiézale.
                    (Get started.)

5 INT. SAFE HOUSE – CONTINUOUS – DAY

The Barber wrings out a towel and puts it in the microwave.

                              BENJAMIN
                    Cuanto tiempo llevas en esto?
                    (How long have you been doing this?)

Startled, the Barber glances at Benjamin. The other man is engrossed in his work. He didn't see the Barber's hand shake. The Barber stirs lather in a cup.

                              BARBER
                    Toda la vida. Me enseño mi papá
                    de chavo. (All my life. My father taught
                    me as a boy.)

                              BENJAMIN
                    A mi tambien me enseñaron de
                    chavo, pero un oficio
                    diferente.
                    (My father also taught me, but a
                    different job.)

The Barber turns to look at Benjamin with the barber's cape in his hands.

The microwave DINGS.

6 INT. SAFE HOUSE – MOMENTS LATER – DAY

The Barber lathers Benjamin's face. Benjamin tinkers with the toy car.

> BENJAMIN
> Tenia rato que no me daba una buena rasurada.
> *(It has been a while since I had a good shave.)*

> BARBER
> ¿Como seis días?
> *(About six days?)*

> BENJAMIN
> ¡Exacto! No, pues tu si le sabes. Andabamos en la loma, persiguiendo a unos cabrones. No tuve tiempo. *(Exactly! You are a good barber. We were in the desert, hunting some people. I didn't have time.)*

The Barber lathers Benjamin's face.

> BENJAMIN
> Mi papá decía que lo que nos separó de los animales fue que nos quitamos el pelo de la cara. Fue lo que nos hizo civilizados. Tonces, de alguna manera, ustedes los barberos son los protectores de la civilización. Bueno … los que le saben.
> *(My father used to say that what separated us from the animals was that we chose to lose the hair on our faces. It was the beginning of civilization. So, in a way, you barbers are the gatekeepers of civilization. Well … those that know it.)*

The siren on the toy car lights up. Benjamin holds it up with a grin for the Barber to see. He puts it on the ground.

The Barber takes out the hot towel and HISSES. He waves it in the air to cool it off.

> BENJAMIN
> No, asi tráetela. Me gusta bien
> caliente.
> *(No, leave it. It's best when it's hot
> like that.)*

The Barber covers Benjamin's face with the towel and sits down, waits.

7 INT. SAFE HOUSE - CONTINUOUS

Benjamin waits in the chair, his face covered, his neck exposed.

The Barber looks down at the bright, sharp edge in his hand.

He looks back at Benjamin, his neck exposed, the building silent. An idea forming …

A7 INT. SAFE HOUSE - CONTINUOUS

The Barber lifts off the towel, adds lather to his face.

> BENJAMIN
> No quieres saber que les paso?
> *(Don't you want to know what
> happened to them?)*

The Barber hesitates with the blade, starts shaving Benjamin.

> BARBER
> ¿A quien?
> *(Who?)*

> BENJAMIN
> A los que andamos persiguiendo.
> *(The people we were chasing.)*

                    BARBER
          Necesito que se recline en la
          silla.
          (I need you to lean your
          head back into the headrest.)

Benjamin tilts his head further back, exposing his neck.

                    BENJAMIN
          Yo creo hasta sale en las
          noticias. Cuatro bultos sin
          cabeza en la Plaza del Sol.
          Hasta el pendejo de Lopez
          Dóriga lo saca. (Watch for it in
          the news tomorrow. Four headless bodies
          in Plaza del Sol still gets the front
          page.)

The blade presses against delicate skin. Every stroke revealing more of it.

                    BENJAMIN
          Pero la gente nos pierde el
          miedo. Ya no se espantan tan
          fácil. Andan acostumbrados. Eso
          no lo podemos permitir: A la
          gente hay que traerla en
          chinga. (But even so people are
          losing their fear. It's getting harder to
          shock them. We can't have that. Next time
          who knows what we'll have to do.)

The Barber pauses, the blade resting against the base of Benjamin's neck. He can practically see the pulse beating.

                    BARBER
          ¿Les van a hacer lo mismo que a
          la periodista? ¿La que
          encontraron los niños? (Will
          it be the same as with the woman
          journalist? The one in Parral that the
          children found.)

Benjamin's eyes stay closed.

>   BENJAMIN
>   Parecido, pero mas lento.
>   *(Similar. But slower.)*

The Barber's blade is still. Sweat gathers on his forehead. The muscles of his arms tense.

A CREAK.

8 INT. SAFE HOUSE - CONTINUOUS

The Barber whips his head towards the door.

A YOUNG BOY (6) stands in the doorway, staring at the Barber with clear eyes.

Benjamin looks at the door.

>   BENJAMIN
>   Andale mijo, ahi ta su juguete.
>   Ya se lo arregé.
>   *(Here's your toy, son. I fixed it.)*

Benjamin rolls the car to the Boy.

>   BENJAMIN
>   Orale cabrón, no andes de
>   metiche.
>   *(Go with your mother, don't be
>   snitching around.)*

The Boy sneaks quick, curious glances around the room.

>   BENJAMIN
>   Vamonos! *(Go!)*

Startled, the Boy runs off.

9 INT. SAFE HOUSE - CONTINUOUS

Benjamin looks around, airs the inside of the robe covering his chest.

                        BENJAMIN
            Este pinche calor nomas no se
            suelta. *(This heat. It just won't
            let up.)*

The Barber wipes sweat from his forehead. He is drenched. A fan in the corner does nothing.

                        BENJAMIN
            Ando forrado de billetes y no
            soy pa' esconderme en un lugar
            con aire acondicionado.
            *(All this money and I can't hide in a
            place with an air conditioner.)*

A crooked smile directed at the Barber. As if they are sharing a private joke.

                        BENJAMIN
            Pero los hoteles apendejan a la
            gente. Hay que andar siempre a
            las vivas, como los coyotes,
            que viven mal, pero viven
            mucho.
            *(But hotels soften people. You've
            got to be like coyotes. They
            live rough, but they live.)*

He waves towards the Barber's station.

                        BENJAMIN
            A ver, pasame una toalla con agua
            fría. *(Get me a cold towel.)*

The Barber wets a towel in the sink and hands it to Benjamin.

Benjamin squeezes the water down the back of his collar.

The Barber's eyes follow the drip of the water. There is something tattooed on the back of Benjamin's neck.

The Holy Death.

Benjamin leans back into the seat, refreshed. From the hallway, the toy car SIREN starts.

The Barber rests the blade against Benjamin's throat and stops. He puts pressure on the blade.

10 INT. SAFE HOUSE - CONTINUOUS

The Barber tenses his jaw. Tiny drops of blood spray IN SLOW MOTION towards his white shirt.

Blood FLOODS down the white towel, across the cement floor.

Benjamin GASPS, his arms grabbing the Barber's shoulders, his legs kicking out. The Barber bears down, all his weight against Benjamin.

Benjamin CHOKES, GURGLES. He strains against the Barber with his remaining strength …

The toy siren still wails. The Barber looks at the door in panic, praying the boy does not reappear.

The Barber holds strong. Benjamin stops moving. His eyes, never leaving the Barber's, glaze over.

SMASH CUT TO:

11 INT. SAFE HOUSE - CONTINUOUS - DAY 11

CLOSE ON the Barber's blade pressing against Benjamin's throat. Benjamin's pulse fluttering under the skin.

The Barber blinks, exhales in relief. His eyes flick towards Benjamin's.

Benjamin calmly meets the Barber's gaze. He knows.

The Barber jerks the blade away, icy realization hitting.

Benjamin's hand calmly pushes the blade back against his throat. He tilts his head back even further. Looks away.

The Barber and Benjamin stay like this for a beat. Each finally aware of the other.

The Barber stretches the skin of Benjamin's neck and slides the blade up towards his chin. The scraping of metal against skin and hair resumes its rhythm.

>   BENJAMIN
>   Cada quien a su chamba, ¿no?
>   *(Each one to his job, right?)*

The Barber shaves Benjamin in silence.

12 INT. SAFE HOUSE - LATER

The Barber wipes his hands and puts away his tools.

Behind him, Benjamin buttons his shirt.

Octavio enters. He crosses to the Barber and smacks a small bottle of aftershave on the dresser.

>   OCTAVIO
>   Ahi esta. *(Here.)*
>
>   BARBER
>   Gracias. *(Thanks.)*
>
>   OCTAVIO
>   Chinga tu madre.
>   *(Go fuck yourself.)*

He walks back to his spot.

The Barber picks up the aftershave. Benjamin indicates to hand it over.

>   BENJAMIN
>   Yo lo hago. Me gusta esta
>   parte. *(I'll do it. I love this part.)*

He splashes on aftershave, studying his face in the mirror.

>   BENJAMIN
>   Quedó bien. Eres tan bueno como
>   dicen.
>   *(It's smooth. You're as good as they
>   say.)* (to Octavio) Págale. *(Pay him.)*

Octavio pulls out a wad of money from his back pocket, saunters towards the Barber counting out bills.

>   OCTAVIO
>   ¿Dólares o pesos?
>   *(Dollars or pesos?)*

                        BARBER
    Pesos.

                        OCTAVIO
    Vamos a pasar por ti una vez a
    la semana.
    (We'll repeat this once a week.)

                        BENJAMIN
    No. Consíguete a otro barbero.
    (No. We won't. Get a different barber.)

                        OCTAVIO
    Pero si acabas de decir que
    este es bueno.
    (Why? You said this one's good.)

                        BENJAMIN
    Por eso.
    (He is.)

13 INT. SAFE HOUSE - CONTINUOUS

The Barber returns his attention to the blade in his hands, starts wiping it with a cloth when he gives a small jerk of his hand. Shocked, he lifts his hand.

A THIN RED LINE OF BLOOD forms along his thumb. A single drop slips free and drips into the bowl on the table, diluting instantly in the soapy water.

14 INT. SAFE HOUSE - CONTINUOUS

From the HALLWAY, SOUNDS of a STRUGGLE - GRUNTING, BOOTS SCRAPING, panicked CRIES and WHIMPERS. Shaken, the Barber looks up.

Two Thugs carry in a bound PRISONER, desperately struggling against his captors and losing.

A powerful SMASH to the back of his head, and the Prisoner is down on the ground.

The Barber watches one of the Thugs bend down over the Prisoner, gun held to the base of his skull.

Hanging from the THUG'S neck a medallion of The Holy Death.

The Barber raises his eyes to the Thug's face, not willing to believe it …

JUAN.

The Barber recoils. His world folds in around him.

Juan glances at the Barber, then back at his comrades. He is speaking, the other men answering. But the Barber does not hear them.

A hand rests on Juan's shoulder. A casual fatherly gesture. It's Benjamin. He passes the gun to Juan.

He steps in front of the Barber, blocking his view.

A BLACK HOOD descends over the Barber's eyes.

CUT TO BLACK

20 *Contrapelo* case study

1 What's the story?

The plot

While shaving a customer, an unnamed barber, proud of his craft, tries to teach his skills to his awkward son. After venting his rage on drugs cartels and their brutality, the Barber discovers that Juan, a youth he employs, is involved with one, and so fires him. Moments later, the sinister Octavio arrives. Soon after, in a safe house belonging to the cartel, Octavio tells the Barber he must shave someone. The Barber demurs, saying he needs lotion to avoid causing rashes, but discovers his customer is none other than cartel boss Benjamin, a man who brooks no refusal. After taking time to prepare, the Barber begins. He considers slitting Benjamin's throat but the sudden appearance of the boss's young son interrupts his thoughts. With the boy gone, he imagines murdering Benjamin, only to realize the boss has understood his fantasy. The shave completed, Benjamin tells Octavio to find a different barber. Juan and another thug drag in a prisoner and Benjamin gives a gun to Juan, who while pointing the weapon at the prisoner, looks toward the Barber …

The story

A barber, proud of his reputation as the best in town, fires Juan for associating with a cartel and as a consequence is ordered to shave its boss Benjamin. In carrying out his assignment, the Barber is torn between pride in his skill and moral anger at the murderous boss. The appearance of Benjamin's young son deters the Barber from murder but when an opportunity to kill the criminal arises, he cannot help but fantasize about the deed, a thought that dooms him.

The approach: Make the plot clear. Tell the story. Emphasize the Barber's moral dilemma and the suspense of his predicament.

The challenges: To create suspense and a foreboding of violence when no violence, even action, is actually shown (until the imagined murder). To avoid stereotypes of gangsters. To convey the stakes of the thriller with few characters and two small interior locations.

2 Premise

When a barber fires an employee for his association with a drugs cartel, he's forced to shave the gang's boss. While performing his assignment he's torn between honoring his craft, on the one hand, and the righteous urge to rid the world of a murderous criminal, on the other. Seeing the opportunity to kill the boss, he faces a question: how can he choose between the two mutually exclusive values that have given meaning to his life without betraying one or the other?

The question the film itself raises might be described thus: "How do we decide between the criteria of meaning?"

The approach: Modulate the flow of energy accordingly. Imbue the prologue with a sense of mystery and menace. Give the scenes in the Barber's shop section an air of dailiness ... until the shot of Juan's medallion, then lace the situation with unease, culminating in the appearance of Octavio.

Empower the next act by rendering the Barber's dilemma visual through the image of the blade, by isolating the Barber in single shots to emphasize his increasingly lonely interior struggle, and by shooting the "visual dialogue" between him and the blade, him and Benjamin's throat.

Use looks between lines of dialogue to express the Barber's inner thoughts and doubts and to convey the subtext between him and Benjamin. Perhaps use tighter, more claustrophobic shots as the sense of inescapable menace builds.

Mark the crescendo of the final scene both by group shots and by cross-cutting between the Barber and Juan.

The challenges: To mark each step of the premise.

3 Theme

Abstract noun: Crime? Justice? Pride? Manhood? Duty?

Conflicting concepts: Morality vs. expediency, integrity vs. power, law vs. crime.

Issue: Narco crime, collapse of law.

Paradox: Together, the imperatives of ritual and justice that each alone provide a sense of meaning, destroy it.

Moral: Pride comes before a fall.

Warning: "We are most in moral danger to ourselves when we are caught up in a righteous fervor against an evil foe" (David Brooks).

Thematic question: How can we act according to our moral values without betraying the rituals that sustain us?

The approach: Bring the audience into the Barber's narrative point of view so that it goes along with his moral rage and pride, and thus itself feels his fall. Build the sense of menace throughout so that the audience also feels increasingly *uneasy* as it holds to the Barber's values.

The challenges: To embody the theme in every scene. To leave the audience with the resonance of the thematic question while delivering the final blow.

4 Genre

Crime drama thriller; revenge thriller/cartel thriller; neo-noir; father–son drama; social issue drama; lament (for the past, for Mexico); tragedy.

The approach: The film might begin with a strong sense of realism and everyday life conveyed by performance, staging, shooting, "natural" lighting, and unobtrusive editing. Once the story moves to the cartel house, however, the movie can take on more of the suspense and threat of a thriller, its style heightened by shot composition, camera angle, more "noirish" lighting to create more shadow and greater contrast in the image. This approach will lead to the visceral imagery of the throat slitting and will culminate in the ominous ending.

The challenges: To convey the stakes of the thriller with few characters, in only two small interior locations, and to deliver the intensity of the Barber's interior personal drama through the depiction of the rituals of his craft and the performance of the actor who will play him, muted as it needs to be but expressive in its containment. To ramp up the tension steadily throughout the film, slowly at first, then with the deliberate acceleration of the thriller as it comes to its conclusion. To incorporate and unify the elements of genre through all aspects of directing craft.

5 World/setting

Period: Contemporary. Place: Parral, Chihuahua, Mexico. A medium-sized town. Conditions: Hot, parched, windless, arid. Sweltering heat. The humidity of the interiors. Locations: Interior car. Interior barber shop. Interior cartel house. Space: Increasingly claustrophobic to emphasize the Barber's worsening sense of entrapment, both from his perilous predicament and in his moral and existential dilemma.

The approach: An initial trip to Parral, then if shooting in this location is not a possibility, the director needs to consider how the setting can be realized elsewhere. Close collaboration with the production designer as to either the building of sets or the selection of more readily available locations is crucial.

The challenges: To combine the authenticity of an actual place with the heightened environment demanded by the film's genre and the pitch of its drama. To give a strong sense of the Barber's character through the set-dressing in his shop. To create the combination of dramatic space and practical utility in the sets or locations—there are several characters in the Barber's shop, so it needs to be spacious enough to allow flexibility of camera placement and angle, but not so large that it might suggest the protagonist has anything more than a modest business. The room in the cartel safe house should be more claustrophobic, offering perhaps one doorway into a passage through which the Barber might escape, if only he could … To decide to use sets or locations. To find the specific nature and appearance of the cartel safe house—what kind of a house is it? How much should the physical constraints of the two interiors and the blocking they necessitate determine the approach to shooting?

6 Cultural, social, and moral canvas

The Barber's ethos enshrines both honor and pride in his craft and the moral primacy of justice. He is self-employed, a one-man enterprise representing the rigid ways and values of the past. For him, respect for, and adherence to, traditional social codes are all-important. In the Barber's culture, the spilling of blood is taboo, an affront to decorum. His is a culture of manhood. Benjamin's canvas, also rooted in preconceptions of manhood, is, however, the polar opposite of the Barber's. A love of power, the ready adoption of amoral expediency and opportunism, and a contempt for the value of human life—rejections of past values—are bolstered by a sense of honor rooted in the loyalty and violence that sustain and bind his criminal organization. In Benjamin's culture, blood must be spilt regularly and without compunction, brutality and the fear it prompts being fundamental to both the functioning of his organization and the meaning of the culture of manhood to which he adheres. Although contrasting, both visions are fiercely male—each character is a domineering father.

The approach: Thorough research in barbering, the contemporary history of Mexico, and the cartel sub-culture is essential. Awareness of how the latter has been depicted in film and TV alone would be insufficient preparation, but might offer useful references. Other film and TV crime and gangster material might be relevant, while documentaries on life in provincial Mexico will prove essential viewing—the nexus of reality and fiction will give the latter greater authority.

The challenges: To convey the cultural canvas of provincial Mexico, the personal ethos of the Barber, and the amoral, opportunistic mindset of Benjamin in a story that takes place in two rooms in a film of around twenty minutes.

7 Tone

The tones suggested by the *Contrapelo* screenplay are largely "minor key":

Tense	Clinical (the showing of the process of preparation for shaving and the shaving itself)
Violent/savage/brutal/angry/cruel	
Darkly comedic	Tender ("major key")
Playful	Poignant
Dark/somber	Congenial ("major key")
Precarious/ominous/portentous	Reverential
Frightening	Humane ("major key")
Menacing	Regretful
Shocking	Nostalgic?
Visceral/tactile	
Oneiric (dreamlike)	(The Barber's shop—"cluttered with a lifetime of collected photos, newspaper clippings, boxing match stubs. A cocoon of possessions.")
Claustrophobic	
Tragic	

The approach: The dissonance of the various tones in the two columns suggests often abrupt tonal oscillation. Like the generic contrast of social realist drama and crime thriller, these opposites can be used to create tension and suspense, the warmth of much of the right-hand column undercut by the chill of the left-hand column. The throat-slitting scene needs to be dreamlike but not so hallucinatory that it doesn't appear real and heart-stopping.

The challenges: All of the above. To shift seamlessly from the dailiness of the opening moments to the threat that builds throughout the scenes in the cartel house. To seed the opening scene with a sense of menace before this becomes evident, perhaps through the introduction of Juan and/or the actor playing him, but at the same time not to exaggerate it or give too much away. To achieve the extreme violence of the throat slitting without prompting the laughs, whether nervous or simply callous, that graphic bloodshed often provokes in audiences. The dark comedy comes from Benjamin, the shock from the Barber's mind. To create shock on the screen in an age of acceptance of shock—to find a new way to achieve this.

8 Structure

There is a teaser preface of just under one page, then three acts—a first set-up of six and a half pages and a second act of almost nine pages, the tension rising, that leads to a third-act denouement, continuous from the second act, of close on one page.

Note: in the teaser, the Barber's voice-over transpires to be dialogue from Scene 2.

The approach: Consider the modulation of rhythm and pace throughout. A steady, business-like pace in the Barber's shop. An acceleration in the opening moments in the cartel safe house, then a teasing deceleration as Benjamin enters and the suspense begins to build until the Barber appears trapped in time as well as space, culminating in the seemingly unending throat-slitting. Thereafter, the pace might pick up as the moment of the Barber's fate moves remorselessly closer.

The challenges: To make one film, not two—one in the Barber's shop, one in the cartel house. To relate the narrative structure to its dramatic and emotional counterpart.

9 Passage of time

Contrapelo begins with an uncontextualized scene before a linear narrative in the Barbershop commences. There is then an ellipsis or time jump mid-way between the Barber's shop in which events, in the main, proceed in real time, and the cartel safe house, in which events also, at least in the main, proceed in real time. Contextualized at the start of the second act, the opening scene is revealed as taking place between the scenes in the Barber shop and those in the safe house. The events of the story take place over one day, a few hours at most.

The approach: Ensure the audience is aware of the film's chronology. Emphasize *real time* at key moments to keep the audience firmly in the Barber's NPOV. Emphasize pauses and silences.

The challenges: To keep a sense of the *clean line of action* by suggesting the passing of real time, even though there are ellipses. To speed up and slow down time as appropriate for suspense and the flow of story.

10 Character breakdown

Main characters

THE BARBER: Protagonist. 40s. Proud. Righteous. Censorious. Stubborn. Brusque. Angry. Rigorous. Tidy. An idealist. He is unnamed—maybe an Everyman.

BENJAMIN: Antagonist. The cartel boss. Late 40s. "A short, wiry man." Manipulative. Sadistic. Callous. Mocking. Proud. Indifferent. Untidy. A bully. A cynic. Brutal. Witty. Clever.

168 *The case study*

Secondary characters

JUAN: 19. Works for the Barber. Thug for the cartel. Vengeful. Innocuous on the surface.
ARTURO: 16. The Barber's son, "a painfully quiet, insecure boy." (Is 16 too old? Make him 13, 12 even? Closer in age to Benjamin's son?)
OCTAVIO: "A big man." Cartel henchman. Menacing. Cruel. Impulsive. Not bright.
BENJAMIN'S SON: 6. Non-speaking. Innocent? Vulnerable?

Minor characters

DON CHAYO: "80s," then "87," "a relic." Crabby. Cantankerous. Does he give a sense of a past world, before the cartels, when tradition held sway?
MIGUEL: Customer. Whiney.

The approach: Ensure contrast in the casting of the Barber and Benjamin, the former perhaps tending to a stolid but not large physique, a man set in his ways, and the latter maybe tending towards slightness in build, a physical element of him at odds with the power he holds and his capacity for violence. The eyes of the Barber will need to project a psychologically and emotionally reflective quality later in the film, those of Benjamin by contrast redolent of a sharp, mischievous, predatory intelligence. Octavio, the antithesis to both, should be taller and bulkier, with little behind his eyes. (Or he might be a younger "hard man"—what Juan might before long become). Arturo's and Benjamin's sons might benefit from an affinity in casting and share a similar look in order to underline the irony of the contrast between their two fathers. Juan should not appear an obvious delinquent or thug. There should be a sense that, given different circumstances, his life might have taken a more felicitous path.

The challenges: The casting of the Barber and Benjamin. To differentiate or choose affinity, as appropriate between other characters. To make Juan seem innocuous yet have the audience recall him clearly when he reappears at the end of the film. To render both Benjamin's evil and his mischief palpable without allowing the latter to undercut the former. To convey the inner dilemma and pain of the Barber, on the surface a steady, stolid man set in his ways, and to make him compelling to an audience—more compelling than Benjamin, who could so easily "steal the show."

11 Narrative point of view

Opening: third-person objective. Then the Barber is the character into whose shoes the audience steps. But there are also instances of third-person objective in his shop when Juan and Don Chayo are seen while the Barber is not looking at them. When the stakes grow and tension escalates, however, the audience is increasingly confined to the Barber's NPOV, just as unable to escape his fear and dilemma as he is himself.

The approach: Adhere rigorously to the Barber's NPOV. Do not reveal characters before he sees them. Use his looks to motivate cuts and camera movement. Design the coverage from his NPOV—he is the fulcrum of the shooting and editing.

The challenges: To tell the story from the Barber's NPOV. To convey necessary information without breaking the bond of the audience to the main character.

12 Introduction of the protagonist and main characters

THE BARBER: His hands are shown in Scene 1, but not his face. Scene 2 begins with the blade of the razor on a whetstone, then "REVEAL the Barber." Not starting on his hands seems to work well. If they were shown there might be a danger he could be identified as the man in Scene 1. That should be avoided.

BENJAMIN: Introduced in Scene 3 by way of his voice off-screen—the voice of the authority that commands the menacing Octavio. Chilling! He's then seen as he comes to the doorway at the start of Scene 4 (from the Barber's NPOV), in need of a shave, his jeans and t-shirt unprepossessing—and yet …. This is an intriguing and unsettling introduction.

JUAN: Introduced early in Scene 2 as he "sweeps the floor in the background." A nicely innocuous introduction to a character whose full significance, understood only at the end of the film, is thus effectively disguised.

OCTAVIO: Introduced at the end of Scene B2 when the audience is expecting Juan to reappear. We see him at the same time as the Barber so that the audience shares the protagonist's moment of surprise, maybe shock. Again, effective.

The approach: Storyboard these introductions. Shot lists are vital. Realize the screenplay description in the shooting. Ensure adequate coverage, with different angles and sizes, for each "announcement." Emphasize suspense before the introduction of Octavio.

The challenges: To differentiate between the introductions. To introduce Juan in an understated manner but with the faintest hint of threat. To introduce Benjamin as slight in physique, casual in demeanor, yet with a terrifying presence.

13 Key images, objects, and motifs

The gold crucifix. The "MEDALLION OF THE HOLY DEATH." The razor on the skin and whiskers of Benjamin. The blood of Benjamin. The blood of the Barber. The toy police car (irony).

The approach: Isolate in the frame the blade of the razor, which should gleam. Isolate in the frame the medallion. Ensure that cutaways of these two elements are seen from the angle of the Barber's POV. Use angle, shot size, and framing to echo the motif of the Holy Death Medallion when later seen on Benjamin's tattoo. The sound of the toy police car should accompany its image. Shoot the blood on the Barber's thumb in three or four alternative close-ups and ensure that it *glistens* as he moves, a factor that will determine the duration of the shot.

The challenges: To capture these images in shots that will intercut seamlessly with the flow of the scene and yet allow for heightened significance and a sense for the audience, as it sees them, that time has stopped.

14 Opening image, frame, shot

"The droning RUMBLE of a CAR in motion. Then—HANDS. Bound by hard plastic bindings."

Sound before image. Question: what is that sound? Hands. Question: whose are those hands? Plastic bindings: why is this person captive?

Meaning in the image. Hands essential to the Barber's work are bound, as is he by his inescapable character conflict.

The approach: Storyboard this.

The challenges: To ensure adequate coverage for storytelling, for the establishing of tone, and for rhythm.

15 Closing image, frame, shot

The black hood descends. Blackness! The death to come …!

The approach: Storyboard this.

The challenges: To capture the moment. Pace. One simple, smooth uninterrupted movement.

16 The ending

The Barber's fate appears to be sealed so that, although he is yet to meet it, there seems to be no further change in the narrative. On the other hand, as the image of the Medallion of the Holy Death reappears, along with Juan, there is the sense that, while the Barber's story is over, the youth's is to continue—Juan has, so to speak, usurped the narrative and is to live the life the Barber despises, in the world he despises, at least for as long as circumstances permit. It is in the brief penultimate scene before Juan's reappearance, however, that the crucial image of the Barber's own blood as he cuts himself reveals the nature of his tragedy and brings his story to its true conclusion. By doing this, by breaking his cultural code, as earlier he broke his moral code by not killing Benjamin, he has destroyed the meaning in his life. Thus he is already in a sense dead when Juan reappears, and so the final scene, while it foretells his physical demise—and certainly the end of his values—functions also as a chilling coda.

The approach: Do not let the audience off the hook. Maintain tension and suspense until the very last frame.

The challenges: To maintain tension and suspense until the very last frame.

17 The step-by-step creative analysis of the screenplay

There follows a step-by-step scene summary, protagonist's journey and audience journey, indicating the turning point and function of each scene.

Scene 1

1. SUMMARY: The Barber is being driven to the Safe House.
2. PROTAGONIST:
   Objective: To survive?
   Obstacle: He is bound, hooded, and held captive by two goons.
   Action: He can do nothing.
3. AUDIENCE: We seem to be in a car but whose hands are those? They've been tied. They appear to be a man's. I don't like the look of this. Seems he's being driven somewhere. Where? Where are we? What is the world of this film? Why is he gripping this satchel? Because he's afraid? Because what it contains is important? What's in it? Cash? Documents? A gun? Why are we being told about shaving? Who is speaking? Is he the one who's speaking or is it someone else? What do these instructions have to do with this man or these circumstances? Who are the other guys? They look like thugs. What's going on? What are they going to do to the hooded guy? I don't feel comfortable with any of this.
4. TURNING POINT: None
5. FUNCTION OF SCENE: To place the audience *in medias res* and make it yearn for context and answers.

Scene 2 (A1)

1. SUMMARY: As he shaves Miguel, the Barber tries to teach his son his craft.
2. PROTAGONIST:
   Objective: To teach Arturo how to give a professional shave.
   Obstacle: Arturo's incompetence. The need to supervise the negligent Juan.
   Action: He chides both boy and youth and presses on.
3. AUDIENCE: A razor! A connection with the shave talk. This is a new scene! Where are we? Look! A barber! So the voice-over was this man speaking. But what happened to the guy in the hood? And where did the thugs go? When will I find out? Will I see any of them again? Have we moved on in time from the previous scene? Or have we gone back? I don't

get it! So what's the connection? Wow, but he's one skillful barber—lucky for his customers, with a razor that sharp! The thing's practically lethal. What if he were to cut someone with it? Like the guy in the chair. I can't see his face because of that towel. Who is he? The guy in the hood I saw in the film's opening? One of the thugs? And who is the boy? From the way the Barber is talking I guess he's his son. The old man waiting looks innocent enough. The kid sweeping the floor too. This place seems a million miles away from the menace of the previous scene. Phew! I feel safe now. I hope I'm not going to be bored though. And it's so claustrophobic here! All that stuff! Old photos. Newspaper clippings. The Barber's living in the past. Seems he's stuck in it and I'm starting to feel trapped myself. Coffee? So Juan makes crap coffee and the old guy's not as sweet as I thought—just listen to his obscenity! What a contrast with the Barber who seems so proper, but look, he smiles at the word "dick"—he's got a human side after all. I could get with this man. Ah! So now I can see the face of the customer. Nothing unusual there. Not one of the thugs. Could be the hooded man maybe? And what a complainer! I've had enough of him already. Oh come on Arturo! Get your act together! Make your dad proud. I want the Barber to succeed in teaching you his trade. Oh! I just realized—this barber must be the main character. Something about him. He's more interesting than the others. Shame about the son—Arturo can't even strop the blade the right way. How's he ever going to shave a customer? But what's with Juan and Arturo? Why did Juan lean in to him? Are they in cahoots? But no, Don Chayo sings his father's praises and Arturo seems proud. So the Barber's a star! Best in town. He's hard on the boy though. Strict. Not sure I like that side of him. But that Juan … he knows how to strop a razor—there's more to him than meets the eye!
4. TURNING POINT: Juan enters the father–son fray.
5. FUNCTION OF SCENE: To set up the Barber's character and world. To introduce Juan.

Scene 2 (A2)

1. SUMMARY: The Barber sees Juan's MEDALLION OF THE HOLY DEATH. Rages at the kid. Tells him to leave.
2. PROTAGONIST:
   Objective: To rid his shop of the medallion.
   Obstacle: Juan's defiance.
   Action: He fires Juan.
3. AUDIENCE: Hey! What did I just say about Juan? What's that medallion he's wearing? Is that a skull? What does it signify? The Barber knows … and he doesn't care for it one bit. "Butchers"? Who's he talking about? Sounds like a gang. Juan's a member of a gang. A violent gang. Wow! The Barber's really letting rip now. Says he'd kill the gang if he could! Should I believe him? But that kid's so defiant. I don't like this. Something bad is

going to happen. Razors? Murderous threats? A sinister medallion? This is not going well. But at least the kid is leaving.
4. TURNING POINT: The Barber sees the medallion.
5. FUNCTION OF SCENE: Sets up the conflict between the Barber and Benjamin.

Scene 2 (B)

1. SUMMARY: A man enters, followed by two others, sinister. (Should the audience recognize them from the opening scene?)
2. PROTAGONIST:
   Objective: To carry on as if nothing happened.
   Obstacle: Three men enter.
   Action: Not shown.
3. AUDIENCE: I'm glad that Juan has left, but even so I'm feeling uneasy. The Barber's got a point about him being a "bad apple," but there's something about his strict condemnation that sticks in my craw. "You have to cut guys like that out. Like dead skin"? Nasty! He sounds like a gangster himself. Oh no! Someone's coming in? Is it Juan? The bell just rang. Look round Barber! You need to see who this is! I need to see too! The others are looking, so look will you! Oh boy, but do I need to see who this is! Ah! At last! He's one clean dude. But ... there's something very cold about him. Too cold! And now there are two more men! Look at their shadows! Long, dark, giving me the creeps. You're in trouble now Barber—and I'm not feeling so good myself either!
4. TURNING POINT: The arrival of the bad guy.
5. FUNCTION OF SCENE: Introduces the menace posed by the cartel. Brings the first act to an end.

Scene 3

1. SUMMARY: The Barber is unhooded and untied in a place belonging to the cartel, and asked to prepare to shave someone—Octavio or someone else? He refuses, saying he needs lotion to avoid rashes.
2. PROTAGONIST:
   Objective: To avoid giving the shave.
   Obstacle: Octavio's insistence.
   Action: To show the broken lotion bottle
3. AUDIENCE: That hood! I saw it at the beginning! So the Barber was the man in the car! Now I know what was going on! But what I don't know, and what I want to know (or do I?), is what is going to happen to him! Because it's not going to be good!
4. TURNING POINT: Praise for the Barber from the unknown voice.
5. FUNCTION OF THE SCENE: Introduces the presence of Benjamin. The actual beginning of the new act.

Scene 4

1. SUMMARY: Cartel boss Benjamin enters, plays nice cop to Octavio's nasty cop, orders him and the other goons to get aftershave lotion while he tells the Barber to start shaving him.
2. PROTAGONIST:
   Objective: To avoid giving the shave.
   Obstacle: The forces marshaled against him are too powerful.
   Action: Not shown.
3. AUDIENCE: Who's this mess of a guy that even Octavio seems scared by? Boy, but does he need a shave! He's so scrawny and disheveled too, but even so there's something menacing about his laid-back manner, and what's he doing with that toy police car? Go figure! Has he got a kid? Is there a kid around somewhere? Is that a good thing or a bad thing? All I know is that I could do with a couple of real-life cops to take care of matters right this minute! Take care Barber! Don't defy him, it will do you no good! But, yes, *DEFY* him! Don't give in to this horrible man. (Horrible, and yet there's something compelling about him!) I'm relieved that he's sending Octavio and his goons away. Although … come to think of it … I'm not, but whatever, I have to watch, I want to stick with this movie … Oh! Here we go, he's told the Barber to start the shave …
4. TURNING POINT: Benjamin deprives the Barber of his excuse by sending Octavio out to get the lotion.
5. FUNCTION OF SCENE: Sets up the character of Benjamin. Sets up the conflict between the Barber and Benjamin.

Scene 5

1. SUMMARY: The Barber prepares.
2. PROTAGONIST:
   Objective: To heat the towel. To stir the lather. (To delay?)
   Obstacle: None.
   Action: To prepare as he always does.
3. AUDIENCE: The Barber is going to have to do this. No way out. These guys are polar opposites. And yet? They have something in common! They're both proud of their professions. Maybe the boss will respect the Barber? Maybe not! What's going to happen? Aagh! That microwave ping made me jump!
4. TURNING POINT: The ping! The shave must start. No turning back for the Barber.
5. FUNCTION OF SCENE: An example of not "cutting to the chase." Instead, the suspense is ramped up. The Barber goes through his pre-shave rituals, but he's never before carried them out in such a perilous situation.

Scene 6

1. SUMMARY: The Barber lathers Benjamin's face, while the latter tinkers with the toy cop car and philosophizes about shaving as marking the beginnings of civilization. The toy's siren goes off. Benjamin opts for the towel while it's still scalding hot.
2. PROTAGONIST:
   Objective: To continue prepping for the shave. (To demonstrate his rigor to Benjamin? To reassure himself with his ritual?)
   Obstacle: Benjamin talks, taunts him with the cop car.
   Action: He goes about his business.
3. AUDIENCE: They seem to be getting on well enough. Even so, I don't feel good about this. Isn't Benjamin paying the Barber TOO MANY compliments? And this philosophizing! What's that about? He's playing with him. What does a cartel boss know about civilization? But hey! Does he have a sense of irony or what? Almost makes me want to laugh. Aagh! That siren made me jump! And where are the real cops when they're needed? But he's some badass, that Benjamin! That towel's scalding hot and he's telling the Barber to put it on his face! Ouch! But he's not flinching. I'm kind of intrigued by this guy. Maybe I even like him ...
4. TURNING POINT: None. The action moves on remorselessly.
5. FUNCTION OF SCENE: To continue to ramp up the tension.

Scene 7

1. SUMMARY: The Barber gets the idea of cutting Benjamin's throat with his razor.
2. PROTAGONIST:
   Objective: To start the shave.
   Obstacle: The notion of killing Benjamin.
   Action: He thinks—does not act.
3. AUDIENCE: Doesn't Benjamin look helpless in that chair! Oh but that blade's sharp! And that neck's there for the slashing. And now the Barber's caught up with me. He's thinking the same thing as I am. This is your chance! Kill him! Kill the bastard! Kill him while you have the chance!
4. TURNING POINT: The Barber gets the idea that he can kill Benjamin.
5. FUNCTION OF SCENE: Sets up Scene 10. Leaves us ambivalent about what we want and what we fear. Presents the Barber with the potential for violence.

Scene A7

1. SUMMARY: Benjamin describes his savagery to the Barber, who begins the shave, the opportunity to slit the boss's throat tempting him.
2. PROTAGONIST:
   Objective: To shave Benjamin.

Obstacle: Intensifying thoughts of murder.
Action: To pause shaving, paralyzed by his dilemma—to shave or to murder …

3. AUDIENCE: The suspense is killing me. Now Benjamin is talking about headless bodies. The guy's a ruthless monster. How could I have said I liked him? (I never really liked him, honest!) Is that what he's going to do to the Barber? Decapitate him? Torture him first? Oh but that neck is there for that blade! You could take him out now Barber! Do it! And yet … Could I do it? Would I??? Aagh! That creak made me jump! Is Octavio back? Uh-oh!
4. TURNING POINT: Someone else arrives.
5. FUNCTION OF SCENE: Reveals the level of Benjamin's ruthless savagery and thus raises the stakes regarding the Barber's moral dilemma.

Scene 8

1. SUMMARY: Benjamin's six-year-old son appears. Benjamin rolls the toy cop car to him and he runs off.
2. PROTAGONIST:
   Objective: None.
   Obstacle: None.
   Action: None.
3. AUDIENCE: It's only a little boy! But this is Benjamin's son. Poor kid! If the Barber had slit his dad's throat he would have seen him die! I'm glad he didn't do it! Did I want him to? I did? Who *me*? At least we seem to have seen the end of that annoying cop car!
4. TURNING POINT: Benjamin sends his son away.
5. FUNCTION OF SCENE: To triangulate the drama. To add a human side to Benjamin. To complicate the Barber's moral predicament.

Scene 9

1. SUMMARY: Benjamin complains about the heat, compares himself to a coyote, demands a cold towel. The Barber complies. The Holy Death motif at the back of Benjamin's neck is shown. As the siren of the toy cop car is heard, the Barber puts the razor on Benjamin's throat and applies pressure.
2. PROTAGONIST:
   Objective: None. (He seems about to decide which way to go.)
   Obstacle: None.
   Action: Finally—to kill Benjamin.
3. AUDIENCE: They're both feeling hot and now I'm sweating myself. And Benjamin's sense of humor is growing less and less funny. Oh look! There's that skull motif again! The one we saw on that kid's medallion. Death! Is that going to be the Barber's fate before the end of the film? And

there's that siren again—the little boy's in the next room, and the Barber's pressing the blade against Benjamin's throat! He's going to do it! NO!!! BUT YES!!! HE'S GOING TO DO IT!!! HE'S GOING TO CUT THE GUY'S THROAT!!!
4. TURNING POINT: The Holy Death tattoo.
5. FUNCTION OF SCENE: To wring each and every possible last bit of suspense from the scenario …

Scene 10

1. SUMMARY: The Barber cuts Benjamin's throat, killing him, while hoping all the while that his son will not reappear.
2. PROTAGONIST:
   Objective: To kill Benjamin.
   Obstacle: Fear that Benjamin's son will reappear.
   Action: He presses ahead with the killing.
3. AUDIENCE: What do those tiny drops of blood spray in slow motion mean? Aagh! I get it! The Barber IS killing Benjamin. He's actually doing it! I never thought he'd actually go through with it! I feel shocked, appalled, exalted, ecstatic, disturbed, transported all at one and the same time … This is ugly! What a horrible death! But it's so compelling! I can't take my eyes off the screen! But the siren! Oh no—the son … what if he comes back now? What if he sees this! Please, please don't let him come back! Oh! Benjamin's stopped struggling … HE'S DEAD! The Barber HAS KILLED HIM!
4. TURNING POINT: Benjamin dies, (A turning point in the scene, not in the story,)
5. FUNCTION OF SCENE:
   1. To meet the audience's expectations of violence. 2. The audience is placed in the Barber's mind. The graphic, oneiric bloodletting privileges it with access to his interior world. 3. The scene evokes deep and complex emotions for which there may be no adequate words.

Scene 11

1. SUMMARY: Matters return to where they stood at the end of Scene 9. The Barber has NOT killed Benjamin. Benjamin grasps what was going through his mind, and defiantly taunts him. The Barber continues the shave; Benjamin is now in complete control.
2. PROTAGONIST:
   Objective: To save himself? (The agency is with Benjamin.)
   Obstacle: He's trapped.
   Action: He does what Benjamin wants—he continues the shave.
3. AUDIENCE: What the … What's happening! Oh, I get it! *The Barber has not killed Benjamin after all.* So what did I just witness? Some kind of

dream or vision? Did I see the murder the Barber wanted to commit? Phew! But that was some ride! Although … help! Benjamin seems to understand what the Barber was thinking. Bad! And now he's put the razor back against his own throat. No movement! Will the Barber cut his neck or will he not? I can't bear the suspense! Ah! So now he's shaving him. Benjamin has taken complete control. "Each to his own job"? If shaving is the Barber's job, murder is Benjamin's. Now I know for sure this is not going to end well!

4. TURNING POINT: Benjamin puts the razor against his own throat.
5. FUNCTION OF SCENE: To snap the audience back into the reality of the story and switch the balance of power back to Benjamin.

Scene 12

1. SUMMARY: The Barber, having finished the shave, puts away his tools. Octavio returns with the aftershave, goes to pay the Barber after Benjamin has complimented him, but Benjamin stops him, explaining that he needs to find a new barber. His response to Octavio's "You said this one's good," "He is," is a death sentence.
2. PROTAGONIST:
   Objective: To escape ASAP.
   Obstacle: Benjamin.
   Action: See next scene …
3. AUDIENCE: It's over. The Barber is putting away his tools. Hey! Maybe he's going to get away after all? But oh no! … Octavio's back. But wait! Benjamin is praising him. Octavio is paying him! The Barber is going to be OK! But wait again! He's not! He's done for! Oh boy but this hurts!
4. TURNING POINT: Benjamin's line "Get a different barber."
5. FUNCTION OF SCENE: To determine the Barber's fate and end any hope for him.

Scene 13

1. SUMMARY: The Barber cuts himself.
2. PROTAGONIST:
   Objective: To wipe his razor clean.
   Obstacle: His realization of his predicament.
   Action: He accidentally cuts himself …
3. AUDIENCE: What's the Barber going to do now? Wipe his razor? OUCH!!! That hurt! And look! He's cut himself! He's spilled blood! The very thing he vowed never to do! And that image! Blood in soapy water! It's haunting! I know it has meaning! But what is it? All I know is that I *feel* it!
4. TURNING POINT: The appearance of the Barber's blood.

5. FUNCTION OF SCENE: There will be blood! And here it is. Like any tragic hero worth his salt, the Barber, victim of his own pride and righteous rage, seals his own fate. By breaking his cultural code by cutting himself as he previously broke his moral code by failing to kill Benjamin, he destroys all sense of meaning in his life.

Scene 14

1. SUMMARY: Two thugs assault a helpless prisoner. The Barber discovers one of them is Juan. Benjamin passes a gun to Juan. The Barber knows the youth will now take his revenge.
2. PROTAGONIST:
   Objective: N/A.
   Obstacle: N/A.
   Action: Realization.
3. AUDIENCE: What's happening? Who's this? *Ow!* But that blow was cruel! Did they kill the guy? Oh no! That skull thing again? What's this? The third time? No, it's the kid's from the shop scene—it's Juan's. So this is Juan himself! *UH-OH!* And Benjamin's passing him a gun … Please no … And the Barber is hooded and …
4. TURNING POINT: Juan takes the gun.
5. FUNCTION OF SCENE: To seal the Barber's fate.
6. AUDIENCE TAKEAWAY: THE FILM HAS ENDED! And before I expected! Like a death. The Barber's—and as I watch the film's end it almost feels like my own!

Credits:

I'm still feeling it. I'm devastated but satisfied at one and the same time. This story will live on in my mind long after its end. The Barber's character proved to be his destiny. Will that be true of all of all of us? Will it be true of me?

(Note: In the completed film of *Contrapelo* the first scene is omitted, the director having preferred to save its ominous tone for later.)

18 Director's statement

There follows a director's statement from Gareth Dunnet-Alcocer, a native of Mexico City:

I don't quite know why I am attracted to something and the searching for that answer is part of the journey. Often when I do find that answer I get bored with whatever I was looking for, or I no longer crave it like the way the soul craves a story … the burning curiosity dulls. Michael Haneke was asked why he makes movies and his answer was something I agreed with: "Don't ask a millipede why it walks, for it will stumble." Although I don't dare compare myself to Haneke, I agree with this statement.

I don't know why I'm attracted to suspense. I know that it makes me feel like I am present. I believe it is one of the most powerful ways to connect a person into a moment. Plucking myself into the intensity of a reality where people's lives were at stake was the only way I could live what they live through, and to try to transmit that to an audience. I experience things very intensely. I was a nervous and fearful kid. Fear is something I know well and have experienced many times. The same goes for ambiguity, for not knowing what is right and what is wrong because reality never seems that straightforward to me. I guess I am a coward, and making this film is the best way I know to help.

Mexico has been in civil war for at least ten years. This drug war has taken the lives of a quarter of a million people, ravaged a country, and sunk a nation into fear, into distrust, into darkness.

Contrapelo is about a barber who achieves understanding. *Contrapelo* should explore what happens when certainty crashes into doubt and encounters wisdom in the process. It's about men trying to survive in the way they can, in the country they have been given.

It is my objective to plunge people into that dilemma, into thinking they're on the right side, tensing into a dangerous conviction and its usual generalizations: Crime must pay. Bad men must be punished.

And then, when we find ourselves most comfortable in that righteousness, I want to slip the viewer into spectrality. Now … why I want to do that is a mystery to me.

21 Conclusion

Every director will develop the approaches and methods that best suit their own purposes, but here is a structured modus operandi to inform those processes. Whether for the director working with a writer's screenplay or the writer-director encountering their script as a director and switching from one challenging mode of filmmaking to another, it offers a means to the deep and rigorous engagement required in translating the blueprint on the page of the screenplay to the progression of image and narrative on the screen. With its comprehensive organization of the seminal facets of dramatic construction as this pertains to film and TV, it provides a framework for further development of the director's method.

Story; premise; theme; genre; world/ setting; cultural, social, and moral canvas; tone; structure; passage of time; character; narrative point of view; introduction of the protagonist and main characters; key images, objects, motifs; opening image, frame, shot; closing image, frame, shot; the film's ending; the summary of the scene; the journey of the protagonist; the journey of the audience; the turning point of the scene; the function of the scene; the director's statement.

Twenty-two factors to steward the passage from page to screen—the heart of the director's duty and craft. A manual. A methodology. A mantra. Above all, a catalyst for the creative vision of the director as they set out to tell their story and reveal, perhaps even start to understand, the complex truths shared by humanity.

References

American Film Institute, "AFI's 100 YEARS ... 100 HEROES & VILLAINS," www.afi.com/afis-100-years-100-heroes-villians/.

Bellow, Saul, *The Adventures of Augie March* (New York: Viking Press, 1953).

Block, Bruce, *The Visual Story: Seeing the Structure of Film, TV and New Media* (Boston: Focal Press, 2001).

Brooks, David, *Meet the Press*, NBC, February 8, 2015.

Byatt, A. S., *Ragnarok: The End of the Gods* (New York: Canongate, 2011).

Calasso, Roberto, *The Marriage of Cadmus and Harmony* (New York: Alfred A. Knopf, 1993).

Egri, Lajos, *The Art of Dramatic Writing: Its Basis in the Creative Interpretation of Human Motives* (New York: Touchstone, 2004 [1942]).

Ferrante, Elena, *The Story of the Lost Child: Neapolitan Novels, Book Four*, trans. Ann Goldstein (New York: Europa Editions, 2015).

Kiarostami, Abbas, *Lessons with Kiarostami*, ed. Paul Cronin (Sticking Place Books, 2015).

Mackendrick, Alexander, *On Film-making: An Introduction to the Craft of the Director*, ed. Paul Cronin (London: Faber & Faber, 2004).

Schopenhauer, Arthur, *The World as Will and Representation* (New York: Dover, 1969 [1819]).

Tarkovsky, Andrey, *Sculpting in Time: Reflections on the Cinema*, revised edition, trans. Kitty Hunter Blair (London: Faber & Faber, 1989).

Bibliography

Campbell, Joseph, *The Hero with a Thousand Faces* (New York: Pantheon Books, 1949).
Corcoran, Nina, "Martin Scorsese calls on theater owners to stop invasion of Marvel movies," *Entertainment News*, October 13, 2019.
Crow, Cameron, *Conversations with Wilder* (New York: Alfred A. Knopf, 1999).
Flood, Alison, "Ursula Le Guin's advice for aspiring writers: 'There are no recipes,'" *The Guardian*, August 3, 2015.
Forster, E. M., "The art of fiction No. 1," *Paris Review*, issue 1 (Spring 1953).
Miller, Henry, *Henry Miller on Writing* (New York: New Directions, 1964).
Nin, Anaïs, *On Writing* (Gremor Press, 1946).
Walser, Robert, "[Untitled, crossed out]," *A Schoolboy's Diary and Other Stories*, trans. Damion Searls (New York: New York Review Books, 2013 [c. 1910]).
Wittgenstein, Ludwig, *Culture and Value*, trans. Peter Winch (Chicago: University of Chicago Press, 1980).
Wittgenstein, Ludwig, *Tractatus Logico-Philosophicus*, trans. C. K. Ogden (London: Routledge & Kegan Paul, 1922 [1921]).

Index

Note: fictional characters are ordered by given name, actual persons by surname. Where a character is based on an actual person of the same name, they are treated as a fictional character, so ordered by their given name. Thus James Joyce as author is listed Joyce, James but as a character in Tom Stoppard's play *Travesties*, James Joyce.

8½ 29
24 67
400 Blows, The 122, 123
1917 63
2001 47, 120

A. S. Byatt 125
About Ellie 31
Achilles 77
Adaptation 37
Adventures of Augie March 84
AFI Conservatory 37
Alcott, John 47
Alex Sebastian (*Notorious*) 17, 80, 96–97, 107, 124, 125, 129
Alex the Droog (*A Clockwork Orange*) 52, 68, 112
Alibar, Lucy 111
Alicia Huberman (*Notorious*) 17, 80, 96, 103, 107, 109, 124, 125
Alien franchise 78
All Falls Down (music video) 93–94
Almodóvar, Pedro 72, 128
Altman, Robert 72, 82, 97
American Film Institute 77
American Honey 18, 21, 27, 46, 74, 80
American Psycho 79
Amis, Martin 65
Amsterdam (*Gangs of New York*) 14, 31, 76
Anderson, Paul Thomas 44, 115
Anderson, Wes 50
Annie (*Bridesmaids*) 126

Another Year 104
Antoine Doinel (*The 400 Blows*) 72, 122
Antonioni, Michelangelo 129
Aparicio, Yalitza 102
Apted, Michael 95
Aristotle 63, 66, 74, 75, 126
Arnold, Andrea 7, 21, 27, 46, 71, 74, 80, 107–108
Aronovsky, Darren 18, 122
Arrival 65
Art of Dramatic Writing, The 10, 16
Aster, Ari 24, 25, 33, 51, 104, 116–117, 122
Atonement 65
Austen, Jane 88

Baron Donati (*Earrings of Madame D …*) 121
Barry Lyndon 29–30, 47, 60, 85
Batmanglij, Zal 127
Beasts of the Southern Wild 111
Beau Travail 122
Beckert (*M*) 79
Beckett, Samuel 73
Before Dawn 61, 67, 128
Before trilogy 63
Bellow, Saul 84
Beowulf 78
Bernie (*Miller's Crossing*) 129
Better Call Saul 69
Big Sick 112
Bigelow, Kathryn 32, 71, 108

Bill the Butcher (*Gangs of New York*) 14, 32, 76, 121
Billi (*The Farewell*) 82
Billy Caspar (*Kes*) 22
Binoche, Juliette 24, 101, 102
Birdman 63
Black, Jack 83
Black Panther 24, 38
Blade Runner 41
Blake, William 79
Block, Bruce 113
Blue Valentine 18
Blue Velvet 117
Boogie Nights 115
Bong, Joon-ho 28, 126
Bourne franchise 25
Boyhood 21–22, 66, 100
Boyle, Danny 71
Breaking Bad 11–13, 18, 46, 60, 69, 83, 127
Bridesmaids 23, 33, 126
Bridge of Spies 30
Buffalo Bill and The Indians, or Sitting Bull's History Lesson 72
Buñuel, Luis 29, 67
Burning 18
Butch Cassidy and the Sundance Kid 122

Calasso, Robert 78
Calvino, Italo 19
Capernaum 27
Carrie Mathison (Homeland) 77
Carrey, Jim 28, 83
Carter, Rick 32
Casino Royale 128
Chaplin, Charlie 83, 126
character: in broad comedy 82–83; configuration of 81–82; contractions of 70–71; in dramatic narrative 73–75; in franchises 83; function of 28, 57, 69, 71, 75, 76, 81; historical characters 71–72; *meta* 72; nature of 69–72; other meanings 69; as proxy for the filmmaker 72; in TV 83
character breakdown: antagonists 76–77; anti–heroes 79; monsters 78–79; protagonists 76; secondary and minor 79–81; shape–shifters 72
Chase, David 127
Chekhov, Anton 10
Children of Men 63
Chinatown 33, 64, 89–90

Chiron (*Moonlight*) 74, 75, 103
Chow Mo-wan (*In the Mood for Love*) 6–7
Cianfrance, Derek 18
cinematographer 8, 32, 33, 47, 106, 109
City Lights 126
Clarice Starling (*Silence of the Lambs*) 78
Cleo (*Roma*) 50–51, 90, 93, 102, 107
Clockwork Orange 52, 68, 112
closing images: as coda 121; freeze frames 122–123; as metaphor 121; obscured by subsequent scene 123; symmetry with opening image 119–120
Coal Miner's Daughter 95–96
Cody, William Frederick "Buffalo Bill" 72
Coen Brothers 129
Come and See 77
Coming of age 22, 26
complicit camera 25
Contrapelo 29, 137
Conversation 63
Coogler, Ryan 24, 38
Coppola, Francis Ford 45, 52, 63
Coppola, Sophia 36, 103
costume designer 8, 71
Crime and Punishment 79
critical camera 25
Cronin, Paul 124
Crowe, Cameron 124
Crowe, Russell 94, 102
Cuaron, Alfonso 23, 36, 50, 63, 90, 93, 102, 107
Curious Case of Benjamin Button 65
Cyril Catoul (*Kid with a Bike*) 70, 81

Dani Ardor (*Midsommar*) 51, 122
Daniel Blake (*I Daniel Blake*) 71
Daniels, Jeff 28
Dardenne Brothers 33, 36, 70, 81
Darth Vader (*Star* Wars) 77
Dave (*Wasp*) 8, 71
David (*The Lobster*) 129
Davies, Terence 72
Davis, Deborah 47
del Toro, Guillermo 38, 91
Demme, Jonathan 78
Denis, Claire 122
Desplat, Alexandre 35
Destroyer 129

186 Index

Devlin (*Notorious*) 17, 80, 96, 103, 104, 107, 109, 124, 125, 132
Dexter 79
Dickinson 72
Dickinson, Emily 72
director's statement 135
Dr. Mabuse 78
Dr. Mabuse the Gambler 78
Don Diego de Zama (*Zama*) 32, 36, 40, 41, 91, 101, 122–123
Doolittle Lynn (*Coal Miner's Daughter*) 96
Dorf, Stephen 103
Dostoevsky, Fyodor 79
Dreyer, Carl 33
Driver, Adam 27
Dumb and Dumber 28, 82
Dunnet-Alcocer, Gareth 137

Earrings of Madame D … 114–115, 120–121
Eastwood, Clint 26
editor 8, 55, 65, 68
Egerton, Taron 27
Egri, Lajos 10, 11, 16, 75
Eisenstein, Sergei 51
Elena (*The Story of the Lost Child*) 135
Eliot, T. S. 117
Ellis, Bret Easton 79
endings: ambiguity in 127; as climax 124; as destination of the story 128; in franchise movies 128; as *fulcrum* scene 129; price of 125; as reflection 124; related to beginnings 124–125; relationship to catharsis 126–127; relationship to genre 129; relationship to narrative point of view 129–130; relationship to thematic paradox 126; surprising and inevitable 125; in TV 128; twist 128–129
English Patient, The 24–25, 40
Ergüven, Deniz Gamze 77
Erin Bell (*Destroyer*) 129
Esmail, Sam 25
Ethan Edwards (*The Searchers*) 119, 122
Evelyn Mulwray (*Chinatown*) 90
Everybody Knows 31
Eyal Spivak (*One Week and a Day*) 79

Farewell 51, 82
Farhadi, Asghar 31
Farrelly Brothers 28, 82

Fassbender, Michael 27
Fast and Furious 27
Favorite 46–47
Feig, Paul 23, 33, 126
Fellini, Federico 29, 72
Ferrante, Elena 135
Ferretti, Dante 31–32
Fincher, David 31, 65
Firmin (*Roma*) 50–51, 102
Fish Tank 27
Fitzgerald, F Scott 73–74, 89
Fletcher, Dexter 27
Flower-Seller (*City Lights*) 126
Flowers of Shanghai 115
Fly (episode in *Breaking Bad*) 60
Fonda, Henry 80
Fonny Hunt (*If Beale Street Could Talk*) 125
Ford, John 103, 119
Forman, Milos 72
Forster E. M. 70
Four Quartets 117
Frank Sheeran (*The Irishman*) 25
French cinema vérité 22
Friday the 13th 78
Full Metal Jacket 36
function of the scene 134
Funny Games 23, 127

Gang of Four 36
Gangs of New York 14, 31–32, 34, 36, 41, 76, 121
genre: definitions of 22; *elevated, hybrid*, multiple, *retro* 37–38
genre as applied to elements of craft: casting 27; characters 26; cinematography 32–34; conflict 28–29; depiction of events 24–25; expectations 22–23; intended audience 23; journey of the protagonist 26; moral universe 26; music 35–37; pay-offs 30–31; performance 27–28; pitch 29; production design 31–32; sound design 34–35; suspension of disbelief 23–24; tonality 29–30; tropes and conventions 25–26
Get Out 38
Gilles (*The Kid with a Bike*) 81
Gilligan, Vince 127
Giuliano, Joshua 68
Godard, Jean-Luc 55
Godfather 45, 52, 64

Goodfellas 64
Gordon, Emily V. 112
Gosford Park 82
Great Beauty 29
Great Gatsby 89
Greene, Graham 129
Grendel 78
Guido Anselmi 72

Hal *(2001)* 120
Halloween 78
Hamlet 19, 74
Hana *(The English Patient)* 24–25
Haneke, Michael 23, 78, 127, 179
Hannibal Lecter *(Silence of the Lambs)* 77, 78
Hannibal Rising 78
Happy as Lazzaro 71
Harris, Thomas 78
Harron, Mary 79
Harry Lime *(The Third Man)* 129
Harry Potter 27, 41
Hecht, Ben 80, 109, 125
Helen *(Bridesmaids)* 126
Hell or High Water 125
Henry Hill *(Goodfellas)* 64
Heraclitus 74
Hereditary 24, 25, 33, 34, 116–117
Hidden Life 65
Highsmith, Patricia 79
Hill, George Roy 122
Hitchcock, Alfred 16–17, 19, 23, 28, 29, 35, 63, 74, 80, 86, 90, 96, 103, 104, 107, 115, 123, 124, 128, 132, 133
Hogarth, Thomas 47
Holly Martins *(The Third Man)* 129–130
Homecoming 25
Homeland 77
Homer 19
Hsiao–hsien, Hou 115

I, Daniel Blake 43–44, 7
If Beale Street Could Talk 125
images: of absence 108–109; of dissonance 108; effect of aspect ratio 110–111; *ikones* 109; opening 110–118; repeated in successive films 108; in the screenplay 106, 111–112; space 111, 113; types of 106–108, 109
In Sound We Live Forever 68

In the Mood for Love 5; plot 5–7
Iñárritu, Alejandro 63
Inception 120
Inglourious Basterds 77
Inland Empire 65
Insider, The 94, 102–103, 111
introduction of main characters: marking of 103–104; misdirection in 102, 103–104; options 99–101; as suspense 104; use of contrasts 102–103
Irishman, The 25, 124
Italian neo-realism 22

Jack Reacher 77
Jackson, Mick 71
Jake Gittes *(Chinatown)* 64, 89–90, 133
Jake La Motta 117–118, 119
James Bond 23, 30, 77, 90, 128
James Gillespie *(Ratcatcher)* 26, 40
James Joyce *(Travesties* play) 72
Jarmusch, Jim 27
Jason Bourne 77
Jay Gatsby 89
Jeffrey Wigand 94–95, 102–103
Jenkins, Barry 18, 74, 75, 103, 125
Jessie Pinkman *(Breaking Bad)* 127
Joe *(You Were Never Really Here)* 125
Johnny Marco *(Somewhere)* 103
Johnson, Rian 111
Joker 77
Jones, Tommy Lee 96
Jonson, Ben 82
Jordan Belfort *(The Wolf of Wall Street)* 65
journey of the audience 132–133
journey of the protagonist 131–132
Joyce, James 88
Julie *(Three Colors: Blue)* 50, 70–71, 92, 101, 104
Jung, Carl 11, 45

Kar-wai, Wong 5, 108
Karen *(Goodfellas)* 64
Kaufmann, Charlie 37
Keaton, Buster 83
Kenyeres, Bálint 61, 128
Kes 21–22
Kevin *(Moonlight)* 74, 103
Kiarostami, Abbas 6, 73, 108, 127, 129, 132
Kid with A Bike 33, 36, 70, 81

Kieślowski, Krzystof 14, 16, 34, 50, 92, 101, 104, 112–113
Klimov, Elem 77
Knight, Stephen 63
Kore-Eda, Hirokazu 30, 46, 82
Krasinski, John 132
Kubrick, Stanley 26, 29–30, 33, 36, 47, 60, 68, 85, 112, 120
Kurosawa, Akira 67, 89, 108, 122
Kusama, Karyn 129

L. B. "Jeff" Jefferies (*Rear Window*) 70, 103, 107, 116, 131
L'Eclisse 129
Labaki, Nadine 27
LaBeouf, Shia 27
Lang, Fritz 41, 78, 79
Lanthimos, Yorgos 25, 46–47, 129
Lazzaro (*Happy as Lazzaro*) 71
Le Carré, John 30
Le Guin, Ursula K 62
Lee, Chang-dong 18
Leigh, Janet 103
Leigh, Mike 24, 72, 104
Lessons with Kiarostami 6
Leviathan 126
Lincoln 32, 71
Linklater, Richard 21–22, 63, 66, 100
Lisa Fremont (*Rear Window*) 70, 131
Loach, Ken 21, 43, 71
Lobster 129
Locke 63
Looper 111
Lord of the Rings 41
Lord Washizu (*Throne of Blood*) 89, 108
Loretta Lynn 95–96
Los Indios Tabajares 36
Los olvidados 29, 67
Loudest Voice 71
Loveless 31, 126
Lowell Bergman (*The Insider*) 94–95, 102, 111
Lucas, George 111
Luck of Barry Lyndon (novel) 30
Luhrman, Baz 89
Lumière Brothers 98
Lynch, David 19, 65, 117

M 79
Macbeth (play) 88
McDowell, Malcolm 52
Mackendrick, Alexander 124–125
Mackenzie, David 125
McLuhan, Marshall 19
McNamara, Tony 47
McQueen, Steve (director) 51, 81
Madame De … 114–115, 120–121
Madden, John 72
Malick, Terrence 19, 47, 65
Mamet, David 10, 125
Manichaean world-view 59
Mann, Michael 94, 102, 111
"Manny" Ballestrero (*The Wrong Man*) 80
Marcus (*A Quiet Place*) 132
Marie Antoinette 36
Marion Crane (*Psycho*) 19, 103–104
Marling, Brit 127
Marriage of Cadmus and Harmony 78–79
Martel, Lucrecia 29, 32, 36, 40, 91, 101, 122
Martha Edwards (*The Searchers*) 119
Martin, Steve 83
Mason Evans Jr (*Boyhood*) 22, 66, 100
Master and Commander 31
Medusa 78
Meisner (technique) 28
Melancholia 30
Memento 6, 56, 65
Mendes, Sam 63
metaphor *see* images, types of
method (acting) 28
Metropolis 41
Midge Wood (*Vertigo*) 107
Midsommar 33–34, 51, 53, 104, 122
Miki (*Throne of Blood*) 108
Milk, Chris 93–94
Miller, Henry 72
Miller's Crossing 129
Milton, John 79
Minghella, Anthony 24, 40, 79
Miss Dennerly (*Notorious*) 80
Mission Impossible 27
Mrs. Mulwray (*Chinatown*) 133
Mr Turner 72
Mr. White (*Casino Royale, Quantum of Solace*) 128
Mon Oncle 28, 33, 82
Monsieur Hulot's Holiday 28
Moonlight 18, 74, 75, 103
motif *see* images, types of
Mulholland Drive 19
Mustang 77
Mystic River 26

Nabokov, Vladimir 106
Nanjiani, Kumail 112
narrative point of view: aspects of audience–character relationship 89–91; categories in literature 87–88; director's articulation of 98; *free indirect discourse* 88; narrative perspective as different concept from 89; other categories of POV in a shot 97–98; in the screenplay 88; *third person limited or intimate* 87–88, 98; use of sound 98
narrative unit 55, 60, 61, 62, 64, 131, 132, 133
Nashville 82
Natural's Not in It (Gang of Four) 36
Nemes, László 45
Newman, Paul 28
Nick Caraway (*Great Gatsby*) 89
Nightmare on Elm Street 78
Nin, Anaïs 74
Nolan, Christopher 6, 65, 120
Norman Bates (*Psycho*) 128
North by Northwest 29
Notorious 17, 35, 80, 96, 103, 107, 109, 123, 124, 125, 129, 132

OA 127
observing camera 25
Odyssey 19
Oedipus Rex 11, 18, 74
Ofelia (*Pan's Labyrinth*) 91
Officer Rhodes *(Bridesmaids)* 126
Oldboy 33, 65
On Film–Making 124
Once Upon a Time in Hollywood 71, 104
One Week and a Day 79, 82
opening shot: complex 112–117; functions of 110; manner of 111; relationship to aspect ratio 110–111; as series of questions 111–115; simple 117; whether specified in screenplay 111–112
Ophüls, Max 114–115, 120–121
Orange is the New Black 77
Osamu (*Shoplifters*) 46
Ostojic, Liska 137

Pacino, Al 94, 102
Pain and Glory 128
Pan's Labyrinth 38, 91
Paradise Lost 79

Parasite 28, 126
Park, Chan-wook 33, 65
passage of time: Aristotelian *unity of time* 63; communication of 66; effects of linear and non–linear narrative 64–65; management of 68; manipulation of 65–66; organization of 64–65; real time 63–64; in short films 67; in TV 67; within the shot 67–68
Paterson 27
Patrick Bateman (*American Psycho*) 79
Paul, Lawrence 41
Paul Prescott (*Notorious*) 80
Peaky Blinders 37
Peckinpah, Sam 67
Peele, Jordan 38
Perseus 78
Peter (*Hereditary*) 116
Phantom Thread 44
Phoenix, Joaquin 77
picaresque 29–30
Piesiewicz, Krzysztof 50
Pinheiro, Renata 32
Piper Chapman (*Orange is the New Black*) 77
Pirates of the Caribbean 31
Poetics 63, 74, 126
Point Break 108
Polanski, Roman 26, 33, 64, 82, 89, 128
Polonsky, Asaph 79, 82
premise: application of 14–15; meanings of 10–14
Priest Vallon (*Gangs of New York*) 14, 31–32, 121
production designer 8, 31, 32, 39, 40, 42, 46, 108, 109
Proust, Marcel 106
Psycho 19, 104, 128
Pugh, Florence 104
Pulp Fiction 6, 56, 65
Purple Noon 79

Quantum of Solace 128
Quiet Passion 72
Quiet Place 132

Raging Bull 117–118, 119
Ragnarok (novel) 125–126
Ragtime 72
Rameau, Jean Philippe 36
Ramsay, Lynne 25, 26, 27, 40, 125

Randy "The Ram" Robinson (*The Wrestler*) 122
Raskolnikov 79
Ratcatcher 26, 27, 32, 40
Rear Window 11–13, 16, 29, 58, 70, 86, 103, 107, 115–116, 131
Reed, Carol 129–130
Regan (*A Quiet Place*) 132
Renoir, Jean 82
Reservoir Dogs 36
Rex (*The Vanishing*) 126
road movie 22
Rocketman 27
Rohrwacher, Alice 71
Roma 23, 36, 50–51, 90, 93, 102, 107
Rules of the Game 82
Russian Ark 63
Ryan, Robbie 47

Salesman 31
Salvador Mallo 72
Sam the Sham and the Pharaohs 36
Samantha (*The Kid with a Bike*) 81
Saul Goodman (*Breaking Bad, Better Call Saul*) 69, 83
Scarlatti, Domenico 36
Schoonmaker, Thelma 65
Schopenhauer, Arthur 81
Scorsese, Martin 14, 19, 31, 36, 41, 64, 65, 85, 86, 117, 121, 124
Scott, Ridley 41, 122
Scottie Ferguson (*Vertigo*) 74, 107
screenwriter 12, 18, 39, 40, 41, 42, 43, 49, 50, 51, 52, 55, 56, 58, 63, 65, 66, 67, 68, 70, 71, 72, 73, 75, 80, 83, 84, 85, 88, 90, 91, 92, 96, 103, 104, 106, 107, 108, 109, 112, 118, 123, 124, 125, 126
Sculpting in Time 64
Searchers, The 119, 120, 122
Sebastião Rodrigues (*Silence*) 121
Separation 31
Sergeant Galoup (*Beau Travail*) 122
Seven Samurai 122
Shakespeare, William 74, 89, 137
Shakespeare in Love 72
Sherlock Holmes 83, 90
Shining 33
Shirin 132–133
Shoplifters 30, 45, 82
Shore, Howard 36
Silas (*Destroyer*) 129
Silence 121
Silence of the Lambs 78

Simone Choule (*The Tenant*) 128, 129
Singing in the Rain (song) 52
Sissako, Abderrahmane 122
Sitting Bull, Chief 72
Sluizer, George 126
Sokurov, Alexander 63
Somewhere 103
Son of Saul 45
Sophocles 74
Sopranos 60, 79, 127
Sorrentino, Paulo 29
Spacek, Sissy 95
Spall, Timothy 72
Spielberg, Steven 30, 32, 71
Star (*American Honey*) 22, 46, 74, 80
Star Wars 35
Star Wars IV – A New Hope 111
Stealer's Wheel 36
Steve (*Hereditary*) 116
Stewart, James 107
Stoppard, Tom 72
story: definition of 5–6; story vs plot 6–8
structure: cultural foundations of three-act structure 58–60; definition of 55; episodic approach 62; flexible structure 60; as map of the film 62; relationship with linear and non-linear storytelling 55–56; in short films 61–62; three-act structure 56–60
Stuck in the Middle with You 36
style: *complementary, subversive* 47
Su Li-zhen (*In the Mood for Love*) 7
summary of the scene 131
symbol see images, types of
synecdoche see images, types of
Szifron, Damian 58

Talented Mr Ripley 79
Tarantino, Quentin 6, 26, 36, 37, 58, 63, 64, 65, 71, 104, 132
Tarkovsky, Andrei 64
Tati, Jacques 28, 33, 82, 83
Temple Grandin 71
Tenant 128, 129
tense in film 68
Tess 82
Thackeray, William Makepeace 30
Thelma and Louise 122
theme: as abstract noun 16; articulation of 18; as conflict 17; difficulty in defining 19–20; encapsulated in a final image 19; as issue 18; as mystery

19; as paradox 18; thematic question 14, 18, 57; as warning 18
There's Something About Mary 82
Thin Red Line 47
Third Man 129
Thorwald *(Rear Window)* 131
Three Colors: Blue 11–13, 14, 16, 34, 50, 70–71, 92, 101, 102, 104, 112–114
Throne of Blood 88, 108
Timbuktu 25, 122
Time's Arrow 65
Tish Rivers *(If Beale Street Could Talk)* 125
Toby Howard *(Hell or High Water)* 125
Tom *(Miller's Crossing)* 129
Tom Ripley 79
tone: definition of 49; developed though process 50; dissonant tone 50–52; effects on elements of craft 52–54; in novels and short stories 49; in screenplays 50; major key 54; minor key 54; modulation of 52; redundancy of 54; through juxtaposition of image and voice–over 51; through parallel action 51–52
Tony Soprano *(The Sopranos)* 79, 127
Torn Curtain 23, 28
Touch of Evil 115
Towne, Robert 90
Toya (Timbuktu)
Tramp *(City Lights)* 126
Travesties (play) 72
Tree of Life 19
Trelkovsky *(The Tenant)* 128, 129
Tristan Tzara *(Travesties* play) 72
Truffaut, Francois 72, 122
Turner, J. M. W. 72
turning point of the scene 133

Uncle Boonmee Who Can Recall His Past Lives 21
unity of time, place, and action 63, 67
Unnameable 73
Unsworth, Geoffrey 47

Vampyr 33
Vanishing 126
Vanity Fair (novel) 30
Verbinski, Gore 31
Vertigo 74, 107, 123
Villeneuve, Denis 65
Visual Story 113

Vivaldi, Antonio 36
Vladimir Ilyich Lenin *(Travesties* play) 72
voice 30, 37, 49
Voldemort *(Harry Potter)* 77
von Trier, Lars 30

Walser, Robert 60
Walter White *(Breaking Bad)* 46, 127
Wang, Lulu 51, 82
Wasp 7; plot of, story of 7–8, 71; images in 107–108
Weerasethakul, Apichatpong 21
Weir, Peter 31
Welles, Orson 115
West, Kanye 93–94
White Ribbon, The 23
Widows 51–52, 81
Wild Tales 58, 67
Wilder, Billy 64, 124
Williams, John 35
Wire 60
Wittgenstein, Ludwig 20, 134
Wolf Hall 71
Wolf of Wall Street 65
Wonder Woman 77
Woolf, Virginia 88
Woolly Bully 36
World as Will and Representation 81
world (human): economics 44; effects on style 47–48; preconceptions of morality 44–45; sense of meaning 45–46; social milieu 43–44; status 44
world (physical): complementary or counter 39; effects on story 39–40; elements of 40; practical considerations of 41; as representation of theme 40; as stages of character journey 40
Wrestler 18, 122
Wright, Joe 65
Wrong Man 35, 80

You Were Never Really Here 25, 125

Zama 29, 32, 34, 36, 40, 91, 101, 122–123
Zeitlin, Benh 111
Zero Dark Thirty 32, 71
Zimmer, Hans 35
Zodiac 31
Zoë *(Wasp)* 7–8, 71, 107
Zvyagintsev, Andrey 31, 126